Rational Praise
and
Natural Lamentation

Also by James L. Battersby:

*Typical Folly: Evaluating Student Performance
in Higher Education*

Rational Praise
and
Natural Lamentation

Johnson, *Lycidas*, and
Principles of Criticism

James L. Battersby

Rutherford • Madison • Teaneck
Fairleigh Dickinson University Press
London: Associated University Presses

Associated University Presses, Inc.
Cranbury, New Jersey 08512

Associated University Presses
Magdalen House
136–148 Tooley Street
London SE1 2TT, England

Library of Congress Cataloging in Publication Data
Battersby, James L.
   Rational praise and natural lamentation.

Bibliography: p.
   1. Johnson, Samuel, 1709-1784—Knowledge—Literature. 2. Johnson, Samuel, 1709-1784—Criticism and interpretation—History. 3. Criticism—History. 4. Literature—History and criticism—Theory, etc. 5. Milton, John, 1608-1674. Lycidas. I. Title.
PR3537.L5B37   828'.6'09   77-89774
ISBN 0-8386-2148-1

PRINTED IN THE UNITED STATES OF AMERICA

for Julie
and to the memory
of my Mother and Father

Contents

Acknowledgments

In the making of this book I have at every stage received generous and helpful assistance from friends, colleagues, and family. To acknowledge publicly those to whom I am indebted is a pleasant task, but not perhaps an entirely gracious one, since by so doing I run the risk of implicating in my errors of omission or commission precisely the people who did most to rescue me from them. Fortunately, by attending to the merit of any larger or smaller element of the book, the reader may quickly differentiate what I am completely or partially responsible for from what I owe to the counsel of others, for in dealing with critical suggestions I have, variously, accepted them fully, accepted them in part, or defiantly neglected them.

My first and continuing debt is to William R. Keast, who taught me long ago that if I aspired to be a Johnsonian I would have to learn to think distinctly and to speak with exactness. Throughout the writing of this work I received support and encouragement from many, but especially from Ralph W. Rader, Sheldon Sacks, and James Kincaid. They read my work carefully and made me wince in pain more than I care to remember. For crucial support at a timely moment I am indebted to Jeffrey Hart. I shamelessly pilfered ideas and information from an embarrassingly large number of friends. They all read the work and urged me by gentle or rough persuasion to make important changes in the study (all such changes were made except when I could honor one friend only by offending another; in such cases I too often offended both). They will recognize their contributions to this book and forgive me for citing them alphabetically. They are: Mark Amsler, Mark Auburn, Betsy Brown, Walter Davis, John Gabel, Lisa Kiser, Ernest Lockridge, Marlene Longenecker, Bernice Rudensky Lubin, Julian Markels, Walter Scheps, and Christian Zacher. This list would be incomplete if I neglected to mention three other friends who debated critical issues with me at length: Morris Beja, W. J. T. Mitchell, and A. E. W. Maurer.

This book was written not only with much "assistance of the learned," but "under the shelter of academic bowers," and I am grateful to the Trustees of the Ohio State University for providing me with two quarters of Assigned Research Duty—one quarter early in the project and one late—so that I could initiate and complete my work.

I thank the following publishers for permission to quote from copyrighted material:

The American Society for Eighteenth-Century Studies, for extracts from Oliver F. Sigworth, "Johnson's *Lycidas:* The End of Renaissance Criticism," *Eighteenth-Century Studies* 1 (1967), and for extracts from Murray Krieger, "Fiction, Nature, and Literary Kinds in Johnson's Criticism of Shakespeare," *Eighteenth-Century Studies* 4 (1971).

Harcourt Brace Jovanovich, Inc., for excerpts from *Samuel Johnson and the Life of Writing*, copyright © 1971 by Paul Fussell. Reprinted by permission of Harcourt Brace Jovanovich, Inc.

Oxford University Press, for extracts from Warren Fleischauer, "Johnson, *Lycidas,* and the Norms of Criticism," *Johnsonian Studies* (Cairo, 1962).

The University of Chicago Press, for excerpts from R. S. Crane, *The Idea of the Humanities* (Chicago: University of Chicago Press, 1967), from R. S. Crane, *Critics and Criticism: Ancient and Modern* (Chicago: University of Chicago Press, 1952), and from W. R. Keast, "The Theoretical Foundations of Johnson's Criticism," in *Critics and Criticism*, ed. R. S. Crane (Chicago: University of Chicago Press, 1952).

University of Minnesota Press, for excerpts from Jean Hagstrum, *Samuel Johnson's Literary Criticism* (Minneapolis: University of Minnesota Press, 1952).

University of Toronto Press, for extracts from R. S. Crane, *The Language of Criticism and the Structure of Poetry* (Toronto: University of Toronto Press, 1953).

Genre, for allowing me to reprint those portions of the Appendix which originally appeared in the Fall, 1977, issue of *Genre* under the title "Coded Media and Genre: A Relation Reargued" (copyright © 1977 by the University of Oklahoma).

Introduction

Johnson's Criticism and the Criticism of Johnson

This book is divided into two separate but related sections, the first, "The Limitations of Dialectical Approaches to Johnson's Thought," concerned chiefly with the cognitive and interpretive inadequacies of a distinct type of critical reasoning, and the second, "Johnson's Criticism: Theory and Practice," chiefly with the coherent body of principles and assumptions governing Johnson's practical, critical judgments. The two sections are related in that they have several topics in common and in that both are preeminently interested in coming to grips with Johnson's critical thought and the relation between practical judgment and critical principle. This introduction is designed to prepare the reader for the process and progress of the argument of the book, for without some preparation the reader might misread or misstress the emphases of the developing structure, especially those in the first section, in which specific modern essays on Johnson are examined in detail. Indeed, it may seem irresponsibly capricious, arbitrarily restrictive, or uselessly petty to focus on a select few modern essays unless the reader recognizes at the outset that the attacks are directed primarily against a commonly accepted set of assumptions and a widely adopted methodological bias.

The first section of the book centers on four fairly recent studies that deal with select aspects of Johnson's thought: Oliver Sigworth's "Johnson's *Lycidas:* The End of Renaissance Criticism";[1] Paul Fussell's "The Facts of Writing and the Johnsonian Senses of Literature";[2] Arieh Sachs's *Passionate Intelligence;*[3] and Murray Krieger's "Fiction, Nature, and Literary Kinds in Johnson's Criticism of Shakespeare."[4] Chapters 1 and 2 focus on the essays of Sigworth and Fussell respectively. Chapter 3 discusses Sachs briefly and Krieger more extensively and, at the end, provides a bridge to the second section. The first section engages in much "destructive" criticism, but it does so under the assumption that destructive criticism is sometimes necessary if one hopes to build or—as I hope to do—rebuild. I have demolished only because I thought that, with the help of other Johnsonians, I could build better. Moreover, in my opinion, destructive criticism as a challenging and testing of hypotheses is as useful and necessary to humanistic as to scientific inquiry. If *knowledge* is possible and capable of advancement in literary interpretation and criticism, then it must be based not only on the development of adequate hypotheses and the construction of sound argruments regarding particular matters of fact, but also on the critical testing of available hypotheses and methods of reasoning. At the present time there is an enormous proliferation of hypotheses but little testing or challenging of them in terms of evidence and logic. We have an abundance of interpretation and a paucity of solid accomplishment. In the absence of any deliberate testing of interpretive hypotheses there can be little advancement or consolidation of critical knowledge. It is not enough to present positive formulations; positive formuations must also be examined in relation to alternative possibilities and common tests of adequacy. Of course, so-called destructive criticism is ultimately "constructive" or "positive," since its end is not to impede inquiry but to reduce the number or redirect the nature of subsequent investigations.

To deal adequately with the positions of the critics discussed, I must examine the essays in some detail, paying close attention to particulars of evidence and logic as well as to matters of interpretive stance, because the case against dialectical approaches has to be founded not only on their theoretical shortcomings but also on their evidentiary and analytic weaknesses. Two positive benefits result from this attention to details, it seems to me. In the first place, by looking closely at specific interpretive details, I am able to show in concrete terms how the "misconstruction" of passages and writings by Johnson is variously dependent upon habits of reading determined by the very hypotheses that the critics are attempting to establish. Second, once local interpretations have been traced back to the exigencies of sponsoring hypotheses, I am able to offer alternative readings of the material and hence to establish a specific interpretive basis for statements made later (in the second section) regarding the principled foundation of Johnson's criticism. Thus the *destructive* section is positive by more than half from beginning to end, constructive at once in an admonitory or heuristic sense and in a positive interpretive sense.

Although the first section concentrates on the methodological imperatives and the argumentative concinnity of four modern studies of Johnson, the reader should bear in mind throughout the first three chapters that I am interested less in inveighing against particular critics than, on the one hand, in disclosing the cognitive inadequacies of a mode of inquiry and argumentation that is becoming once again alarmingly frequent in literary studies and in Johnsonian studies in particular and, on the other hand, in relating a variety of particular passages from Johnson's works to what I take to be the radical terms, distinctions, assumptions, and principles determining their significance and meaning. My interest in these critics and studies is entirely subordinated to a concern with specific critical approaches, with, more exactly, the theoretical and practical weaknesses of "dialectical" approaches to critical problems and the inability of such approaches to advance our knowledge of the nature and bases of Johnson's thought. Indeed, the writings on which I concentrate in the first section were selected primarily because they present in clear and striking forms virtually all the argumentative permutations of the dialectical mode of reasoning; they exhibit the mode in virtually the full range of its possibilities.

At the center of all four studies is a conception of polarity, inconsistency, or contradiction in Johnson's thought. The studies distinguish themselves from one another in various ways—in terms, for example, of the questions or problems they address, the kinds of discordancy they detect, the texts on which they rely for evidence, the assumptions they make about the importance of the discordancy to Johnson's thought and the relation in which it stands to other things (poetry, history, etc.); but they all begin the process of reasoning from some basic set of antithetical terms and argue to "proofs" by adjusting isolated passages from Johnson's writings to the terms of their primary categories. In short, these critics not only exhibit but attribute to Johnson precisely the sort of critical procedure that he, like Hume, always distrusted and consistently challenged, as he does, for instance, in his various remarks on legislated demands for certain poetic topics or kinds of diction in the various genres.

Sigworth emphasizes tergiversation, the movement of Johnson's mind from apodictic, Renaissance standards of judgment to standards of the heart based on Johnson's surveys of life. Johnson's switching of allegiances is the focus of his study, the turn from one to another standard being signalized most notably in the disparity between his analysis of pastoral in *Rambler* 36 and his critique of *Lycidas* in the *Life of Milton*, where he demands "an expression of racking grief," not simply "a manipulation of artistic form."[4] By virtue of this critical realignment, Johnson becomes a pivotal figure in the transition from Renaissance standards to a "Romantic—a modern—point of view." To Paul Fussell, on the other hand, Johnson's critical thought is characterized by a perdurable oscillation between two antithetical poles of attraction. Here the emphasis is not on the abandonment of one and adoption of another standard, but on a persistent and fretful appeal to conflicting and antipodal standards, Johnson at one time asking for a literature that is "akin to legal argument and implies a similar objective process: a canvass of received formulations and devices which will work . . . because they are familiar" and at another for a literature of "genuine self-expression" that "emanates from a motive which shuns the familiar in favor of the unique, the authentic."[6] To Fussell, Johnson causes so much trouble as a critic because he regularly asks a single work—*Lycidas*, for example—to be both one thing and another at the same time. Ultimately, the central contradiction in Johnson's critical thought has its etiology in a larger encompassing contradiction: the subsumptive contradiction is between Johnson's "social sense that literature is a mere rhetorical artifice akin to legacy advocacy" and the "religious sense that for the literarily gifted the production of literature and the living of the life of writing are very much like a Christian sacrament."[7] From this a priori, dialectical base, Fussell proceeds to the documentation of claims by reading isolated passages in terms of his antithetical categories.

Both Sigworth and Fussell treat Johnson's critique of *Lycidas* as a document of central critical significance to which appeal can be made in the justification and substantiation of their views, and for both, analysis begins after a basic contradiction or inconsistency has been identified. More important, however, is the fact that both rely on a common method of reasoning, though in going their predictable ways Sigworth is obliged to show that in the course of time Johnson altered his basic critical orientation radically, whereas Fussell must maintain that Johnson hopped erratically from pole to pole throughout his life. In a certain sense Sigworth's apodictic standards/standards-of-the-heart division is roughly equivalent to or consonant with Fussell's rhetorico-legal/self-expressive dichotomy. But for my purposes the two essays are valuable to the extent that they illustrate different aspects of a single mode of reasoning. The categories may be analagous in some respects, but by virtue of their commitments to different conceptions of Johnson's temporal engagement with literary problems, they must perforce engage in different tasks and satisfy different argumentative ends. Similar categories and different ends function at the command of an identical system of inference.

When at the beginning of chapter 3 I turn to a brief examination of Arieh Sachs's *Passionate Intelligence,* I am principally interested in another wrinkle in the dialectical fabric. For Sachs the basic polarity is in Johnson's conception of the faculties of man, not in Johnson himself, as Fussell would have it. In Fussell's analysis, Johnson is "madly irrational" and "impulsive," bounding with amazing agility and uncommon celerity between his two senses of literature without any apparent reason, and this activity can be traced back to a division within the man himself. Sachs, on the other hand, is interested in showing that Johnson's thought on various subjects reflects a conception of a basic polarity in the faculties of man. Sachs begins with the assertion of a prefabricated formulation of Johnson's thought: the rich complexity of that thought is discussed in relation to two faculties, reason and imagination. And the essential features of his thought are determined by an a priori notion of what the nature, function, and relation of those faculties were to Johnson. In Sachs's terms: "I shall argue that Johnson's satire on man (especially in *Rasselas*) springs from the view that in human nature reason and passion [Sachs often uses "passion" interchangeably with "imagination"], the angelic and bestial are intermixed. . . ."[8] And to Sachs this notion of the polarity of faculties "equally underlies the religious, the moral, the political, the aesthetic, and the psychological phases of his thought."⁹ Here again, once the basic polarity is established, reasoning becomes a matter primarily of selecting passages from a variety of texts that can be read in some fashion as commensurate with the powers enfolded in the abstract categories initiating discussion. For my purposes Sach's argument is instructive as a variation on the sort of procedure examined in detail in the chapter on Fussell.

Murray Krieger's essay on the "Preface to Shakespeare," discussed in chapter 3, brings us to the end of the argumentative possibilities, since beyond his approach there are only modifications of types previously examined. His essay is especially useful to the book inasmuch as, in addition to betraying the features of a characteristic kind of reasoning, it deals centrally with a major critical document and hence provides an efficient link to the next section of the book, a detailed investigation of the coherent body of principles and assumptions informing Johnson's practical judgment and evaluation of literature. With Sigworth and others, Krieger emphasizes binary operations, beginning his discussion with the idea that there is at the heart of the "Preface" a central contradiction respecting, in this case, the nature of reality. According to Krieger the world of experience inherent in the "Preface" alternately reflects *causality* or *casualty*, one or the other being stressed as Johnson confusedly changes his ontological hats. On the side of *causality* we have the "mirror universe of universals," the "assumption that there surely *is*, beneath the infinite variety of individuated nature and of the individual human responses to it, a general nature and a general core of human nature."¹⁰ On the other side, the side of *casualty*, Johnson "continually calls for endless variety or diversity, apparently forgetting about the unity which is the central quality of the causally controlled system he called for earlier."¹¹ For a while Johnson wavers uncertainly between the horns of his metaphysical dilemma, now inclining toward causality, now toward casualty until, in the "unities of the drama" section of the "Preface," he adopts a new mood. This mood, captured in the demand for unity of action and in Johnson's recognition of our "consciousness of fiction," resolves the metaphysical problem by transforming the *casual* into a "real" reality and the *causal* into an "art" reality; in his causal mood

Johnson had subordinated nature to art, whereas in his casual
mood he had subordinated art to nature. Thus we discover in the
unities section that the ontological problem had been more apparent than real all along. Here, at any rate, the universal and the
particular function cooperatively. The new general system is "the
system created by the poet as his fictional unity of the endless
variety found 'in the real state of sublunary nature,' a unity freed of
all artifice but that required to be 'a just picture of a real
original.' "[12] Here then is the dialectical mode in the form of a
"progress piece," complete with thesis, antithesis, and synthesis.
Johnson moves from a naive conception of universal system to a
conception of the unregulated diversity in the real world, and then
achieves a fuller and higher innocence with his notion of artistic
unity. In true apocalyptic fashion harmony is achieved by a marriage settlement: experiential diversity consents to live amicably
with artistic unity in the world of fiction.

By the end of the analysis of the Krieger essay, the reader should
have a clear sense of the range of dialectical discourse, since the
four critics give expression to the three major possibilities of the
type: (1) *resolution without conflict* (Sigworth; Johnson switches
allegiances and, by so doing, aligns himself with "a Romantic—a
modern—point of view"; the key here is *inconsistency*); (2) *conflict
without resolution* (Fussell and Sachs; everything in Johnson's
thought can be discussed in terms of an oscillation between antithetical poles of attraction or in terms of a basic polarity of faculties; the key term here is *contradiction*); (3) *conflict with resolution*
(Krieger; intransigent contradiction becomes the basis of cooperation at a higher level of integration; the key term is *synthesis*).

The focus of this book is on Johnson's criticism and the criticism
of Johnson, but every reader should recognize and understand that
the first section throws into relief studies that are but special
avatars of a kind of critical procedure that speaks with authority
and power in virtually every area of literary study. It is the mode of
reasoning that at present prevails in criticism, and wherever we
look—whether in distinctions between style and content, form and
content, the latent and the manifest, historical forces and form,
logical structure and poetic texture, poetry and drama, archetypal
pattern and artistic form, sign and symbol, literary and nonliterary
discourse, and the like—it is flexing its muscles and "demonstrat-

ing," among other things, by positive and negative analogy, that *this* is really *this* or that *this* is just the opposite of *this*. On the purely positive side the first section of the book, looking ahead to the second, is designed to establish concrete and specific alternatives to interpretations uninformed by an adequate working conception of the theoretical bases of Johnson's critical thought. The positive aims of the destructive criticism are to expose the cognitive and interpretive inadequacies of certain kinds of approaches to Johnson's critical thought and, more generally, to enable readers to resist the seductive charms of critical arguments based on dialectical principles, abstract terms, and mystical entities.

Having briefly outlined differences among the approaches of the four critics, I shall now summarize their common dialectical tendencies or qualities. For all their manifold differences in specific aim, subject matter, and preferred dichotomy, the critical opinions examined in this book betray a common tendency to begin critical reasoning, not from some empirically distinguishable event or effect that it is then the business of criticism to explain in all its particularity in terms of necessary and sufficient conditions, but from some basic proposition or truth concerning, say, the modern point of view, Johnson's bifurcated sensibility, or his "thought." An abstract or general principle—with its attendant, correlative, or adjunct terms and distinctions—is first established, and then particular passages or works are discussed in terms of their peculiar or specialized participation in the assumed proposition or principle, so that in the end what is explained is an aspect or implication of the explanatory hypothesis.

In all the writings that I have selected for particular examination, "analysis" begins with the postulation of a central contradiction or inconsistency in Johnson's thought or of two antithetical terms to one or the other of which various expressions of thought or opinion significantly Johnsonian can be reduced. Once the ruling hypothesis has been selected, the next effort of mind in this mode of reasoning is to demonstrate that wherever the critic looks the special inconsistency or the distinguishing antithesis is manifestly and volubly present. What has been predicated of one passage is predicated of another similar to the first in some terminological or doctrinal respect, but throughout, the meanings of the passages are relative to the possibilities of meaning implicated in the ruling hypothesis, the agency of double predication (not relative to any particular question, problem, context, or any coherent set of premises only on the assumption of which could we account for the full particularity of the work from which the selected passages are taken). Reasoning is from like to like, like to unlike, unlike to unlike—*likeness* being determined in general by the persistence of analogous terms or of categorical habits of interpretation, even in the absence of *like* terms—and not, as is the case with Johnson's criticism, from effect to cause, from some identifiable result or feature of a text to the necessary and sufficient conditions of its existence. Reasoning, in short, proceeds by means of logical combination and division within the limits established by the differentiating categories of the sponsoring hypothesis. Argument thus is essentially paratactic or anaphoric, with closure achieved (1) by reasserting as a conclusion—following the citation of a number of exemplary passages—the hypothesis with which analysis began (Sigworth, Fussell); (2) by claiming on the basis generally of some arbitrary standard that either the "good" or the "bad"—the high or the low, the natural or the supernatural, the rational or the imaginational—pole is ultimately more highly esteemed (Sachs); or (3) by altering, just when opposition seems most intransigent, the terms of the conflict slightly so that the antagonists can be translated into mutually dependent constituents of a final integrative hypothesis (Krieger). In the end the procedure achieves neither *explanation*—nothing "external" to the hypothesis (a particular text, say) can really be explained by a hypothesis accountable only to itself—nor *description*—the "facts" of the text have no status as precisely those facts independently of categorical coercion. From first to last the procedure is an exercise in saving the hypothesis, not the facts.

One of the subsidiary ends of three of these recent studies is to define Johnson in relation to his critical successors, to save him, in effect, from identification with the Dragon of Error, neoclassicism. Thus Sigworth attempts to enlist Johnson in the romantic—modern point of view. According to Sigworth "modern criticism begins with Johnson."[13] Krieger is interested in highlighting in the "Preface" adumbrations of the Wordsworthian spirit and in detecting in the call for unity of action anticipations of Coleridgean organicism. And Fussell's work is, in a sense, one long effort to endow the theme "Johnson, Our Contemporary" with credibility. In each case the means by which Johnson is linked to the future and separated from the past is precisely the means by which Johnson is made to participate in the demands of a ruling hypothesis, namely, by double predication or doctrinal analogy. In short, these critics simply focus on terms or doctrines that, when considered in isolation, appear clearly to signalize Johnson's association with views and categories distinctly nonneoclassical; they then proceed to find in subsequent critical documents terms or doctrines that, when divorced from the conceptual frameworks informing them with determinate significance, appear to run parallel to or to exhibit some positive correlation with those extracted from Johnson's writings. The overarching idea apparently is that Johnson rises in esteem as he advances toward our period. What we lose in the process, I think, is Johnson's specific contribution to literary criticism, the specific intellectual integrity of a kind of criticism that is permanently useful (as I attempt to demonstrate in section 2) to readers who are interested in the sorts of questions and problems with which Johnson was concerned and with which his assumptions and principles of reasoning were peculiarly equipped to deal. The enterprise of placing Johnson in this place or that—in this or that "ism"—is always successful and always fruitless, and it will remain so as long as critics are determined to ascertain Johnson's whereabouts by juxtaposing passages of "similar" doctrinal significance; as long as this system of distribution is in use, Johnson will continue to live restlessly, taking up residences at the command of successsive categorical instructions.

Further, in emphasizing isolated passages and doctrines, these critics, unintentionally but necessarily, bring back into prominence the Johnson of the *aperçu*, of the brilliant insight, the Johnson of sensibility who needs no system, the Johnson, at any rate, who is best understood in terms of general and reductive categories of thought. Returned to center stage is the great Cham who, by sheer force of personality, stands as a power to be reckoned with in spite of—indeed, perhaps because of—his massive contradictions and glaring inconsistencies. This Johnson is no system-monger, no retailer of systematic theories, but a man infinitely adjustable to various emergent occasions or, on the contrary (and even more damaging), a man who regularly adjusted various and complex emergent occasions to the dimensions of a severely limited set of categories.

That Johnson distrusted abstract schemes and theories, there can be no doubt, as there can be none about the fact that Johnson is sometimes inconsistent or that he at times disagrees with himself. But lest the persuasive power of articles and books in the dialectical mode and the demonstrable fact of real inconsistency or contradiction in Johnson's works overwhelm judgment, it is perhaps useful to remember that neither a distrust of abstract systems nor occasional inconsistency establishes sufficient grounds for supposing that Johnson was as a critic either unsystematic or incoherent. The absence of any lengthy and systematic theory of art in Johnson's writings obliges us, as Jean Hagstrum noted some years ago, to "make explicit what is implicit and to deduce theory from practice."[14] Additionally, if we hope to achieve some adequate understanding of Johnson's critical thought, we must first recognize and then attempt to demonstrate that Johnson was a man ready for all occasions primarily because, in general, he avoids "arbitrary decision and general exclamation . . . by asserting nothing without a reason and establishing all [his] principles of judgment on [what he takes to be] unalterable and evident truth."[15] Only when the a priori way has been abandoned will it be possible to put the Johnson of sensibility to rest and to initiate investigations that have a fair chance of offering something answerable to or commensurate with the richness and complexity of Johnson's critical thought.

For all its faults, however, the dialectical mode continues to be popular, and this is so primarily because it is easy to manipulate and persuasive in its effect. Its simplicity can be attributed to its restriction to antithetical categories. Its persuasive power is a consequence of the fact that it produces statements that are both *confirmable* and *nonfalsifiable*, in a manner of speaking. For example, all the views examined in section 1, though failing to satisfy rigorous standards of substantiation, provide for a kind of "confirmation," in that they all "demonstrate" that actual details in Johnsons's writings can be read in such a way as to participate in the kinds of meanings compatible with the terms of the ruling hypothesis. (It should be remembered, however, that confirmation is the easiest part of hypothesis-testing; it is never enough that a hypothesis can make some sense out of the facts of a text, for any hypothesis can do this in one way or another.) Similarly, none of the studies examined can be "falsified," inasmuch as every time the selected facts of Johnson's writing are examined in accordance with the imperatives of the sponsoring hypothesis, they will be capable of bearing the meanings of the hypothesis. Indeed, the facts confronted are subject to prior restraint. Since generally the facts have no functions in larger or smaller contexts independently of the hypothesis, the "facts" supporting the hypothesis are really facts *of* the hypothesis. Confirmable and nonfalsifiable though they may be, the views examined cannot meet the principal tests of adequacy, if only because, in addition to being circular and self referential, they are incapable of explaining why what is said should be said as it is said at any specific moment, or, on the other hand, of explaining what are the necessary and sufficient conditions, internal and external, of any particular exemplification of the preferred categories at a specific point in a particular text.

Such then are the common tendencies and qualities of the views scrutinized in the first three chapters. The fully orchestrated attack against the dialectical mode is presented in chapter 3, following the discussion of Krieger's essay. As the reader goes through the first section he should perhaps keep one caution in mind. At no point am I suggesting that critics cannot legitimately discuss Johnson's criticism in relation to our time or Coleridge's, or in relation to anything conceivable, for that matter. Throughout the first section I take quite seriously E. D. Hirsch's distinction between *textual meaning* and *textual significance,* between the changeless, self-identical meaning of the text and the *meaning-fulness* of the text, that is, "the changing contexts in which that meaning is applied."[16] My argument is not immediately with those who wish to consider the possible relations in which Johnson's writings may stand to other things (including society, history, psychology, etc.), but with the radical shortcomings of certain critical positions and methods that attempt to establish or enrich our understanding of Johnson's meaning and that assume that textual meaning is knowable, stable, and determinate. My arguments are directed only at certain kinds of efforts to identify that determinacy. What is ultimately at issue is the fundamental difference between explanations that are designed to satisfy minimum demands of demonstration and proof in particular matters of fact (those offered alternatively in the first section and systematically in the second section) and explanations that are not (those of the dialectical variety).

For the second section of the book, which is thoroughly positive or constructive, the reader requires little preparation. Nevertheless he should understand that the section moves deliberately and steadily from considerations of theory and principles of judgment to matters of practical interpretation and ends more or less where the book began, with Johnson's critique of *Lycidas*. This section begins with an attempt (in chapter 4) to establish the theoretical framework governing Johnson's criticism generally, then examines Johnson's conceptions of pastoral (chapter 5) and elegy (chapter 6) in relation to his coherent view of literature, and concludes with an analysis of the critique of *Lycidas* in relation to Johnson's criteria for excellence in pastoral elegy. The analysis of the critique comes last (as it must, since I am moving from theory to practice), but the reader should understand that my interest in the critique is subordinated to an interest in the body of principles and assumptions informing Johnson's critical thought. The critique of *Lycidas* is a special instance of the kind of judgment implicated in Johnson's principled conception of pastoral elegy, and Johnson's conceptions of pastoral and elegy are special reflections of his basic critical framework. For this section one caution is perhaps necessary. The reader should not assume that one of the aims of the analysis of Johnson's critique is to demonstrate that the final or best judgment of *Lycidas* was given almost two hundred years ago in the *Life of Milton*. At most I am attempting to show that, given Johnson's critical framework and his conception of the nature, value, and ends of art, the critique is sensible, defensible, respectable, and *inevitable*.

At the end of chapter 3 I attempt to bridge the sections with a brief discussion of the standards that an adequate working understanding of Johnson's theoretical framework would have to satisfy. An adequate hypothesis would be one that with maximal precision and economy accounted for the specific judgments that Johnson made on specific occasions in the process of dealing with specific issues or problems. The hypothesis would enable one to demonstrate both that Johnson's practical decisions follow of necessity from or are compatible with a determinate set of principles and assumptions, and that the textual material could be as it is only on the supposition of that set of principles and assumptions. Such a hypothesis would focus, not on the persistence of terms and doctrines (though it would be able to deal with and account for significant terminological or doctrinal repetition), but on the regular and flexible adaptation of basic principles and criteria of value to the demands of specific problems, the adequacy of the hypothesis being regularly tested against the details of the texts examined and against possible alternative conceptions of the same material.

At the opening of chapter 4 I distinguish between the critics examined in the first section and critics such as Hagstrum, Keast, Crane, Wimsatt, and Abrams, who have contributed substantially to our understanding of the systematic operations of Johnson's critical intelligence. Building on the positive accomplishments of my predecessors and keeping the standards defined at the end of the preceding chapter clearly in mind, I conclude the fourth chapter with what I take to be a reasonably adequate working formulation of the first-order critical priorities and assumptions governing Johnson's critical reasoning. Throughout this section attention is directed primarily to those papers and essays in which Johnson addresses himself to large questions of critical theory (*Ramblers* 37, 60, 156, 158, e.g., and the "Preface to Shakespeare").

Chapter 5, dealing with Johnson's conception of the pastoral, focuses on *Ramblers* 36 and 37, in which Johnson attempts to arrive at a "distinct and exact idea" of pastoral writing, advancing principles that, as he says, have their "foundation in the nature of things." Having shown that Johnson derives his principles "from reason and not from precedent," I conclude with an examination of his critical remarks on Virgil's contribution to pastoral in *Adventurer* 92 and on the history of pastoral composition in the "Life of Ambrose Philips."

In the concluding chapter the focus is on elegy, pastoral elegy, and, finally, *Lycidas*. Although Johnson wrote no extended essay on the elegy, I argue that we can arrive at an adequate understanding of his generalized working conception of the form by attending to those brief definitions and practical statements in his writings which both imply and are implied by Johnson's fundamental critical assumptions and his coherent view of literature. At any rate, it is from these brief definitions and practical comments on specific elegies that we must derive Johnson's conception of the special demands of elegy. From an examination of these we come to understand that what is central to elegy is the occasion and that what the occasion demands is the expression of rational praise and natural lamentation. The diversity of elegy, like that of biography, is relative to the character of the person praised. And to Johnson, fondness, pity, admiration, and a desire to emulate virtue should be the natural emotive consequences of full empathetic perception of the character of the deceased. Just before the critique of *Lycidas* is discussed (but with the critique in mind) I comment on diction, rhyme, and numbers in reference to Johnson's prosodic principles and on his notion of "easy" poetry, giving special attention to the word *harsh* in Johnson's criticism of poetry in the *Lives* and to his analysis of rhyme and numbers in the series of *Rambler* papers on Milton's poetry. Once the critique of *Lycidas* is placed within the context of the *Life of Milton* and the framework of Johnson's critical priorities, it can properly be understood, not as a monumental critical mistake occasioned by extraordinarily naive standards of sincerity, but as the ineluctable consequence of those principles and assumptions which early and late guided Johnson's judgment of particular works. In the end I argue that the critique is no less the natural offspring of Johnson's critical genius than the "Preface to Shakespeare," and both—to change metaphors—take us to the manor of principles to which Johnson came early and in which he stayed late.

In general terms I am saying throughout the book that without some reasonably adequate working understanding of the intellectual bases of Johnson's thought it is impossible to advance our knowledge of his positive and enduring contribution to criticism. What I am suggesting in practical terms is that the modern critic should approach Johnson's writings with the understanding that the meanings of particular remarks, however striking and interesting considered independently of or in relation to statements made elsewhere (by Johnson or others), are most immediately relative to the specific questions and problems with which Johnson is concerned and to the critical framework within which he habitually works. His persistent interest in certain questions and problems reflects the durability in his thought of certain primary assumptions about the nature, value, and ends of art. Johnson's judgment of literary works emerges from prior considerations of the nature of artistic selectivity, the general features of human life (to which everything that aspires to please must be accommodated), and the general conditions of pleasure in truth and novelty or variety, and his reasoning always proceeds from some identifiable empirical effect to artistic cause, the general end of critical discussion being to learn something about the capacities of man, about how far man may extend his designs in his endeavors to make life more endurable or more enjoyable.

I noted earlier that on the positive side the two sections of this book were linked in part by common topics or issues. The most obvious link of this sort is the critique of *Lycidas;* the first and last two chapters give special prominence to Johnson's review of the poem. Indeed, the essays by Sigworth and Fussell were chosen in part because of their focus on the critique and its relation to Johnson's critical priorities. In addition to displaying different aspects of a particular kind of reasoning, both deal at length with a piece of criticism that has for Johnsonians and others a peculiar appeal or attraction. It is, according to most critics, a "howler," an instance, in many eyes, of the triumph of prejudice over reason (common sense, good taste, or whatever); at the very least, it is a classic instance of naive standards of sincerity and a passing fair example of the genetic fallacy in its elemental state. It is, after all, the critical review that even Johnson's warmest admirers have rather shunned than greeted warmly. It is not easy to have the critique and respect for Johnson's critical acuity at one and the same time, it would seem. I have chosen to discuss the critique in relation to Johnson's fundamental critical principles precisely because it is such a challenging piece of criticism. Whatever else it may be, it can serve as a sort of acid test for any hypothesis affirming the essential coherence and integrity of Johnson's critical thought. It may be an anomaly, but I have never thought so. At any rate, the essays by Sigworth and Fussell provide an opportunity to deal at length with matters of theoretical and practical criticism (with theory, method, and explication), to reexamine the bases of Johnson's thought, and to determine whether the critique in relation to a determinate body of principles and assumptions is indeed anomalous. In the first two chapters, then, the reader will find several passages of locally efficient commentary that will be enlarged upon and related systematically to Johnson's primary critical assumptions in section 2.

Beyond the brief presentation of alternative readings of aspects of Johnson's critique in the first two chapters, there are throughout the first section of the book comments on a large number of issues of central importance to Johnson's critical thought and to his relation to past and future criticism. Since the major subject of the second section is the nature and integrity of Johnson's criticism, all the earlier discussions of particular critical matters, instigated by local interpretive exigencies, are useful to the purpose of the second section to the extent that they disclose aspects of Johnson's thought that are consonant with or capable of subsumption by the theoretical principles established later. Of particular relevance to section 2 are the discussions of "truth" and "nature" in the first three chapters, of "sincerity" in chapter 2, of the "rules" and the "unities" in chapters 1 and 3, of "genius" and "self-expression" in chapter 2, of the bases of the emotional response to art in chapter 3, and finally, of "love poetry" and "epistolary composition" in chapter 2. Each of these commentaries should contribute something to the reader's developing sense of the consistency, durability, and coherence of Johnson's conception of literature and something to the legitimacy and validity of the views expressed in section 2. When examined in relation to the second section, the local passages of interpretation resonate with larger significance. Essentially, the progression of the book is not so much additive in the arithmetic sense (1, 2, 3, 4, 5, etc.) as cumulative in the geometric sense (1, 2, 4, 8, 16, etc.); at least the reader should see that much of the positive commentary in the first section is there to support the position, fully articulated later, that, although Johnson wrote no lengthy and systematic treatise on art, he had nevertheless a systematic mind and worked from a stable body of critical assumptions.

Whatever the deficiencies or merits of this book, it will have satisfied its author if in some way it advances an understanding of Johnson's criticism as a powerful and enduringly useful instrument of inquiry and judgment.[17]

Rational Praise
and
Natural Lamentation

Johnson's Criticism:
From Apodictic Standards
to Standards of the Heart

Two recent discussions of Johnson's critique of *Lycidas*, for all their various and manifest differences, reach remarkably similar conclusions about some aspects of Johnson's criticism and find strikingly similar grounds for justifying an admiration either of Johnson's acuity or his prescience. In the first place, both writers affirm (what others have also noted) that Johnson is an empiricist. To Paul Fussell, "Any lingering superstition that Johnson can be meaningfully described as, in some way, a 'neo-classic' critic . . . will be evaporated by a close scrutiny of his remarks on *Lycidas*. . . . Johnson is not a neo-classicist but an empiricist."[1] And Oliver Sigworth is convinced that Johnson's criticism of *Lycidas* represents "a move from rationalism to empiricism, a move also from the apodictic standards of received Renaissance criticism to the standards of the heart."[2] Additionally, both writers, in documenting the empirical sensibility, attach crucial importance to Johnson's remarks on "sincerity," one seeing them as a call for "an expression of racking grief . . . an effusion of real passion . . . [a demand for] not just a manipulation of artistic form . . . but new matter, personal and sincere . . . ,"[3] the other as an indication of Johnson's sense that "literature is what happens when genuine self-expression occurs: it emanates from a motive which shuns the familiar in favor of the unique, the 'authentic.' "[4]

It would be possible to cite several other parallel passages that imply a conformity of opinion in the two critics, but such an exercise would deflect attention from the different purposes of the two essays and the different critical assumptions underlying the whole arguments from which the isolated passages were taken. As it happens, the two essays employ similar methods of reasoning but argue from different fundamental assumptions about the nature of Johnson's engagement with critical problems. In what follows I shall consider each essay separately, taking up Sigworth's essay in this chapter and Fussell's in the next, reserving comment on the common argumentative tendencies of both pieces until chapter 3.

For Sigworth, Johnson's review of *Lycidas* not only differs from the evaluation of pastoral in *Rambler* 36, but also signifies a turn to a new criterion of literary excellence and value; it is his demand, made late in life—"when he had lived much and suffered much, and forgotten nothing of his suffering"—for "new matter, personal and sincere" that makes Johnson, it seems, "a pivot in the transition from a Renaissance to a 'romantic'—a modern—point of view; modern criticism begins with Johnson."[5] Early in the essay, after suggesting, by implication at least, that there are discrepancies between *Rambler* 36 and the review of *Lycidas*, Sigworth asserts that his purpose is not to trace the evolution of Johnson's thought or the "evolution of his ideas on pastoral" (we are to take evolution for granted), but rather "to suggest, first, that by the time he came to look again at *Lycidas* he might have neglected to remember what the Renaissance pastoral really was, and, second, that the impulses behind such a neglect are worth scrutiny."[6] A close examination of Johnson's demand for the "effusion of real passion," as instigated by a lifetime of suffering, enables the reader to see that "Johnson was a man with a Renaissance education whose experience in life had forced him to doubt most of the literary precepts of that education . . . [and that] those fruitful tensions in his thought anticipate the literary ideas we now assume without examination: that literature should be the expression of 'life' and of the author's passion, that we can somehow look through the poem to the man."[7]

On the face of matters, Sigworth's essay would appear to provide the occasion for much celebration among students of Johnson. No longer is he a prop for the crumbling edifice of neoclassicism, the last great spokesman for Renaissance-Augustan standards in an age rapidly on the way to the "romantic" period but, indeed, a herald of the greatness to come, an instigator of the aesthetic revolution that came to ripeness in the early nineteenth century and from the fruits of which we are even today enjoying the salubrious benefits. What former critics, fond of Johnson, generally felt obliged to explain away as an embarrassing critical oddity, Johnson's extraordinarily naive emphasis on sincerity, is in fact precisely what secures our enduring admiration for him, for this emphasis represents a turning point in critical history. And if Sigworth's claim reaches no farther than the facts will allow, our understanding of critical history and of Johnson's role in that history will be greatly enhanced, but our enthusiasm for this new Johnson with the modern point of view will have to be moderated if conclusions too weighty are derived from evidence too insubstantial. It may be that in attributing so much to so little Sigworth misrepresents critical history and trivializes Johnson's place in it.

Sigworth clearly presupposes in the reader a functional understanding of both received Renaissance criticism and empiricism, but an understanding that must remain uncritical and satisfied with vague, undefined content. There are perhaps few today who would find anything particularly remarkable in the assertion that Johnson had an empirical cast of mind, in the sense that he tested report and doctrine against experience, his own and that of others, and attempted to regulate imagination by reality, attending, additionally, to "facts" as recorded in documents, exhibited in conversation, or clearly implicated in artifacts and behavior. But *empiricism* is a large umbrella, under which a rich diversity of intellectual principles and critical premises may take shelter. Separated from a consideration of the particular questions a writer attempts to answer, the assumptions he makes about the subject matters he investigates, the ends his arguments serve, and the system of inference he regularly employs in the solution of particular problems, *empiricism* is little more than a broad, general category, providing in itself no means of discriminating among fundamentally different kinds of criticism or analysis.

Even if we were to accept the term in its broadest signification, however, in what sense is Johnson's *empiricism* meaningfully related to the intellectual bases of the writings of Blake, Wordsworth, Coleridge, Shelley, to, that is, the "romantic," modern point of view? How does Johnson's empiricism serve as the pivot in the turn from received Renaissance criticism to romanticism (another term that we are asked to accept in a general, undefined sense)? Should we begin to think of the major critical documents of the "Romantic" period as monuments of empiricism? Apparently for Sigworth a demand for the "effusion of real passion" can be considered a nexus uniting Johnson with all that follows in critical history; it is this demand that clearly signals the move from the apodictic standards of received Renaissance criticism to the standards of the heart, that informs us that Johnson "argues his critical appeal in modern terms, for what he demands from literature in this respect is exactly what we demand from it, and most exactly what Renaissance, that is neo-classic, criticism generally did not demand."[8]

I submit that *standards of the heart* stands in very uncertain opposition to neoclassic criticism and in equally uncertain relation to "empiricism," "romanticism," and "modern demands." The reader, of course, would look long and hard before he found a critic whom history had consigned to neoclassicism making an appeal to standards of the heart, but the persuasive force of this phrase is somewhat abated when we recognize that it is not Johnson's, but Sigworth's. (Johnson would undoubtedly prefer a discussion of emotions in terms of the uniform and universal principles of the human mind, since for Johnson—and many of his "neoclassical" contemporaries—emotions, though triggered by infinitely various local circumstances and thus widely diversified in both form and intensity, reflected the stable and knowable operations of our common intellectual nature).[9] As Sigworth's account unfolds, the reader begins to suspect, I think, that the buckling of Johnson to "romanticism" depends very heavily upon the positive (but unexpressed) correlation of *effusion of real passion* and that celebrated phrase, which only a kind regard for the genius of posterity prevented Johnson from bringing to full, if premature, articulation, namely, that all good poetry involves "the spontaneous overflow of powerful feelings." Johnson would seem, then, to be on the verge of great but, from the perspective of history, untimely utterance.

In fairness to Sigworth, it should be noted that he brings us to standards of the heart only after recalling Johnson's handling of the unities in the "Preface to Shakespeare" and of the "Great Chain of Being" in the review of Soame Jenyns's *Free Enquiry into the Nature and Origin of Evil.* According to Sigworth, Johnson "demolishes the unities by making his appeal to 'nature,' in this case to the theatrical experience of any sensible man, forgetting the literary form as an abstract artistic construct . . ." and bases his refutation of Jenyns's views "ultimately upon . . . [his] 'surveys of life.' "[10] Notice, however, that being fair to Sigworth's argument unwittingly discloses a flaw in his primary thesis, for if the demand for real passion can be subsumed under the class of critical values contained in the attacks against the unities and the Great Chain, then the distinctiveness of the critique of *Lycidas* must be abandoned. Johnson's review of *Lycidas* does not signal the "end of Renaissance Criticism" if it is grounded in priorities intellectually consonant with those expressed in 1757 ("Review" of *Free Enquiry*) and 1765 ("Preface to Shakespeare"). Novelty succumbs to consistency; the new is congruent with the old. The response to *Lycidas* exhibits a form of critical redundancy, for it merely gives locally efficient and appropriate expression to a persistent principle. In short, the object, not the basis, of critical judgment has changed in the movement from the unities to *Lycidas*. The remarks on *Lycidas* become simply one more example of Johnson's habitual (or at least regular) appeal to the standards of the heart.

But this revision, this recognition of consistency, undermines the validity of Sigworth's secondary thesis, offered as incidental speculation in the last four pages of the article but actually occasioned by the argumentative imperatives of the first part of the essay, namely, that Johnson's unequivocal request for genuine passion is a natural consequence of a lifetime of suffering. Recourse to biography here is perhaps partially justified by the detection of a breakdown or a breakthrough in Johnsonian poetics: by the impossibility of accounting for what is taken to be new in Johnson's criticism in terms of antecedent judgments or of those poetic principles which have governed past critical practice. However, the novelty attributed to the critique of *Lycidas* and absolutely essential to the biographical conjecture is not, as we have seen, consistently maintained by Sigworth. An explanatory hypothesis originating in biographical details can be employed, of course, at any time in a polemical discourse, but it is a peculiarly serviceable resource whenever the critic detects something anomalous, new, or discontinuous in the works of a writer. For Sigworth the critique of *Lycidas* apparently is curiously allied to but also somewhat distinct from antecedent judgments.

Moreover, the native charm of the biographical explanation of Johnson's demand is undercut by intrinsic weaknesses. That Johnson suffered is unquestionably true; that in the *Life of Milton* he stated that *Lycidas* is not to be considered an effusion of real passion is also undeniably true. But when the first fact is juxtaposed to the second fact, the first does not necessarily become the cause of or the motive for the second. Personal suffering is neither a necessary nor a sufficient precondition of the demand for real passion. Juxtaposition insures contiguity, but it does not establish causation. Moreover, if personal suffering were the necessary or probable condition of a call for passion in literature, one wonders why a man like Johnson—painfully aware of human existence as a state in which much is to be endured and little to be enjoyed, a state furthermore radically conditional and of uncertain duration—did not make such a demand earlier, at least by 1755, when he had experienced and suffered much and "most of those whom [he had] wished to please [had] sunk into the grave."[11] Perhaps he could have, but the crucial passage in the *Life of Milton*, on the novelty of which much of Sigworth's argument depends, was not yet written.[12]

Sigworth's ancillary hypothesis is not to be denied its appeal, for clearly it gives us not the Great Bear, the forbidding, arrogant, aggressive, petulant dictator, but an approachable sufferer, who at the end of his life exemplified in his critique what he had come to demand from literature: Johnson's review of *Lycidas* is a cry, personal and sincere, for a Miltonian cry, personal and sincere. On the other hand, what we are given does not compensate us for our loss, for the tendency of Sigworth's explanation is to emphasize Johnson's sensibility and to drive from the field of active contemplation that Johnson who asserted that it is

the task of criticism to establish principles; to improve opinion into knowledge; and to distinguish those means of pleasing which depend upon known causes and rational deduction, from the nameless and inexplicable elegancies which appeal wholly to the fancy. . . . Criticism reduces those regions of literature under the dominion of science, which have hitherto known only the anarchy of ignorance, the caprices of fancy, and the tyranny of prescription;[13]

who informed us that Dryden

> may be properly considered as the father of English criticism, as
> the writer who first taught us to determine upon principles the
> merit of composition;[14]

who wrote in the final *Rambler:*

> Arbitrary decision and general exclamation I have carefully
> avoided, by asserting nothing without a reason, and establishing
> all my principles of judgment on unalterable and evident truth;[15]

who, referring to *Reflexion* vii, asserted:

> Boileau justly remarks, that the books which have stood the test
> of time, and been admired through all the changes which the
> mind of man has suffered from the various revolutions of knowl-
> edge, and the prevalence of contrary customs, have a better
> claim to our regard than any modern can boast, because the long
> continuance of their reputation proves that they are adequate to
> our faculties, and agreeable to nature;[16]

and who, early in the *Journey to the Western Islands of Scotland,*
wrote:

> It is true that of far the greater part of things, we must content
> ourselves with such knowledge as description may exhibit, or
> analogy supply; but it is true likewise, that these ideas are
> always incomplete, and that at least, till we have compared them
> with realities, we do not know them to be just. As we see more,
> we become possessed of more certainties, and consequently
> gain more principles of reasoning, and found a wider basis of
> analogy.[17]

This list of quotations could, of course, be greatly extended, but the
point is that, taken together, these (and other) statements incite us
to consider Johnson's critical pronouncements in terms of critical
principles and a reasoned understanding of the nature of literature
and of pleasure (whether deriving from literature or life), not in
terms of biography.

Of course, a critic might still argue that, persistent professions of
allegiance to principles of reasoning notwithstanding, Johnson was

ignorant of the "real" basis of his demand for something new in literature, but before acceding to that explanation the skeptical reader might reasonably request what Sigworth consistently fails to supply, namely, a careful examination of the precise means by which Johnson disassociates himself from neoclassicism and attaches himself to a romantic, a modern point of view, and a detailed account of the nature of Johnson's particular kind of empiricism. Sigworth fails, however, to show how or to indicate whether the remarks on the unities, the Chain of Being, or *Lycidas* are to be subordinated to any specific set of primary precepts, assumptions, or intellectual priorities. Are the various critical judgments logically implicated in a determinate and knowable theoretical or intellectual framework, distinguishable by some term more refined than *empiricism?* When Johnson says that in *Lycidas* "there is no art, for there is nothing new," can we legitimately assume that "what for Johnson constituted 'art' at this time of his life was something 'new' in what certainly appears to be our sense of the term . . ."?[18] Is Johnson the first, foremost, most prominent critical empiricist (at least one of the first empiricists), or the critic who most regularly asked poetry to accord with nature as it was experienced by the generality of mankind? Would most so-called neoclassic critics be inclined to praise a poetic passage describing or expressing human emotion that did *not* accord with human nature, with what every sensible reader would recognize as being adequate, under given circumstances, to either the speaker or the occasion? Lacking any careful delineation of Johnson's peculiar relationship to literary history or to a distinguishable form of empiricism, the Johnsonian must find comfort in a Johnson who, at the end of his life, turned to real passion and aligned himself with the interests of the future as a result of his suffering, the turn amounting finally to a kind of emotional reflex action. If the critique can be discussed in terms of critical principles, why must we resort to biographical material that begs more questions than it resolves? And if the critique is related to the appeal of nature ("Preface") and to "surveys of life" (Review of Jenyns), why should we give any particular preeminence to the critique of *Lycidas* or accept the suggestion that it is a historical marker announcing "the end of Renaissance criticism in England." Finally, if in the critique Johnson demolishes one aspect of Renaissance criticism, as he demolishes other aspects in the "Preface" and the review of Jenyns, and if he carries on this demolition work by referring steadily to "new" standards of the heart, then where amidst this persistence can we locate his inconsistency? Our confidence that at the end of his life Johnson severed all ties with the tradition with which he was formerly associated must apparently be founded on no more secure a basis than the silent concatenation of real passion—standards of the heart—romantic (modern) point of view.

Sigworth, of course, does not explicitly deny to Johnson's criticism a theoretical foundation or to Johnson a principled understanding of literary effects, but he never invites us to consider the relationship of the critique to any relatively stable body of principles or assumptions underlying his criticism and hence determining the specific content of his practical critical pronouncements. Nor are we made to understand how complete and thoroughgoing was Johnson's rejection of what is "conventionally" placed under the rubric of neoclassicism; nor are we specifically enjoined to look upon the review of *Lycidas* as but one of the many instances in which Johnson differentiates himself from his critical predecessors, thus highlighting another significant moment in the process of rotating toward a Romantic viewpoint. Such efforts are perhaps beyond the scope of Sigworth's interests; in their absence, however, we are obliged to accept the call for passion as something both fundamentally new and generally persistent in Johnson's criticism, to give inordinate importance to one specific segment of one isolated passage in one particular biography, to grant the essential romanticism of the call, and to attribute its late occurrence, at least tentatively, to remembrance of protracted suffering.

Although Sigworth begins by asserting that he is interested in supplementing the efforts of Warren Fleischauer (who, in "Johnson, *Lycidas*, and the Norms of Criticism,"[19] emphasizes the principled basis of Johnson's critique), he ends by directing attention to sensibility rather than to principle, buttressing his "philosophical" case throughout with references to neoclassicism, romanticism, and empiricism, vague, general terms that we are to accept as largely self-defining. Yet, to take up just one of these terms, to what conception of neoclassicism must we appeal or from what neoclassical critics and works do we understand Johnson to be turning, if we assume that his critique is a pivot in the transition from a Renaissance to a romantic point of view? The truth is that the reader, looking beyond the chestnuts accumulated in a survey course, can find virtually no single English critic among Johnson's predecessors who supports wholeheartedly the severely restricted form of "neoclassicism" on which Sigworth, who nowhere explains exactly what he means by the term, seems to rely. Wherever we look, the neoclassical beast is elsewhere. He is not residing in Addison's "Pleasures of the Imagination" papers (1712), in Pope's "Preface to the *Iliad*" (1720), in Hume's "Of Tragedy" (1757) and "Of the Standard of Taste" (1757), in Hutcheson's *Inquiry into the Origin of Our Ideas of Beauty and Virtue* (1725), in Shaftesbury's *Characteristics* (1711), in Burke's *Philosophical Enquiry* (1759), in Gerard's *Essay on Taste* (1759), Kames's *Elements of Criticism* (1762), Hogarth's *Analysis of Beauty* (1753), to name a few works of critical and "historical" importance. Also it is clear that, to change metaphors, Dryden is not a regular and completely dependable celebrant of the "neoclassical" ritual; Pope practices only occasional conformity.

Moreover, in the large and steadily increasing number of modern studies of eighteenth-century aesthetics, we find little support for the view that Johnson occupies a pivotal position in the history of taste. For example, in his penetrating study of empirico-sensationist critical theories *(The Beautiful, the Sublime, and the Picturesque)*, Hipple analyzes the formal imperatives implicated in a wide variety of distinctly non-"neoclassical," eighteenth-century writings,[20] and Robert Marsh, to cite only one other critic, has offered a comparable study of "dialectical" theories of poetry in the eighteenth century.[21] (As Marsh suggests, the reader interested in discovering Coleridgean principles of aesthetic reasoning in the eighteenth century would be better advised to look to Hutcheson, Akenside, Harris, and Hartley than to Johnson.) In the aggregate the labor of criticism and scholarship in our century has made all of us uncomfortable with any casual use of neoclassicism as a term of definition, for, as a recent analyst of Dryden's criticism understatedly remarks, "The variety of meanings given to 'neoclassicism' can be exceedingly confusing."[22] In short, the term no longer automatically stimulates in us any very clear, distinct, or stable set of ideas, norms, or standards that can be fruitfully employed in distinguishing a kind of criticism to which a significant number of eighteenth-century writiers steadfastly adhered. Deviation from, not unwavering adherence to, a rigid neoclassical orthodoxy (however defined) is the rule in English criticism from Dryden to Johnson.[23]

No one familiar with the critical output of the Restoration and eighteenth century and with modern discussions of that output would have much difficulty (after adopting Sigworth's method of reasoning) in transferring to, say, Dryden, Addison, Hume, Burke, Hutcheson, or Akenside the critical distinction that Sigworth is willing to attribute to Johnson—modernity. Indeed, the procedure by which one demonstrates that some or many critics were attempting to liberate themselves from the chains of neoclassical orthodoxy is now painfully familiar. One simply abstracts from the writings of selected critics statements or doctrines that on the face of matters cannot be accommodated to the dimensions of neoclassicism as one defines it.[24] To demonstrate an attachment to the future, one simply defines *romanticism* or *modernity* in such a way as to be capable of including the opinions or doctrines that one has abstracted from selected eighteenth-century texts. Nevertheless, my remarks should not be interpreted as an invitation to students of the period to do unto Dryden or Addison what Sigworth has done to Johnson, an invitation, that is, to relocate the pivotal point in the transition from apodictic standards to a romantic—modern—point of view. On the contrary, one of the chief purposes of this chapter is to demonstrate that neither Johnson's nor any other critic's contribution to criticism or place in critical history can be established by means of the system of inference adopted by Sigworth.

Apparently underlying much of Sigworth's argument are the related assumptions that critical history unfolds in accordance with some principle of entelechy; that the richness of Johnson's criticism must be understood, if it is to be respected and respectable, in terms of its fulfillment in the nineteenth century; that, teleologically considered, the mid-eighteenth century has value in proportion to its purposeful commitment to full realization in the future; and that critics (in this case Johnson) deserve admiration or obloquy as they advance or retard progress toward romanticism. Now, if we reason from assumptions such as these to the procedures of argument necessary to their substantiation, we find that the space between belief and proof is most easily abridged by noting parallel passages that immediately convey doctrinal similarity or difference.

The citation of parallel passages for the purpose of indicating correspondence or disparity of opinion is a common device of critical argumentation, but the more consistently and exclusively it is used, the less conclusive are the conclusions that it yields (it accumulates evidence with more facility than it establishes proofs), because it is a device peculiarly suited to the task of finding what needs to be found, and because the reader persistently suspects (rightly, more often than not) that the meanings that run parallel reflect exigencies of a sponsoring hypothesis, not the "intentions" of the works from which the "parallel" passages are extracted. By this procedure, of course, every critic can be made to disagree with himself and to concur with everyone or anyone else; isolated statements achieve meanings independently of the contexts (large and small) in which they were made to function. Meaning of statement is thus relative to an interpreter's thesis, not to the determinate purpose of the argument in which the statement appears.

The peculiar rhetorical weakness (as distinct from intellectual weakness) of this system of inference, of course, is that it allows those who reject the conclusions that it produces (and that govern the hunt for and selection of evidence) the easiest of intellectual victories, the citation of additional parallels that serve, presumptively, to support contradictory or conflicting conclusions. More important, the procedure assumes that substantial uniformity or disparity of opinion can be determined by the congruent or divergent content of isolated passages of criticism. Similarity or disparity is established without considering the intellectual bases or the specific purposes of the arguments of which the passages are constituent parts.[25] Of course, it is frequently the case that genuine, radical differences in distinct essays are obscured by terminological or propositional similarities. The limits of meaning tolerated by statements are determined, not by the possible lexical meanings of the words constituting the statements, or by the meanings the statements will support when considered independently, but by the whole meanings in relation to which the statements function as determinate parts and from which they, of course, derive their functions.

If it had formerly been fashionable for students of Johnson to identify Johnsonian pasages that squared with selected aspects of a previously defined neoclassicism, it now seems to be the fashion to find in Johnson's criticism adumbrations of romantic doctrine.[26] Sigworth depends upon the method outlined above, but in general he leaves it to the reader to find the correspondences between Johnson's remarks and those of romantic-modern critics or, with regard to Johnson's refutation or rejection of Renaissance criticism, allows the reader to extrapolate from his suggestions the detailed nature of Johnson's break with the past; the parallels and contrasts, though generally implicit, are nevertheless central to the substantiation of his case.

At this point it might be useful to look closely at how Sigworth goes about differentiating Johnson from his neoclassical forebears. He says, for example, that Johnson "demolishes the unities by making his appeal to 'nature,' in this case to the theatrical experience of any sensible man, forgetting the literary form as an abstract artistic construct, and referring it rather to our knowledge of life."[27] In the first place, Johnson is not, of course, the first to challenge the unities; he had been anticipated by Nicholas Rowe, Farquhar, and others. Second, Johnson most definitely does not forget the abstract, artistic construct; indeed, tragedy could produce no pleasure, according to Johnson, if the spectator forgot that he was watching an abstract artistic construct, that is, a play. "It is false, that any representation is mistaken for reality; that any dramatick fable *in its materiality* was ever credible, or, for a single moment, was ever credited."[28] Later in the "Preface to Shakespeare," Johnson says: "It will be asked, how the drama moves, if it is not credited. It is credited with all the credit due to a drama. It is credited *whenever it moves*, as a just picture of a real original. . . ." For Johnson, "Imitations produce pain or pleasure, not because they are mistaken for realities, but because they bring realities to mind" ("Preface"). And "The delight of tragedy proceeds from our consciousness of fiction . . ." ("Preface"). Johnson certainly refers to life (the source, end, and test of art), but the reference presupposes a persistent distinction between the realities brought to mind and the *fable in its materiality*, between what is possible or probable in human life and the abstract, artistic construct, consciousness of fiction being a necessary condition of the pleasure we derive from the representation of painful realities. To forget the abstract, artistic construct would be to set the stage of the mind for a representation that would provoke either unendurable pain or uncontrollable laughter, for that which we could not humanly tolerate (as, say, in the case of *Lear*) or could not possibly credit (except in the case of the most rigorously "correct" drama).

Absolutely essential to Johnson's discussion of the unities is the determination of what the mind is ready and willing to suppose about the *materiality of fiction*, passages of time and changes of location being part of the materiality for which the imagination of the playgoer can make suitable and necessary mental accommodations. Johnson does not exactly say, as Hume does in explaining the "conversion" principle in the essay "Of Tragedy," that the pleasure we derive from representations of painful events depends primarily upon our awareness of the artistic manipulation of diction, verse, metaphor, and so on, but, as does Hume, he emphasizes that in the relationship between pleasure and awareness of fictional construct, the latter is an integral component of the former, is a prior condition of the former. If actors and spectators are always in their senses, as Johnson firmly believes, then they must be persistently aware, at some level of consciousness, of the distinction between representation and life.[29] Clearly, what is new in Johnson's excursus on the unities is not the appeal to nature or to the theatrical experience of any sensible man, but the fundamental distinction he makes between "material" aspects of representation and the emotional realities ("those pains and pleasures" which we recognize "as once our own" or consider "as naturally incident to our state of life")[30] that representations bring to mind.

To extend and refine our notions of what the imagination of the spectator may properly suppose, Johnson must first make clear what can and cannot be credited in drama; at stake in his discussion of the unities issue are the bases of credibility in dramatic imitations. Most previous writers, who also—it should be noted—made their appeal to *nature*, assumed that no sensible man could reasonably be expected to believe that within three hours days could elapse and continents be traversed. The unities of time and place were endorsed because they guaranteed or insured the credibility of the dramatic representation, and in defending them the critics *made their appeal to human nature, to the theatrical experi-ence of any sensible man;* no sensible man could reasonably be asked to believe that the same place could stand in one act for Alexandria and for Rome in the next, or that a young prince could become an old king in the time it took to watch a play. To be truly a mirror of life, drama must of necessity avoid anything that the widest reaches of credulity could not conceivably credit in life. Unquestionably, the assumptions on which many defenses of the unities were based are naive and, in general, psychologically unsophisticated, but Johnson simply does not differentiate himself from his predecessors by making his appeal to nature, to the theatrical experience of any man.

And what is true of the unities is true likewise of many other "neoclassical" matters. For example, rules concerning propriety, decorum, poetic justice, and so on, had their final authority, at least theoretically, in the nature of man, and even though venera-tion of the "ancients" was widespread (which is not to say uni-versal), that veneration was generally buttressed by a confident belief in the conformity of revered practices to the requirements of art and the real nature of man; the practices were tested against lived experience and received notions (philosophical, practical, and commonsensical) about the mind of man, which was generally assumed to be essentially the same in all places and in all ages. With regard to the source and authority of the natural principles on which the rules of art are founded, if we ask whether they were "to be sought . . . directly in the mind as known by common observa-tion or philosophy, or indirectly through study of the great works of art which owed their permanent appeal to conformity with them," we find that "there were few, if any, writers on criticism from the beginning to the end of the [Restoration, eighteenth century] period who did not . . . think it essential to combine the two ap-proaches."[31] Johnson may yet be distinguished from other critics of the Restoration and eighteenth century, but the criteria of "nature" and "surveys of life," as handled by Sigworth, facilitate not at all the task of differentiation.

Early in the essay Sigworth uses the following quotation from Pope's "Discourse on Pastoral" to define what the "Renaissance considered the pastoral, as a kind of poetry, to be":

A Pastoral is an imitation of the action of a shepherd, or one considered under that character. The form of this imitation is dramatic, or narrative, or mix'd of both; the fable simple, the manners not too polite nor too rustic: The thoughts are plain, yet admit a little quickness and passion, but that short and flowing: The expression humble, yet as pure as the language will afford; neat, but not florid; easy, and yet lively. In short, the fable, manners, thoughts, and expressions, are full of the greatest simplicity in nature. . . .

If we would copy Nature, it may be useful to take this Idea along with us, that pastoral is an image of what they call the Golden Age. So that we are not to describe our shepherds as shepherds at this day really are, but as they may be conceiv'd then to have been; when the best of men follow'd the employment.[32]

This is the conception of pastoral from which Johnson presumably frees himself. Now, there is much in this definition to which Johnson takes exception, the remarks on the Golden age, for example, but instead of turning immediately to Johnson, let us look at how Sigworth uses the definition to separate Johnson from the Renaissance tradition. He says: "We note here the clichés of Renaissance criticism: 'Imitation,' 'fable,' 'manners, thoughts, and expressions' (the usual route of a Renaissance critic in approaching a poem), 'copy Nature,' 'Golden age.' There is nothing in this definition which Scaliger, Vida, Boileau, or indeed Horace would have found remarkable. Nor would Sidney, who in his brief discussion of the pastoral is concerned to prove that, as all Renaissance poetry was supposed to be, it also could be a vehicle for instruction. . . ."[33] From these remarks we are allowed, if not obliged, to infer that at least some part of Johnson's liberation from the restraints of Renaissance criticism is attributable to his terminological independence and, it would seem by implication, to his unwillingness to believe that pastoral poetry could also be a vehicle for instruction. The latter, if implied, needs no refutation here, for every reader has, I assume, a ready arsenal of quotations with which to explode the suggestion.

As for the terms, it should be obvious that if Renaissance criticism can be identified by the regularity of their occurrence, then Johnson everywhere betrays his affiliation, and nowhere so frequently as in the critical sections of the *Lives of the Poets*. Indeed, readers will have to look no further than the *Life of Milton* to find examples of their employment by Johnson. From Dryden to Thomas Twining, from Dennis to Richard Hurd, there is nothing about Restoration, eighteenth-century criticism so strikingly apparent as its steady reliance on a relatively stable critical vocabulary, from which Sigworth has selected for notice only some of the most frequently recurring terms. Critical vocabulary is in fact one of the distinguishing signs of the criticism of the period, and although no period in critical history can perhaps produce more evidence of diversity in critical approach than the eighteenth century, its critics (however different their critical assumptions, problems, emphases, and ends) shared, for the most part, an immediately identifiable lexicon of critical terms. Johnson cannot conveniently be distinguished from "Renaissance" critics on the basis of critical vocabulary. On the other hand, egregious mis-representation of critical productivity in this period would be the only result of taking this terminological compatibility as a clear indication of intellectual homogeneity. Just as apparent similar-ities or differences in doctrinal content do not establish a sufficient basis for determining whether two critics either agree or disagree with one another in any essential way, so the prevalence in various critical writings of the same discrete set of working terms does not preclude the use of that set for radically different aesthetic purposes, in support of fundamentally different critical approaches, reflecting disparate primary frames of reference, modes of analysis, and methods of argumentation. The recurrence of identical terms, indeed, often obscures crucial differences among eighteenth-century critical approaches.

In charting Johnson's break with the past, Sigworth repeatedly invites us to attend to Johnson's forgetfulness; with amazing regu-larity he punctuates his essay with references to lapses of memory in the writer whose "prodigious memory" had formerly struck the accomplished, inveterate cynic with astonishment. Early in the essay, we are told in cautious terms that when Johnson looked again at *Lycidas* he "might have *neglected to remember* what the Renaissance pastoral really was."[34] At the bottom of the same page, however, we are assertively informed that *Lycidas* was a "perfectly respectable adaptation" of the Renaissance pastoral elegy, "the respectability of which Johnson *had forgotten* when he complained that 'With these trifling fictions are mingled the most awful and sacred truths, such as ought never to be polluted with such irreverent combinations.' "[35] Later we are reminded that in expecting from *Lycidas* an effusion of real passion, Johnson "had allowed himself *to forget,* what he probably knew as a scholar no matter how little he sympathized with the view as a reader of poetry, that to effuse real passion was not the function of the Renaissance pastoral."[36] Finally, when Johnson says of Pope's juvenile "Pastorals" that the writer "evidently means rather to shew his literature than his wit," he is *"forgetting* that Pope himself had been rather proud of the fact . . . that such virtues as might be ascribed to his verses were to be attributed to his assiduous imitation of the ancient and Renaissance masters of the *form. . . ."*[37]

With respect to Johnson's forgetfulness concerning *Lycidas* (the first three instances of forgetfulness cited), it is perhaps sufficient to say at present that Johnson cannot legitimately be accused of forgetting what his criteria of literary evaluation do not invite him to "remember." Johnson, by theoretical or principled commitment, was not interested in *Lycidas* as a distinct kind of poem (as Sigworth says elsewhere), valued and valuable only to the extent that it meets a long list of specific genre requirements. A poem perfect in its kind (according to standards laid down by critical legislators or sanctioned by previous practice) may divert the "learned" for a while (just as the contemporary popularity of Addison's *Cato* may stand, allowing for its violation of poetic justice, as a monument to the inability of formula-bound literature to produce lasting pleasure), but as a candidate for literary fame, *Lycidas* must be judged according to the pleasure it is capable of evoking in readers both familiar with and ignorant of the historical development of the pastoral elegy—according, that is, to its capacity to satisfy the general conditions of pleasure, truth and novelty (or variety). Johnson does not forget what a Renaissance pastoral really was; he simply brings to his evaluation of *Lycidas* the critical standards that he generally applies to literature.[38]

As for Pope's "Pastorals," one legitimately wonders why Johnson should be obliged to remember, in a review, that Pope was proud of his imitations, as imitations. At any rate, it is clear that Johnson does not neglect to mention virtues that Pope would willingly have ascribed to his "Pastorals." Indeed, Johnson finds in them merits to which Pope had made no claim. The passage from which Sigworth quotes reads in full:

> To charge these Pastorals with want of invention, is to require what was never intended. The imitations are so ambitiously frequent, that the writer evidently means rather to shew his literature than his wit. It is surely sufficient for an author of sixteen not only to be able to copy the poems of antiquity with judicious selection, but to have obtained a sufficient power of language, and skill in metre, to exhibit a series of versification, which had in English *no precedent,* nor has since had an imitation.[39]

What Johnson says in the last sentence of this passage throws into relief, I think, one of the chief interpretive errors in Sigworth's major argument, an error that of necessity affects the value of the evidence appropriated to sustain that argument. Much of Sigworth's case depends upon the reader's acceptance of his explication of Johnson's remark that in *Lycidas* "there is no art, for there is nothing new." To Sigworth, the newness that Johnson is calling for here is "new matter, personal and sincere"; this remark tells us that Johnson wants from Milton an effusion of real passion. Now, I submit, alternatively and competitively, that we can best understand the point of Johnson's remark on *Lycidas* by recognizing that Johnson finds in Pope's "Pastorals" a *novelty* that the reader will look for in vain in *Lycidas,* that the novelty called for is located, not in emotion or passion, but in rhyme, meter, and diction (the components of versification), and that Johnson recalls us to the absence of real passion when he says that in *Lycidas* "there is no nature, for there is no truth." In *Lycidas* we find harsh diction, uncertain rhymes, and unpleasing numbers, whereas Pope's "Pastorals" disclose a power of language and skill in meter sufficient to exhibit a series of versification that had in English *no precedent.* If Johnson discovered no nature (and thus no truth) in Pope's "Pastorals" (which, "not professing to imitate real life, require no experience, and exhibiting only the simple operations of unmingled passions, admit no subtle reasoning or deep inquiry"), he nevertheless detected something new, at least in English, in the *art* with which the imitations were composed.[40] And if the demand for an effusion of real passion can be subordinated—as it can be—to Johnson's general call for natural truth, for expressions dictated by nature (and hence compatible with common human experience), then there is nothing new in the demand.

In directing us to Pope's "pastorals" Sigworth may have done himself an additional disservice. By way of cautious supposition, let us infer from what in the nature of passion Johnson did not expect to find in Pope's "pastorals" what sort of passion he might conceivably expect to find in poetry professing to imitate real life. To "enchain the heart by irresistable interest" (*Rambler* 60), the writer should at least communicate his sentiments in such a way as to promote the conception or excitation of "the pains and pleasures of other minds" *(Life of Cowley)*. And since real life is complex, emotional agitation (assumed or genuine) should exhibit something more than the simple operations of unmingled passions and, consequently, disclose in its expression the results of either subtle reasoning or deep inquiry. The effusion of real passion will thus be commensurate with general human experience (with what the general reader can readily suppose and, hence, credit) and adequate to the particular circumstances provoking it.

Using the above as a general working hypothesis, I am willing to suppose that what Johnson wants from *Lycidas* is a fine delineation of the ideas and feelings that the death of an honored and meritorious schoolfellow excites in the mind of a sensitive, deeply affected man, a delineation full of refined sentiment and personally distinguished by those particular associations of thought which the reader might easily imagine as possible or probable under the specified circumstances of friendship and irreparable loss. In short, Johnson, I think, allows extensive room for the expression of whatever is personal and sincere, but the writer must find the means in language by which the unique (or personally sincere) may be legitimately constituted within the possibilities of a "recognizable" type of experience (otherwise, nothing determinate is communicated), without at the same time sacrificing those peculiar nuances on which satisfactory or adequate delineation principally depends. Personal and sincere, yes; spontaneous, no. Sigworth's phrase, "new matter, personal and sincere," is perplexingly ambiguous enough to support a rich multiplicity of specific formulations of its precise meaning, but to the extent that "emotional spontaneity" can be enfolded within its ambiguity, it admits to legitimacy a conspicuously fallacious signification.[41]

One question perhaps begged by the preceding discussion is why Johnson brings to *Lycidas* expectations and standards that he is willing to forgo in his evaluation of Pope's "Pastorals," why, that is, he expects real passion from *Lycidas* and judges the poem according to its conformity to truth and nature. An immediate answer would seem to be that *Lycidas* provokes the application of Johnson's general criteria of literary excellence, because it is an elegy, indeed, a personal elegy (at least purportedly), a type of composition from which it is reasonable to expect some expression of fondness, some natural lamentation. As with the unities, we are here dealing with the issue of credibility, and to be credited as an elegy a poem must either express or excite emotion in a manner naturally consonant with its peculiar occasion; a poem that meets all the requirements that critical legislators, abstracting rules from the selective habits of previous writers, have deemed necessary to the perfection of pastoral elegy may result in a literary curiosity, but unless it reflects or generates feelings that can be recognized as naturally incident to its motivation, the reader contemplates the work in a state of frigid tranquillity. The "rules" for pastoral elegy, like the unities of time and place, are tolerable only to the extent that, as a consequence of their observance, they do not prevent or inhibit the poem from doing its proper work or achieving its proper effect. It is one of the marks of Johnson's critical genius that in spite of virtually comprehensive knowledge of "Renaissance" literary practice, he always asks whether the rules are right because they are established or established because they are right.[42] Johnson's standards of rightness may not be acceptable to every modern reader, but they are those to which he makes consistent appeal and on which his judgments are persistently grounded. Here as elsewhere, his criticism reflects his practice of separating the necessary from the accidental or adventitious.

More generally, Johnson subjected *Lycidas*, but not Pope's "Pastorals," to a "nice examination" because he felt that Milton's poem was praised beyond its worth, acquiring in time a value that, as far as Johnson was concerned, owed more to Milton's reputation for genius than to its intrinsic merits. The dangers involved in fostering by silence the perpetuation of unmerited esteem were, to

Johnson, manifold. Silence is a partisan of deceit when it is the effect of paying respect to the memory of the dead and the authority of a name and of suppressing the voice of truth and of disregarding the loud exclamations of experience. Also, in attempting, by his standards, to improve opinion into knowledge, Johnson prevents Milton's securely based greatness from being too fatally bound to the qualities of his lesser achievements, thus precluding the easy triumph possible to a critic who, in the absence of clearly defined principles or useful working distinctions, confounds the lesser with the greater. And in subjecting *Lycidas* to close scrutiny, Johnson reminds us, lest the impulse to emulate greatness be overwhelmed by blind admiration or corrupted by the fatal attractions of work of inferior quality, that Milton's genius, whatever the unparalleled heights to which it soared, was not always on the wing or always able to fly beyond the boundaries within which mere mortals work.[43] At any rate, it is clear that, however we read the tone of Johnson's remarks on Pope's "Pastorals," he is not "complaining" about the absence in them of new matter, personal and sincere, but articulating a rational and manly praise of the two bases of their literary worth: (1) as fine imitations of ancient (not Renaissance) masters, and (2) as examples of versification without a precedent in English.

Sigworth's abiding, but nevertheless vague sense of "real passion" regularly leads him into oversimplifications or distortions of Johnson's meaning. For example, in support of his contention that Johnson wanted "new, genuine, unfeigned passion" in poetry as early as the 1750's, he quotes the following from *Rambler* 36 and the review of Warton's *Essay on the Genius and Writings of Pope:*

> nor will a man, after the perusal of thousands of these [pastoral] performances, find his knowledge enlarged with a single view of nature not produced before, or his imagination amused with any new application of the views to moral purposes. (*Rambler* 36)

> with too much justice [Warton has remarked] that there is not a single new thought in the pastorals. (Review of *Essay*)

Interested as I am in the consistency of Johnson's views, I find it difficult to read these two passages, even with Sigworth's urgent prompting, as desiderative of "new, genuine, unfeigned passion" in pastoral poetry. When restored to their contexts, the passages are even less amenable to Sigworth's purposes than they are in isolation. The referent of "nature" in "single view of nature" is *physical,* external nature (i.e., trees, shrubs, rocks, etc.); although new views of physical nature are necessarily rare, still, "as each age makes some discoveries, and those discoveries are by degrees generally known, as new plants or modes of culture are introduced, and by little and little become common, pastoral might receive, from time to time, small augmentations, and exhibit once in a century a scene somewhat varied" (*Rambler* 36). As for the "application of those views to moral purposes" and, in the review of Warton's *Essay,* "a single new thought," Johnson would appear to be speaking of sentiments (as in "my sentiments exactly," as in "sentiments to which every bosom returns an echo"), not of sentiment (as in the man of sentiment, i.e., feeling).

Over and over again we are struck by flaws in the foundation on which Sigworth has chosen to erect Johnson's critical perspicacity. Even on the matter of sincerity, Johnson cannot easily be distinguished from his predecessors and contemporaries, if the testimony of passages containing similar doctrinal content can be trusted. According to Jean Hagstrum, Johnson nowhere more clearly reveals his attachment to his age and, implicitly, to a critical tradition than in his application to *Lycidas* of the doctrine of "sincerity." Hagstrum reminds us that

Fielding had done no more than utter a contemporary critical commonplace when he wrote: "The author who will make me weep, says Horace [*Ars Poetica* 11.102-3], must first weep himself. In reality, no man can paint a distress well, which he doth not feel while he is painting it; nor do I doubt, but that the most pathetic and affecting scenes have been writ in tears" [*Tom Jones,* bk. 9, chap. 1]. Dennis, the aesthetician of the passions, had drawn a most typical conclusion about the implications for language when he said that similes are not natural in the language of grief, since the mind, in producing them and other similar adornments, must exercise faculties "utterly inconsistent" with grief, a state in which the soul is confined and the imagination straitened [see E. N. Hooker, *Dennis's Criticism* 1.2]. For similar psychological reasons, Hume had found wit and passion "entirely incompatible" ["Of Simplicity and Refinement in Writing"].[43]

Of course, the doctrine can be traced back as far as "chapter 17" of Aristotle's *Poetics*.

Far from being a harbinger of the romantic period, Johnson is, it would seem, something of a stick-in-the-mud; we would be justified in concluding so, at least, if the presence of analagous doctrine in the writings of his contemporaries and forebears could force judgment.[45] But the evidence of analagous doctrine no more justifies our equating Johnson's criticism with that of Dennis, Hume, or Fielding than it obliges us to link it with that of Tolstoy, who speaks thus enthusiastically on the issue of sincerity:

> Sincerity, that is to say that the author should himself vividly feel what he expresses. Without this condition there can be no work of art, as the essence of art consists in the infection of the contemplator of a work by the author's feeling. If the author has not felt what he is expressing, the recipient cannot become infected by the author's feeling, and the production cannot be classified as a work of art.[46]

And it may well be, as Sigworth says, that "*Nature* and *passion* . . . did not mean to Johnson, nor do they mean to us, what they meant to Boileau when he translated Longinus or to Rymer, for both of whom the word [Sigworth does not indicate which of the two words he is referring to] had referred more to rhetoric than to human passions," but here as elsewhere he gives us distinctions without notifying us of differences. Sigworth goes on to assure us that appeals to nature and passion had been common enough in the criticism produced prior to the mid-eighteenth century, but "it was . . . in their changed semantic relations in the mid-eighteenth century that such traditional appeals turned interest away from instead of directing it toward the traditional forms."[47] Now, *changed semantic relations* is another frustratingly ambiguous phrase that functionally can be used to cover a multitude of sins or virtues, thus allowing Sigworth to mean more or less than he means to different readers. But by implying so much, the phrase tells us nothing very meaningful about the mid-eighteenth century. At best, *changed semantic relations* points to symptoms of change, without elucidating the nature of change. To get at the nature of change, Sigworth would have to examine in detail changes in critical emphases as they were governed by changes in critical subject matters, methods, and purposes. And such an examination would lead inevitably to the discrimination of a wide variety of discrete systems of critical thought in the mid-eighteenth century, systems in which the appearance of analogous doctrines in diverse critical essays would count for little in the enterprise of associating critics with one another (though doctrinal similarities and common tendencies of thought might certainly be noted and discussed).

The pertinence of *changed semantic relations* to Johnson would seem to be explained by the following: "Johnson, . . . just as we today, was not very interested in the 'kinds' of literature as such, and demanded that poetry accord with 'nature,' the accordance to be tested by 'my surveys of life.' "[48] Whatever may be the case today, it is certainly true that Johnson was not very much interested in the "kinds" of literature as such, but this lack of interest cannot serve to differentiate Johnson neatly from many pre-mid-century critics, as we have seen; nor can it discriminate Johnson's peculiar critical choices from those of many critics, who, like him, were not very interested in "kinds," but in such general qualities of art and nature as the beautiful, the sublime, the pathetic, and, additionally, in "an empirical, genetic, and usually associationist psychology [that sought] philosophic principles . . . in human nature [and grounded] philosophic method . . . in a mental atomism of elements and laws of combination,"[49] from all those, in short, who focused on the perceiving mind, not, as Coleridge would later, on the creative mind. Further, I am not sure that our understanding is much enlarged when we are informed that Johnson tested nature according to his surveys of life, since, separated from any precise specification of the nature and practical implications of such a test, "surveys of life" is a standard in search of a determinate meaning. In its general signification, however, this standard is virtually coextensive with critical thought. Previous arguments need not be repeated here, but to previous examples of appeals to nature might be added the testimony of Addison, who in 1711 assumed that the critic should make some reference to his surveys of life when he said that the arts "were to deduce their Laws and Rules from the general Sense and Taste of Mankind, and not from the Principles of those Arts themselves."[50] In sum, Sigworth's evidence simply is not calculated to enforce the conclusion that Johnson is a pivot in the transition from a Renaissance to a "romantic—a modern— point of view."[51]

This review of Sigworth's case can be brought to conclusion with a few brief comments on the penultimate sentence, the sentence that initiated discussion:

> Thus by perceiving that Johnson was a man with a Renaissance education whose experience in life had forced him to doubt most of the literary precepts of that education, we are able to see that those fruitful tensions in his thought anticipate the literary ideas we now assume without examination: that literature should be the expression of "life" and of the author's passion, that we can somehow look through the poem to the man.[52]

In the first place, Sigworth has devoted virtually no space to a discussion of fruitful tensions; his focus has been on event, not process, and he has been concerned not so much with tension as with tergiversation. We had been led to believe throughout the article that the fertility was not in the "tension" but in the rejection or abandonment of apodictic standards.

Second, I am at a loss to understand what revolution in critical thought is triggered by the notion that "literature should be the expression of life." I see in this no very exclusive standard; indeed, it is a flag that all sorts of critics and poets could heartily salute without fear of being vilified as disloyal reprobates, including Aristotle, Horace, Quintillian, Sidney, Robertello, Corneille, Dryden, Boileau, Bossu, Hume, Burke, Hurd, Shelley, and Arnold, and not excluding poets expressionist, impressionist, symbolist, naturalist, imagist, obscurantist, propagandist, occultist, or existentialist.

Finally, I can find very little in modern critical writing even inclining toward the view that today we regularly assume that literature should be the expression of the author's passion or that we can look through the poem to the man.[53] Is it reasonable to assume that the extraordinary richness and diversity of critical thought and literary practice from Johnson's day to our own can be comprehended under Sigworth's "common denominators"? Can critics from Coleridge to Eliot, Blackmur, Empson, Winters, Frye, and Bloom, or poets from Blake to Wallace Stevens, from Mac-

pherson to Ginsberg be best understood as so many advocates of
the artistic criteria cited by Sigworth? Can we conceivably hope to
find the modern correlatives of Johnson's demands, as Sigworth
formulates them, in the writings of critics who stress the importance in literature of paradox, ambiguity, logical structure and
irrelevant local texture, primal myth, mythic displacement,
metaphoric core, stylistic kernel, patterns of imagery, morphemic
iteration, Apophrades, and on and on? Can we not, in fact, more
confidently assert, with fewer fears of being immediately contra-
dicted, that readers today, with the possible exception of some few
phenomenological and psychological critics (with whom, even at
the farthest reaches of my temerity, I hesitate to associate Johnson)
generally do not look in literature for an expression of the author's
passion or assume that we can somehow look through the poem to
the man (few critics, at any rate, set out deliberately with such
purposes in mind)? Have those painstaking modern analyses of the
various means by which creative writers have successfully
removed the author from direct contemplation (of which Wayne
Booth's of narrative prose and Robert Langbaum's of poetry are
among the most notable) been only so many articles of deceit and
chicanery, designed to lead a somnolent public by cogent argument
and detailed documentation of claims away from the home truths
that are here restored to light? This series of self-answerable
questions could, of course, be greatly extended and, in extension,
enforce, of course, the same point—that Sigworth has not identified those literary ideas which we now assume without
examination.

Moreover, it should be recognized that even if what he says were
in some general sense true, we would still be left with a set of
assumptions that can in no way facilitate an appreciation or understanding of the literary and critical practice of writers from Johnson's day to the present; assumptions so general are practically
useless. Furthermore, they are not even assumptions of the first
order. Because of their inherent indefiniteness, they cannot serve
as the constitutive bases of any single coherent system of thought.
Any critic who attempted to use them as the bases of critical
reasoning in a sustained argument would necessarily be obliged to
restrict their range of allowable implications by concentrating on
selected aspects of their potentiality. As presented, the assump-

tions are capable of generating a wide diversity of different or contradictory criticisms, very few of which would be compatible with Johnson's critical position, and in differentiating these disparate criticisms from one another, we would be forced to direct attention to the additional (i.e., the refined, the truly generative) assumptions that make possible each criticism as a coherent, self-justifying system. Thus the Freudian and the, say, socialist critic, reasoning from the same general assumptions, would depend, in constructing their arguments, upon radically different primary assumptions about, for example, art, life, nature, passions—about, that is, all the key terms in the ideas assumed without examination. The point is that a rich plurality of disparate views is legitimately contained within the "constitutive" power of Sigworth's stated "assumptions." In the final analysis, however, the "literary ideas" noted are less assumptions capable of generating coherent views of literary product or process than isolated doctrines, doctrines divorced from the intellectual foundations that would inform them with determinate meaning and value.

Beginning with a putative instance of inconsistency in Johnson's views on pastoral (prerequisite to a discussion of the move from apodictic standards to a modern point of view, which in turn leads to the discussion of the biographical etiology of that transition), relying throughout on implied doctrinal differences or similarities to separate Johnson from past or to link him to future critical endeavor, and concluding with the citation of several doctrines that are patently neither modern nor Johnsonian, Sigworth has chosen, it seems to me, one of the means least likely to confer lasting honor on the critical acuity of Samuel Johnson (or of any other critic, for that matter). To have distinction on the terms specified and as a result of the method of argument adopted by Sigworth is to be forever subservient to the doctrinal preferences or prejudices of successive generations of critical historians.[54]

Johnson's Criticism: Stable Instability

At the opening of the first chapter, I noted certain doctrinal similarities in the writings of Sigworth and Fussell on Johnson's critique of *Lycidas*. In what follows, it should be clear that, doctrinal similarities notwithstanding, the two critics have different purposes in view, address fundamentally different problems, and proceed to "proofs" from basically different assumptions about literature and Johnson's criticism, though they rely on a common method of reasoning.

Fussell's discussion of the *Lycidas* review dominates the central section of a chapter entitled "The Facts of Writing and the Johnsonian Senses of Literature," in which we discover that Johnson's *two* senses of literature—as *self-expression* and as *rhetoric*—simply mirror prominent aspects of the major conflict intrinsic to the "facts of writing" and that Johnson erratically oscillates between the two antithetical senses of literature, making judgments as he inclines, unpredictably, to one or the other pole.

The theoretical base of the discussion of Johnson's senses of literature is found in the opening section of the chapter where, in response to the question "what constitutes literature," Fussell states:

> Simply this: the decision of an audience that a piece of writing is "literary." An act of what observers will consent to consider literature can take place only when an *individual talent* engages and, as it were, fills in the shape of a *pre-existing form* that a particular audience is willing to regard as belonging to the world of literature.[1]

A shorter and slightly refined version of the formula states that "the making of literature is a matter of the engagement of a *vulnerable self* with a fairly *rigid coded medium*. . . . The idea of the 'coded medium' is a modern way of conceiving of a relatively *fixed literary genre*."[2] These then are the basic "facts of writing." Once the crucial definition of "facts" is achieved, Fussell can proceed to discuss Johnson in the light of talent and medium: the definition serves as the stable foundation of subsequent binary operations. With his "facts" of writing established, Fussell directs his attention to Johnson, discovering, not very surprisingly, in his "acts" of writing the practical display of the "facts" as antecedently defined.

Just prior to his detailed discussion of Johnson's senses of literature, Fussell makes the following important remarks: "by scrutinizing his intercourse with genres we can thus recover, I think, something like an *orthodox literary sense* of the *relation* between a writer's *individual uniqueness* and the *objective sameness* that characterizes the world of genres. And as I focus from time to time on Johnson's way with genres, I am going to be suggesting that *his way is really the way of all writers*, despite their often colorful statements to the contrary."[3] With these comments Fussell carries to Johnson the distinctions and categories (in slightly transmuted form) previously "established" as essential to writing. As the essay unfolds, however, the reader comes to recognize that while it is held together by the persistence of dialectical terms having class affinities, its argument is, finally, incoherent, inconsistent, and confusing, since the individual talent and the rigid coded medium (upon the fusion of which—so the "theoretical" argument runs—all writing depends) become ultimately for Johnson the *antithetical* bases of demands for two distinct, radically different *kinds* of writing. Thus, although Johnson's *two* "senses of literature" (in Fussell's terms, his "rhetorical" and his "self-expressive" conceptions of writing) are "terminologically" compatible with Fussell's governing categories (i.e., coded medium and individual talent), they lead finally to appeals for incompatible, indeed contradictory literatures. In Fussell's words: "These, then, are the poles defining the Johnsonian senses of literature. On the one hand, *literature is* akin to legal argument and implies a similar objective process: a canvass of received formulations and devices which will work— that is persuade—because they are familiar. On the other hand, *literature is* what happens when genuine self-expression occurs: it emanates from a motive which shuns the familar in favor of the unique, the 'authentic.' "[4] What makes Johnson such a devilishly

perverse critic, of course, is his habit of asking a single work—
Lycidas, for example—to satisfy antithetical demands, to be both
one thing and another at the same time. Nevertheless, it is important to recognize at the outset that although Fussell consistently
grounds his explanations in a pair of primary categories, he ultimately creates a Johnson who fails to confirm the hypothesis about
writing for which his example was introduced.

Moreover, even if Fussell were to assert—which he nowhere
does—that Johnson is simply asking at one time for a literature
with more individual and less code and at another for one with less
individual and more code, the "theoretical" problems would remain unresolved, for in the absence of adequate or universally
accepted definitions of literary forms, we have no way of determining (again, by Fussell's standard) the critical legitimacy of Johnson's demands, especially the demand for self-expression.[5] In his
postulation of the facts of writing, Fussell has made no very precise
provisions for the more or less of the one or the other (and, of
course, absolutely no provision has been made for their independence); not only do we have no stable means of determining what
kinds and degrees of combination can be tolerated by the forces of
recognition, but we also have no means, finally, of distinguishing
talent from medium. What Fussell posits as the two fundamental
components of any piece of writing, Johnson transforms into the
grounds of two distinct kinds of literature; what Fussell has joined
together, Johnson has brought asunder, allowing a possibility (if we
accept as valid the assertion that for Johnson literature is what
happens when genuine self-expression occurs) that Fussell's theoretical scheme cannot accommodate. At any rate, nowhere in the
discussion of Johnson's two senses of literature does Fussell suggest that as a critic *Johnson* demands the happy *collocation* or
fusion of talent and medium. In Fussell's essay the illusion of
consistency is, at best, the accidental effect of terminological
persistency.

If "an *orthodox* literary sense of the relation between a writer's
individual uniqueness and the objective sameness that characterizes the world of genres" can be recovered by scrutinizing "Johnson's intercourse with genres," then Fussell should move directly
from analysis of the "facts" (the elemental rocks on which the
orthodoxy is founded) to an investigation of Johnson's writings,

but, complicating matters unnecessarily, he insists that "learning to read Johnson requires first a look at what literature seemed to him to be."[6] However, if the "facts" are indeed *facts,* a prior examination of what Johnson understood literature to be is clearly no necessary prerequisite to a discussion of the operation of those facts in Johnson's writings; such a look is critically superfluous, since corroboration of the hypothesized facts is in no way dependent upon establishing a positive correlation between Johnson's critical views and those of Fussell. The facts obtain whether Johnson, as a critic, happens to endorse them or not. In short, the "facts of writing" impose necessary limitations not on Johnson's critical principles and assumptions, but only on his existential dilemma as a man in the act of writing. Thus, unless in his critical pronouncements Johnson betrays an unmistakable intellectual affiliation with Fussell's hypothesis, there is no point whatsoever in looking at what literature seemed to him to be. The argument does not require this look; the look testifies to the fact that Fussell requires (and believes he finds in Johnson) a co-religionist. At best, however, Johnson is a heretic, an apostate, for, according to Fussell's account, he never seems to contemplate the possibility of any mystical union of the father (coded medium) and son (self-expression) of writing. Instead of disclosing the nature of the relation between individual uniqueness and the objective sameness characterizing the world of genres, Johnson switches allegiance from one to the other primary category erratically, now asserting that literature is characterized by objective sameness and now that it is characterized by self-expression.

Turning to an examination of the bases of Johnson's conceptions of writing, Fussell discovers that they originate in a "central contradiction that we would not be surprised to meet if we had not simplified him out of all recognition. This contradiction is one between the social sense that literature is a mere rhetorical artifice akin to legal advocacy, and the religious sense that for the literarily gifted the production of literature and the living of the life of writing are very like a Christian sacrament."[7] In other words, "This opposition is between a cunning knowingness and an almost unbelievable innocence." To understand Johnson's criticism without oversimplifying it, it is important to remember "that both are fully developed in Johnson and that both senses are likely to operate at almost the same time."[8] From this a priori, dialectical base (comprised of two sets of coordinate terms, with social sense, legal advocacy, and cunning knowingness on one side, and religious sense, Christian sacrament, and unbelievable innocence on the other), we are led by dialectical necessity (i.e., by analogical reasoning, the system of inference and method of "demonstration" available to dialectical argument) to Johnson's antithetical senses of literature, each sense an extension into criticism of one set of coordinates; hence, social sense is critically fulfilled in the conception of literature as rhetoric, necessary artifice, and the religious sense in the conception of writing as self-expression. It is between these polar conceptions of literature that Johnson oscillates; thus all particular critical remarks can be construed as locally efficient and locally appropriate deployments of terms compatible with and determined by one or the other governing conception. But if this much is granted, it is clear that we cannot move by any very easy transition from Johnson's polar antitheses to an understanding of the *relation* between individual uniqueness and generic sameness or to a confirmation of the view that literature is a matter of engaging the vulnerable self with a coded medium. What Fussell exhibits is a kind of terminological "cloning," one pair of primary terms producing another pair (and so on), with each pair not exactly identical to its forebear but sufficiently similar to establish unmistakable family resemblance, the whole system of inference supported, not by any regular concatenation of necessary propositions, any demonstration of necessary relation, but by means of analogical insinuation. In the end we must recognize that the polar senses of literature attributed to Johnson offer no independent testimony to the validity of Fussell's hypothesis concerning the facts of writing and that Johnson's relation to Fussell's orthodoxy is not that of an exegete (or a paraclete), but that of an excommunicant.

Having discussed the argument in terms of its primary dialectical terms and its system of inference, I shall now examine Fussell's grounds for assigning conflicting, contradictory senses of literature to Johnson and for contending that in the critique of *Lycidas* (and elsewhere) both senses are in operation. In dealing with these matters I shall be more frequently interested in demonstrating that Fussell has not established necessary or sufficient

justifications for his assertions than in developing a fully articulated alternative account of the matters under discussion, focusing here on the unreliability of the evidence on which Fussell's case
is based and reserving for later a presentation, in my own terms, of
an alternative approach to the principles governing Johnson's critical judgment, especially of *Lycidas*.[9] Further, in order to confine
this section to manageable limits, I shall concentrate on a select
few (but salient) items of evidence in Fussell's case, a procedure
justified by the twin facts that Fussell's argument is not progres-
sive, with one assertion following naturally from its predecessor
and leading naturally to its successor, and that a few examples
exhaust the *kinds* of evidence to be found in the "argument."

In the first place, it should be evident to every reader that the two
senses of literature attributed to Johnson are not constitutive principles of critical thought to which we can consistently appeal
whenever we wish to understand the radical significance of or the
underlying bases of Johnson's various critical remarks, or from
which, after the fact of a given statement, we can reason to the
necessity of the statement, demonstrating that it is contained
within one of the senses as a legitimate implication. Indeed, we can
go further and say that we never encounter in Johnson's criticism
anything approaching an exclusive demand either for mere rhetorical artifice or for genuine self-expression; neither demand makes
any provision, in and of itself, for (at the very least) that "pleasing
instruction" which has its foundation in truth; both demands, if
allowable at all must be subordinated to and understood as significant in relation to more radical principles respecting, among other
things, subject matters, ends, conditions of pleasure. Mere artifice
divorced from truth, or novelty, does not necessarily satisfy the
conditions of pleasure or owe any allegiance to the nature of things
or the known (or knowable) operations of the human mind; genuine
self-expression, unless adjusted to linguistic conventions that
allow the reader to recognize what is expressed as coextensive with
rational existence under certain conditions, has no independent
value and cannot evoke response commensurate with the occasion
or circumstances provoking expression. Further, allowing the
categories the widest latitude of implication, we are, I think,
unable to find the means by which such characteristic remarks as

the following can be comprehended under their class authority. Which pole triggers:

> Nothing can please many, and please long but just representations of general nature; ("Preface to Shakespeare")

or

> From poetry the reader justly expects, and from good poetry always obtains, the enlargement of his comprehension and elevation of his fancy; (*Lives*, 1:291–92)

or

> The noblest beauties of art are those of which the effect is coextended with rational nature. . . ;" (*Lives*, 3:333)

or

> Arbitrary decision and general exclamation I have carefully avoided by asserting nothing without a reason, and establishing all my principles of judgment on unalterable and evident truth; (*Rambler* 208)

or

> all true poetry requires that the sentiments be natural; (*Idler* 77)

or

> There is scarcely any species of writing, of which we can tell what is its essence, or what are its constituents. (*Rambler* 125)

The two senses of literature *aspire* to integrate more than is within their power to bring together.

In describing the religious sense that leads to the self-expressive concept of writing, Fussell asserts that for the "literarily gifted" the production of literature is very much like a Christian sacrament. Conspicuous in this statement is the particularly odd phrase *literarily gifted*, which seems to imply that writers have either special faculties or general faculties in a special degree and, by extension, that the varieties of mental powers correspond perfectly to the varieties of special employments; in short, the phrase suggests a divinely instituted classification of men based on the inherence in our separate natures of a propensity for one kind of excellence or of a natural suitability for a specific form of endeavor. In such a world the business of man, of course, is to identify that work for which he is naturally adapted. However, if such were in fact the case, one wonders by what manner of enterprise destitution could be eluded by the man who, *carpentarily gifted,* was born into or transported to a land without trees, an Arab rover, say, or, trusting Johnson's account in the *Journey to the Western Islands* of the paucity of vegetable exuberance in the north country, a Scot.

The notion of peculiar genius (suggested by Fussell's phrase) is, of course, everywhere resisted and rejected by Johnson: "The true Genius is a mind of large general powers, accidentally determined to some particular direction."[10] One man may have more mind than another, Johnson admits, but "no, Sir . . . people are not born with a particular genius for particular employments or studies, for it would be like saying that a man could see a great way east, but could not west. It is good sense applied with diligence to what was at first a mere accident, and which, by great application, grew to be called, by the generality of mankind, a particular genius."[11] Lest the reference to the carpenter above be considered far-fetched, the reader will recall what Johnson, illustrating the same point on another occasion, had said: "Suppose you show me a man who is a very expert carpenter, another will say he was born to be a carpenter—but what if he had never seen wood? Let two men, one with genius, the other with none, look at an overturned wagon: —he who has no genius, will think of the wagon only as he sees it, overturned, and walk on; he who has genius, will paint it to himself before it was overturned, —standing still, and moving on, and heavy loaded, and empty. . . ."[12] Mental powers are certainly distributed unequally, but there is, according to Johnson, no unequal distribution of discrete powers or faculties.

The reader might be inclined to allow Fussell's "literarily gifted" an alternative reading when he discovers later in the chapter the following quotation from Boswell's *Journal of a Tour to the Hebrides:*

Robertson said, one man had more judgment, another more
imagination. Johnson. "No, Sir; it is only, one man has more
mind than another. He may direct it differently; he may by
accident see the success of one kind of study and take a desire to
excel in it. I am persuaded that, had Sir Isaac Newton applied to
poetry, he would have made a very fine epick poem. I could as
easily apply to law as to tragic poetry." Boswell. "Yet, Sir, you
did apply to tragic poetry, not to law." Johnson. "Because, Sir, I
had not money to study law." (August 15)[13]

What Johnson says here squares perfectly, of course, with his
views on genius (a mind of large general powers accidentally turned
to a particular direction). Fussell, however, does not see in this
passage anything tending to undermine the patent implication of
the phrase *literarily gifted*. He is at this point concerned with
documenting the claim that the law greatly influenced Johnson's
critical sensibility, fostering the notion of literature as quasi-legal
argument—as, that is, mere rhetorical artifice. To Fussell, Johnson is here equating advocacy with the arts of epic and tragedy, a
notion that Fussell hopes to buttress with the "concurring" opinion
of Jean Hagstrum: "Of this virtual equation of advocacy with the
arts of epic and tragedy Jean Hagstrum has rightly said: 'In this
lively interchange of opinion Johnson denies any special position to
literature and removes from it the mystification that has often
surrounded it. He relates it to the law, to mathematics, and to other
coordinate disciplines. The assumption is that literature . . . is an
austere and rigorous mental pursuit.' "[14] This is but one particularly felicitous example of Fussell's habitual practice of filtering
uncongenial evidence through his ruling hypothesis, thereby arriving at "proofs" in spite of the facts. Clear to every reader, I think, is
the fact that Hagstrum's remarks—perceptive and just—refute
rather than confirm the opinion that introduces them.

The mediating concept in the Boswell passage, as Hagstrum
clearly understands, is not argument (legal or any other kind), but
the powers of mind requisite to excellence in any challenging
human enterprise. As men of genius are accidentally turned to
different pursuits, so the materials, objects, and ends of their labor
and thought will differ, but no particular study or endeavor can be
carried to excellence without the cooperative functioning of reason
and imagination, of all of the faculties of the mind. Johnson is not

asserting that the *arts* of epic and tragedy are to be equated with *advocacy;* he is saying clearly and forcefully that, however different and various arts and employments may be in however many different respects, excellence in any one endeavor results from the application of the full resources of the mind to the specific problems of that endeavor. And as "the basis of all excellence is truth," so in the production of truth imagination must come to the aid of reason and reason to the aid of imagination. In the case of the man of genius confronting an overturned wagon, it is clear that he could never have *reasoned* to an understanding of the proper relation of object to road unless he had *imagined* the wagon as an object capable of rolling; and, of course, he was able to *reason* to a means of putting the wagon "right" only when he *imagined* it, not as it was—heavily loaded—but as it could be—empty. Whether the man of genius walks to the east or to the west, he brings his whole mind with him. If the equation of advocacy with the arts of epic and tragedy were ever an article of Johnsonian belief, the self-evident fact is that he did not take this occasion to give it memorable expression.[15]

In an effort to provide the "mere artifice" side of the hypothesis with life-sustaining nourishment, Fussell is not above milking the bull of idle speculation. That pole of Johnson's critical sensibility calling for a literature of mere rhetorical artifice akin to legal advocacy—the side of the polarity "where literature appears as a social, argumentative, and (merely) affective function"—is to be understood, we are assured, as an indication of the impact that the law and lawyers had upon Johnson. Where there is a demand for literature akin to legal advocacy, there must be (it is assumed) some basis for it in the particulars of Johnson's life.

Convinced of the demand and of the necessary relation between it and personal history, Fussell notes: "His boyish introduction to learning took place in the legal atmosphere of the Lichfield Grammar School, proud of its record of producing lawyers and justices. A boy attending such a school would never have been allowed to forget what he was there for."[16] Lichfield Grammar School did, of course, produce many distinguished lawyers and justices (and clergymen, statesmen, and physicians), but neither from Johnson's own record of his training nor from any other authority do we

learn of anything peculiarly *legal* in the program of instruction or
the interests of the master and the instructors. Addison, perhaps
the most famous graduate, was not a lawyer. Edmund Hector was
not a lawyer, and John Taylor, Johnson's other lifelong school
friend, was more reverend cattleman than reverend lawyer. Neither Gilbert Walmesley nor Cornelius Ford, perhaps the two most
important figures in Johnson's early life, seems to have won Johnson's esteem and respect as a consequence of his knowledge of the
law. Why a bookseller's son living in a cathedral and garrison town
would be more influenced by the law than by some other branch of
learning, inquiry, or service, I am unable to guess.

Nevertheless, Fussell goes on: "As an adult he selected London
lodgings very near the Inns of Court and the bulk of his middle-
class friends were lawyers.[17] As an adult, Johnson, of course, lived
in various parts of London, but even if Fussell's remarks were
generally true, we would still have to know *why* Johnson selected
such lodgings (whether choice was governed by legal impulse). Can
we unequivocally state that the cause of selection is in a desire to
dwell in the vicinity of aspiring lawyers? And if so, upon what
compelling evidence is such an idea based? And even if the evidence were irrefutable, by what ineluctable train of reasoning
could we bring the congregated evidence to bear directly upon
Johnson's critical principles or sensibility? And, to switch to the
second part of the assertion, by what complicated system of com-
putation do we arrive at the conclusion that the bulk of Johnson's
middle-class friends were lawyers (and, implicitly, that Johnson
was associated with them *because* they were lawyers)? When we
look at the members of any of the clubs with which Johnson was
affiliated, we notice no predominance of lawyers. Similarly, when
we quickly compile from the tops of our heads a list of middle-class
friends (e.g., Burke, Goldsmith, Garrick, Reynolds, Richardson,
Thomas Warton, Joseph Warton, Percy, Henry Thrale, Hester
Thrale, Stevens, Charles Burney, Fanny Burney, Edmund Hector,
John Taylor, Tom Davies, Baretti, William Strahan, etc.), we
discover no very impressive preponderence of lawyers in the
group. That many of Johnson's friends were lawyers is certainly
true, but unless Fussell can demonstrate that the nexus of friendship is a common interest in the law and that this mutual interest is

somehow directly related to Johnson's critical sensibility, the fact of friendship with lawyers is little more than an interesting piece of biographical information.

From the bulk of legal friends Fussell selects two for particular attention: "It is no accident that his two main biographers, Boswell and Sir John Hawkins, were lawyer and judge respectively: as legally trained professionals, both were drawn to a mind which so ably could conceive of literature in terms they too could understand, namely, as quasi-legal argument."[18] In response to this it is worth remarking perhaps that when they met Johnson, the one was not a lawyer and the other was not a judge, that at the time of meeting Boswell was actively resisting the congregated force propelling him toward the law, that both Boswell and Hawkins fail to emphasize the legal foundation of their attraction to Johnson, that they both neglect to mention how their own conceptions of literature as quasi-legal argument were reinforced by Johnson's literary and critical practice, and so forth. Among other curious things, are we henceforth invited to assume—by analogical extension—that Hawkins was motivated to write a history of music *because* he saw in that history something approximating the form of a legal argument? Can we extend this reasoning to other friends and rightly assume that Reynolds was irresistably attracted to Johnson because he responded to Johnson's conception of literature as quasi-painting, as a verbal artifact aspiring to the condition of a painting, or that Henry Thrale looked to Johnson as the champion of the idea that literature is business, an idea that only a blockhead would have the temerity to challenge? By this means we arrive at as many conceptions of writing as there are friends with different primary interests. From all the available evidence we can only conclude that Boswell and Hawkins were biographers of Johnson *and,* incidentally it would seem, legal professionals.

Johnson was certainly interested in the law (as he was in medicine, chemistry, politics, intellectual history, literature, religion, commerce, and much else), but Fussell establishes no very secure biographical foundation for Johnson's critical views when to speculation he adds that Johnson wrote Parliamentary debates for Cave, that he wrote what amounted to legal briefs for Boswell, that he wrote law lectures for Robert Chambers. When measured against a lifetime of writing and literary assistance, these "facts" have no singular distinction or value. Nor is the case much advanced when, in an effort to document Johnson's practical experience with as well as theoretical knowledge of the law, Fussell enlists the support of William Bowles, who has informed us that "at one period of his life he used to frequent the office of a Justice of the Peace, under the idea that much of real life is learned at such places."[19] If we attend to Bowles's report, what we learn from it, of course, is that Johnson regularly went to the office of the justice of the peace, not for legal information, but for information relating to real life and the condition of man, doubtless believing that from such attendance he could learn something important about the springs of contention, the sources and objects of vanity, the common causes of unhappiness. The office of the justice exposes strikingly graphic examples of the raw nerves and bare bones of human perplexity and discontent. Whatever practical experience and knowledge of the law Johnson obtained at the office must be interpreted as surplus and adventitious dividends accruing to a primary investment of concern in real life, in the motives of human action, the bases of human strife.

Throughout the rhetorico-legal section, Fussell imposes unnecessary limitations on his case by maintaining that legal argument is for Johnson the quintessential mode of rhetoric. Had he taken rhetoric as the subsuming category, he would have been able to use law and legal influences to supplement his general argument, noting additionally that Johnson's fondness for the legal aspects of rhetoric (or the rhetorical aspects of law) is perfectly consistent with his general tendency to find his primary critical terms and distinctions in the vocabulary of rhetoric. If the law had been regularly subordinated to rhetoric and if Johnson had been presented as a critic who lucidly and powerfully expressed the bias of the age for a rhetorically oriented literature and criticism (acquiring friends and foes in proportion to the forcefulness of his expression of the bias), then Fussell's argument would have been, if not less incorrect, more plausible. The simple and inescapable fact is that we have no reason to assume that Johnson expected most literature to approximate the conditions of an argument, legal or otherwise; for example, the reader would look in vain in the *Preface* or *Notes to Shakespeare* for a demand for a literature akin to legal advocacy; the plays move to the extent that they are credited, and

they are credited to the extent that they appear to be just representations of life, moving exhibitions of the dilemmas, pains, and
pleasures to which we, as participants in the general condition that
is represented before us in particular circumstances, may be
exposed.

Since his primary object is to illuminate the critical consequences of Johnson's legal-literary sensibility, Fussell is obliged to
go beyond biographical particulars to actual critical pronouncements. And we are quickly informed that "from this legal, rhetorical, and affective conception of writing emerge many of Johnson's
most impressive literary perceptions."[20] The reader who naturally
expects Fussell to go directly to the "Preface to Shakespeare" or to
those *Rambler* papers in which Johnson addresses large critical
questions and from which the assumptions and principles determining his judgment can best be discovered (e.g., *Ramblers* 36, 37,
125, 156, 158) is immediately disappointed, for Fussell places his
primary emphasis on Johnson's attitude toward letters (as
expressed in a few brief remarks), on his—really Savage's—notion
of the biographical import of Thomson's writings, and, finally, on
the "equation of advocacy and epic" passage in Boswell's Hebrides
Journal.[21]

He goes about the business of establishing Johnson's "legal
mood" (in which "he is deeply suspicious of any conception of
literature which would—naively and preposterously, in his view—
associate the literary act with the impulse toward uncoded self-
expression")[23] by notifying us that "one of the most delightful
moments in the *Life of Pope* . . . is his dogged refusal to admit that
the private letter is anything but a formal and objective literary
genre whose conventions are such that, given the depravity of
human nature, almost anything *but* the actual truth about the
writer can be disclosed in it."[22] The passage on which Fussell's
judgment is based reads:

> Very few can boast of hearts which they dare lay open to them-
> selves, and of which, by whatever accident exposed, they do not
> shun a distinct and continued view; and certainly what we hide
> from ourselves we do not show to our friends. There is, indeed,
> no transaction which offers stronger temptations to fallacy and
> sophistication than epistolary intercourse. (*Lives*, 3:207)

In reading this passage, the reader should bear in mind that here—
just before he scrutinizes *Pope's character* as it is represented in
his personal letters—Johnson is puncturing the foolish, common
assumption that the "true characters of men [are necessarily to] be
found in their letters, . . . that he who writes to his friend [nec-
essarily] lays his heart open before him." Johnson is attacking a
silly belief; he is not positively asserting that epistolary communication precludes truthful representations of facts, attitudes, feelings, states of mind, or whatever. Johnson has no illusions about
the necessary and unimpeachable veracity of the personal letter,
but in his remarks in the *Life of Pope* he says very little about the
private letter as a formal and objective genre (as I make clear
below, the private letter is considered formally and objectively in
Rambler 152), affirms no belief in the natural depravity of man,
stops considerably short of saying that almost anything but the
actual truth about the writer can be disclosed in the private letter,
and nowhere asserts that truth of character is always, deliberately,
and necessarily misrepresented in private correspondence. Moreover, it is worth noting that, even in the context of an attack against
a common, false assumption, Johnson observes not only that
"friendship has no tendency to secure veracity, for by whom can a
man so much wish to be thought better than he is as by him whose
kindness he desires to gain or keep," but also that

> to charge those favorable representations, which men give of
> their own minds, with the guilt of hypocritical falsehood, would
> shew more severity than knowledge. The writer commonly
> believes himself. Almost every man's thoughts, while they are
> general, are right; and most hearts are pure while temptation is
> away. It is easy to awaken generous sentiments in privacy; . . .
> to glow with benevolence when there is nothing to be given.
> While such ideas are formed they are felt, and self-love does not
> suspect the gleam of virtue to be the meteor of fancy. (*Lives*,
> 3:207−8).

Nevertheless, the passage in the *Life of Pope* that speaks most
forcibly and tellingly to Fussell can lead him to but one "inescapable conclusion": that, to Johnson, "the personal letter is exactly
the *least* sincere of all the genres." Johnson rejects one foolish
assumption only to adopt another.

One of Fussell's major shortcomings here is his determination to collapse all distinctions into one frame of reference and to invest the local-general with general-general significance. What is true of one topic possible to epistolary discourse is not necessarily true of all possible topics. When the subject of a letter is the writer's own life (the writer's estimate or assessment of his own ethical, social, intellectual character), the impartial reader *may* justly refuse to accept the account, in the absence of independent testimony, as *entirely* reliable, and this is so for the general reasons specified and suggested by Johnson; we do not write such epistles as disinterested witnesses, and we are not naturally inclined to disclose to those whom we esteem (and those whose trust and confidence we would not willingly lose) aspects of our character that, since they have not our approbation and supply no encouragement to self-esteem, cannot be expected to strengthen our friendship. (And such partial or selective disclosure has its basis generally, not in depravity but in virtue, mutual affection, esteem, etc.) Nevertheless, it is also true that "the writer of his own life has at least the first qualification of an historian, the knowledge of the truth; and though it may be plausibly objected that his temptations to disguise it are equal to his opportunities of knowing it, yet I cannot but think that impartiality may be expected with equal confidence from him that relates the passages of his own life [especially when he does not write with the prospect of eventual publication in view] as from him that delivers the transactions of another" (*Idller* 84). Also, the temptations to fallacy and sophistication, though strong and generally persuasive, are not necessarily irresistable, and what few *can* actually do is not, Johnson allows, impossible to all.

However, the real problem with self-evaluative reports, whether presented in letters or autobiographies, is an epistemological one. Without corroborating testimony from other sources, we generally have no way of knowing whether the report is fair or just. Whether the writer rates his character high or low, the circumspect reader—after considering and assessing the probable betrayers of fairness, objectivity, precision, comprehensiveness—will not hastily determine that there is an absolutely positive correlation between report and fact. The central issue concerns the grounds on which we can know "character" with reasonable certainty. Sincerity is a false issue. Whatever the substance of his remarks, the letter-writer may sincerely believe that he is telling the truth (he may also lie sincerely) and sincerely express what he sincerely believes. Moreover, self estimation is but one of a virtually infinite number of subjects to which the letter-writer may turn his attention. As occasion, need, and circumstances alter, the letter-writer will find opportunities to express *sincerely* his thoughts, feelings, attitudes, and values on a variety of subjects, to state *sincerely* his condolences, his good wishes, his love, to plead *sincerely* for a benefit, to ask *sincerely* for assistance, and so on. Apparently, "sincerity" belongs to the "self-expressive" side of the polarity and thus cannot be allowed in letters, which, by Fussell's analysis, are members of the rhetorico-legal world of discourse.

If Fussell were seriously interested in coming to grips with the critical principles governing Johnson's judgment of letters, he would not concentrate on a single passage in the *Life of Pope*; he would also make some attempt to account for *Rambler* 152, in which Johnson distinguishes among kinds of personal letters, noting, among other things, how differences in style, diction, and imagery are determined by differences in topics, correspondents, ends, and occasions. Nowhere in this paper does Johnson suggest —what to Fussell is inescapable—that the personal letter is "exactly" the *least* sincere and natural of all genres. To Johnson it is clear that "as letters are written on all subjects, in all states of mind, they cannot be properly reduced to settled rules, or described by any single characteristic . . . " (*Rambler* 152). Nevertheless, "letters should be written with strict conformity to nature, because nothing but conformity to nature can make any composition beautiful or just" (*Rambler* 152).[24]

A careful examination of Johnson's attempt to advance principles commensurate with the nature of letters, radically considered, in *Rambler* 152 reveals no postulate capable of generating the idea that the conventions of the personal letter are such that "almost anything *but* the actual truth about the writer can be disclosed in it." Whenever a person writes, he discloses "truths" about himself, directly or indirectly, especially when he expresses his attitudes, opinions, feelings, which he may certainly do in a letter. Of course we disclose aspects of ourselves even when we are not writing *about* ourselves, and what we may wish to conceal may be legitimately and rightly inferred from what we actually say. As is frequently the case, Fussell supplies in defense of his proposition evidence that undermines it. To the Bishop of St. Asaph's remark that "it appeared from Horace's writings that he was a cheerful, contented man," Johnson, Fussell reminds us, replied: "We have no reason to believe that, my Lord. Are we to think Pope was happy, because he says so in his writings? We see in his writings [including, and perhaps particularly, his letters] what he wished the state of his mind to appear."[25] Refusing to infer "quality" of mind or condition of life directly from statement (and working undoubtedly from a governing conception of Pope's character, based on and informed by a rich accumulation of resonant biographical particulars), Johnson can nevertheless state with considerable assurance what truth about Pope is actually and *sincerely* disclosed in those writings in which personal happiness is expressed.

To bring his point home, Fussell goes to a letter written by Johnson to Mrs. Thrale (October 27, 1777) on the subject, at least ostensibly, of letter writing, in which, according to our critic, "Johnson takes pains to explode the common myth that a genre like the letter, because it uses the conventions of sincerity and openness, is thus a vehicle of genuine self-disclosure."[26] Fussell calls our attention to the second paragraph of the following letter, which reads in full:

Dear Madam
    You talk of writing and writing as if you had all the writing to yourself. If our Correspondence were printed I am sure Posterity, for Posterity is always the authours favourite, would say that I am a good writer too. Anch' io sonô Pittore. To sit down so often with nothing to say, to say something so often, almost without consciousness of saying, and without any remembrance of having said, is a power of which I will not violate my modesty by boasting, but I do not believe that every body has it.
    Some when they write to their friends are all affection, some are wise and sententious, some strain their powers for efforts of gayety, some write news, and some write secrets, but to make a letter without affection, without wisdom, without gayety, without news, and without a secret', is, doubtless, the great epistolick art.
    In a Man's Letters you know, Madam, his soul lies naked, his letters are only the mirrour of his breast, whatever passes within

is shown undisguised in its natural process. Nothing is inverted, nothing distorted, you see systems in their elements, you discover actions in their motives.

Of this great truth sounded by the knowing to the ignorant, and so echoed by the ignorant to the knowing, what evidence have you now before you. Is not my soul laid open in these veracious pages? do not you see me reduced to my first principles? This is the pleasure of corresponding with a friend, where doubt and distrust have no place, and everything is said as it is thought. The original Idea is laid down in its simple purity, and all the supervenient conceptions, are spread over it stratum super stratum, as they happen to be formed. These are the letters by which souls are united, and by which Minds naturally in unison move each other as they are moved themselves. I know, dearest Lady, that in the perusal of this such is the consanguinity of our intellects, you will be touched as I am touched. I have indeed concealed nothing from you, nor do I expect ever to repent of having thus opened my heart.

I am, Madam, Your most humble servant,
Sam: Johnson[27]

In this letter Johnson expresses "the sort of sardonic irony possible only to those whose sense of genre is exquisitely developed. . . ."[28] It seems to me that Fussell here misreads both the tone and the content of the letter. There is no time in this chapter to examine the multiple ironies of this letter, but every reader surely notices that the tone is playful and that Johnson discloses and expresses his affection for Mrs. Thrale, making clear in the process the easy and familiar terms on which they have their warm friendship. (We see in this letter the genuine "pleasure of corresponding with a friend, where doubt and distrust have no place.") Johnson, it is true, is not seen reduced to his first principles, and he certainly attacks (playfully) the popular view (a view that Mrs. Thrale is perhaps too willing to credit) that letters of necessity discover actions in their motives, confirming his point by writing a letter on the *subject* of letter writing, thereby precluding—so it would seem—the appearance of what many believe letters are peculiarly suited to convey. The letter is not characterized, however, by sardonic irony (the end of sardonic irony would be, assuming that Mrs. Thrale missed it, the gratification of a mean pride or superiority or, assuming that Mrs. Thrale understood it, the humiliation or distress of the correspondent), but by lively wit, ebullient good humor, and affection; it is a tour de force of verbal legerdemain, and we miss some of its central ironies if we believe, as Johnson invites us to, that it is written "without affection, without wisdom, without gaiety, without news, and without a secret"; Johnson displays "great epistolick art" by both satisfying and *not* satisfying the ironically specified conditions of great epistolic art.

Concentrating on surface statement, Fussell overlooks the fun and joyous deviousness of Johnson's ironies. As soon as we ask to whom Johnson could write such a letter, we recognize immediately that it would have to be someone with whom he was on good terms and whom he wished to please (not offend). Mrs. Thrale will have a letter, and Johnson—always reluctant to write for the sake of writing, or when he had nothing to say, no business to transact, no inducement or opportunity to rectify an opinion, fortify a resolution, support a proposal, solicit aid for the distressed or deserving—complies with her wish, writing an epistle perfectly designed to force her forgiveness and to preserve her love and esteem. Briefly, the letter delightfully satisfies the requirements of letters of this *sort:* "The purpose for which letters are written when no intelligence is communicated, or business transacted, is to preserve in the minds of the absent either love or esteem; to excite love we must impart pleasure, and to raise esteem we must discover abilities" (*Rambler* 152).

With effortless gaiety Johnson reminds Mrs. Thrale that he has not been a hopelessly unresponsive and lax correspondent, conveys the news that there is no news, imparts wisdom by indirection (perhaps hectoring her own opinions at the same time), while expressing his fondness for her throughout. And as for a secret, it is in the relationship itself, which allows Johnson to write as he does and which guarantees that the good feeling and affection animating the whole will not be misread; it is in the mutual esteem, to which the whole letter testifies. At least part of the "secret" inheres in the irony enfolded in the irony of the remark that "such is the consanguinity of our intellects [that] you will be touched as I am touched." (They will be touched in their respective risibilities.) We have here irony turning back on itself, an instance of double irony. "Consanguinity of intellects" (along with "united souls," etc.) is, of course, an ironic phrase following naturally from antecedent claims and perfectly appropriate to the prevailing ironic tone and context. But it is also clear that the pleasure that the whole letter imparts is founded on a genuine consanguinity of intellects at some level. In spite of his lively ridicule of the opinion that personal letters necessarily display the essential man, Johnson nevertheless writes a *personal* letter, in which he discloses, if not his first principles, at least his sincere and genuine affection.

Focusing on the "statements," we tend to forget that it is a personal letter written on a specific occasion expressly for Mrs. Thrale. The trouble is that in going to the letter to discover what Johnson says *about* letters, we neglect what Johnson *is saying* sincerely and clearly (though sometimes indirectly) to Mrs. Thrale *in* the letter. There is *in* the letter—in its tone and content— genuine self-disclosure, which Fussell's restrictive conception of self-expression prevents him from detecting. In the end, Johnson's letter to Mrs. Thrale and his comments on Pope's letters cannot actively support the "very eighteenth-century idea that the act of literature is necessarily an act of argument, that the writer, even when he assumes the role of poet, is most comparable to a barrister arguing a case" (Fussell, p. 46). Avoiding the major critical documents (and hence the radical critical postulates in relation to which Johnson's particular critical judgments are instances of consequential reasoning), Fussell goes a great distance to find particular passages that, even under the pressure of categorical coercion, adamantly refuse aid to his controlling assumptions.

I shall conclude this examination of the evidence enlisted to support the "legal" pole of Johnson's critical thought with a few comments on Fussell's interpretation of a section of the *Life of Thomson*. Fussell asserts that "the letter is only one of the genres whose operation makes 'self-expression' either a ridiculous image or a dangerous and ultimately self-destructive illusion. The poem [presumably all poems, of whatever kind] is another." The point is confirmed by noting that "as Johnson observes in the *Life of Pope*, 'Poets do not always express their own thoughts.' "[29] And Fussell finds a "clinching" illustration of his point in the *Life of Thomson*:

Savage, who lived much with Thomson, once told me he heard a lady remarking that she could gather from his works three parts of his character, that he was "a great lover, and great swimmer, and rigorously abstinent"; but, said Savage, he knows not any love but that of the sex; he was perhaps never in cold water in his life; and he indulges in all the luxury that comes within his reach. (*Lives*, 3:297—98)

Allowing for the fact that it is Savage's rejoinder (not Johnson's) and that the sprightliness of the sally is what impresses us most, we can still recognize that it implies views with which Johnson concurs: first, the reader ought not on all occasions to interpret the views, opinions, and preferences of a poetic speaker as those of the poet himself; and second, it is generally unwise, in the absence of additional and irrefutable evidence, to assume that a poet's personal actions are always comformable to his precepts, or that very precise biographical information—relating to nonpoetic activity—is directly inferable from the particulars of poems. The problem with the lady of Savage's acquaintance is that she arrives at conclusions too precise and substantial from evidence too insubstantial or ambiguous and translates signs relating to one order of significance into meanings within an entirely different order of significance. But what does all this have to do, finally, with the social, argumentative, and affective function of literature, and how does this passage help to demonstrate that this function is one of the two between which Johnson's judgment oscillates? The social, argumentative, affective function can be realized as effectively when the poet is expressing his own thoughts and feelings as when he is not.

Because Johnson notes that poets "do not always express their own thoughts," we ought not to conclude that he thinks they never do or that he believes that they express their own thoughts only when he is in his nonlegal mood. Moreover, even when a poet does not express his own thoughts, he necessarily discloses aspects of his intellectual and poetic character, revealing by his poetic actions characteristic habits and processes of thought, tendencies of mind, dictional preferences, analytic powers, skills, and so forth, every particular work contributing something to our understanding of the peculiar range and power of individual genius. When our attention is focused on intellectual or poetic character, as Johnson's regularly is, the particular works, as they are confronted successively, fulfill, extend, or alter our type conception of character, which becomes more trustworthy and stable as each successive work exhibits more "redundancy" or is more regularly consistent with what is expressed or implicated in its antecedents.

As a critic who regularly referred from works to human abilities and from psychological effects to psychological causes, Johnson brought to his reading of a particular work a functional type conception (derived, in large part, from previous reading or induced while reading) of the writer's characteristic habits and powers.[30] Furthermore, he brought to each work a functional, relatively stable conception of what was possible to human effort within the chosen "form," a flexible but relatively stable conception of the capabilities of man, derived from experience with a long succession of endeavors, against which particular "new" works, in their various aspects, were measured. Long before psychoanalytic speculation deflected attention from the ethical-intellectual-personal nature of poetic activity, many critics, Johnson among them, recognized that even when the poet does not express his own thoughts he necessarily discloses aspects of himself as he writes; he discloses his literary "character." Moreover, there are some forms of literary expression that, at least in some of their manifestations, not only allow for, but seem by nature to require, the articulation of the writer's own thoughts—elegies occasioned by personal loss and amorous verses directed to a certain *she* (not to a publisher) being two forms from which the reader may legitimately expect an expression of personal feeling and thought.[31] Johnson regularly reads character, power, skill, and the like *out of* works, but he rarely reads particular biographical detail *into* works, in the manner of the lady in the "Savage" passage.

When all of Fussell's evidence is brought together, we are forced to conclude that the assembled elements of illumination simply do not demonstrate "that Johnson fully understands that the relation between poet and poem is not the relation between penitent and confessor: it is rather [when Johnson is in his legal mood] the relation between barrister and client." To Johnson, the relation is neither the one nor the other, and Fussell's evidence cannot inform his hypothesis with anything approaching cognitive adequacy. The terms with which he is content to work are not adequate to the task of accounting for the variety of accurate and nice discriminations that Johnson makes or of delineating the principled bases of his various judgments. No satisfactory provisions are made in his antipodal scheme for, among other things, truth, novelty, variety, nature, probability, pleasing instruction, the expression and excitation of emotion, and so on—all the major terms and concepts, that is, with which every critic must deal if he hopes finally to distinguish the underlying and constitutive principles of Johnson's critical practice. Although Fussell stresses (indeed, bases his whole argument on) Johnson's inconsistent, wildly erratic oscillation between poles, he fails to demonstrate that these are precisely the poles of attraction.[32] To do that Fussell would have to go on to show—which he fails to do—either that *within* the elected categories of attraction Johnson *consistently* adduces the same criteria of judgment *or* that in the full articulation of the separate demands in a variety of contexts Johnson's "arguments" are internally *coherent, consistency* being reflected in the noncontradictory nature of the various terms and distinctions by which the same point is asserted of many works over the years and *coherence* being manifested in the "logical" relatedness of the terms by which the point is regularly enforced over the years. In all the evidence cited by Fussell, I detect neither consistency of term, phrase, or concept nor coherence of critical argument.

The other side of the polarity—the self-expressive side—is no more securely established than its antipode. As before, Fussell goes for his proofs, not to critical texts of central significance (i.e., those texts in which Johnson discusses critical principles rather than applying them to specific works), but to the critique of *Lycidas* and, secondarily, to Johnson's comments on Prior's amorous verses. What we are asked to accept as one of the two distinguishing poles of Johnson's critical sensibility, Fussell finds in two brief sections of the *Lives of the Poets,* sections dealing with only two *kinds* of writing. Evidence for this "demand" is drawn from a severely limited selection of texts written late in Johnson's career and dealing with kinds of poems peculiarly and naturally limited in purpose and project. Without considering whether, to Johnson, elegies and amorous verses accomplish the general task of poetry under special conditions or limitations, Fussell, armed with his dialectical scheme, proceeds on the assumption that we can best understand Johnson's remarks on these works if we accept them as consequences of an a priori class demand for "self-expression."[33]

By Fussell's standards, the critique of *Lycidas* deserves particular attention because it displays Johnson at his inconsistent best,
hopping with amazing agility and with uncommon celerity from one
pole to the other; it is here that both poles of his critical sensibility
operate at almost the same time, here that we find, not argumentative concinnity, but the racy syncopation of discordant, disjunctive
critical demands. Since the critique is also for Fussell the chief
source of evidence for the self-expressive mood, his interpretation
of it deserves particular scrutiny. Fussell begins:

> We must now consider the other pole, which we will find him
> embracing no less seriously. Our text now is his *Life of Milton*,
> especially the passage embodying the well-known denigration of
> *Lycidas*. And when considering Johnson on *Lycidas*, we must
> remember that his depreciation of that poem occurs within a
> context of critical praise of Milton's epic achievement so lavish
> and enthusiastic that it seems hardly to belong to the familar
> Johnson at all. . . . This is a remarkable flux of enthusiasm from
> Johnson.[34]

Fussell has the distinction, I think, of being the first to suggest that
Johnson's review of *Paradise Lost* is strikingly un-Johnsonian. And
I am almost frightened at my own temerity when I suggest, alternatively, that the flux to which Fussell refers can perhaps be attributed to differences in the objects examined and that Johnson,
unwilling to subordinate his critical mind to the authority of a name
(unlike many of his contemporaries), subjects both works to
rational and manly review. At any rate, I see no reason to believe
that the different evaluations imply radically different and
incommensurate standards of value or principles of reasoning. By
focusing on "flux of enthusiasm," Fussell deflects attention from
Johnson's specific commentary and towards his erratic behavior,
thus preparing us for further disclosures of flightiness; in short,
these remarks, deliberate but unsubtle, have an insidious intent: to
fix us in a state of receptiveness for what follows (in particular, for a
discussion of Johnson's spasmodic nature as evidenced in contradictory utterances). We have been prepared for the ensuing
"argument," but we have been given, it is useful to remember, no
compelling reason to assume that in moving from praise to blame
Johnson has changed his base of intellectual operation.

According to Fussell, the first sentence of the critique is "well within the boundaries ordained by his sense of literature as rhetoric. 'One of the poems on which much praise has been bestowed ["much praise" of anything always triggers Johnson's skeptical contrariness] is *Lycidas,* of which the diction is harsh, the rhymes uncertain, and the numbers unpleasing.' "[35] Now, since diction, rhyme, and numbers are necessary parts of poetry (rhyme being the allowable, if not highly approved—by Johnson—exception) whether the poet chooses to express "himself" or something akin to legal argument, there is no irresistible reason why we should associate these three *material* parts of poetry with rhetoric; clearly Johnson could determine that a poem *sincerely* expressing the poet's intimate thoughts and feelings exhibited harsh diction, uncertain rhymes, and unpleasing numbers, unless we admit, as perhaps we must, that a "self-expressive poem" is a contradiction in terms, that is, a poem without diction, rhyme, and numbers. The first sentence must adhere to the "legal" pole *only because* Fussell has *only* two poles of reference; since Johnson is not calling for "self-expression," he *must,* by dialectical necessity, be saying something that falls within the range of statements constituted by his "legal" conception of literature.[36]

What Johnson seems to be saying in his opening remark—quite clearly, I think—is that since those secondary or ancillary pleasures of poetry which diction and melody are capable of producing are not in fact excited by this poem, we must look elsewhere in the poem for elements sufficiently excellent to justify the praise bestowed on it. Implicit in the statement is the idea that the pastoral mode is an exhausted mode, incapable of offering much that is both "new" and "natural" in the way of imagery and sentiment, to which, however, we must turn, inasmuch as there is nothing in the rhyme, diction, or numbers to detain the reader interested in identifying and illuminating the sources of poetic pleasure in *Lycidas.* Unlike Pope's pastorals, *Lycidas* offers nothing in the way of versification that is both pleasing and without a precedent. Considered in terms of their independent merits—in terms, that is, of their power to please independently of the thought, imagery, and feeling that they express or support—the rhyme, numbers, and diction are deficient. Or, in other words, these *material* components of *Lycidas* are not sufficiently beautiful in themselves to compensate for or to excuse deficiencies of thought or imagery.

According to Fussell the next sentence ("What beauty there is we must therefore seek in the sentiments and images") "maintains the affective," rhetorical focus: "We notice that Johnson's eye is still on that part of the process of literary transmission where rhetoric presides; that is, on the relation, necessarily social as well as artistic, between speaker and audience."[37] Again, since the writer must employ some imagery and express some sentiments in the process of constructing an artifice of rhetoric or expressing his own thoughts and feelings, I fail to see why—unless a "self-expressive poem" is to be understood as subsisting without imagery or sentiment—we should assign this remark to the legal pole. If the relation between speaker and audience is crucial, then, of course, it is crucial to self-expressive as well as to legal literature, albeit perhaps in different ways (otherwise, how could we talk about what the self is expressing or know indeed whether a self had been expressed?). Presumably, even the most self-expressive writing permits—since it cannot forbid—discussion in terms of the writer-audience relation, and if any "meaning" is communicated and shared, some determinate relation between the two must obtain. (And a discussion of that relation does not necessarily commit a critic to a rhetorico-legal conception of literature.) The division of the first two sentences of the critique from the rest of the paragraph is determined by Fussell's categorical conception and not, I think, by the sense of the paragraph, considered independently of that conception.

When, moving into a discussion of *sentiments* and *imagery*, Johnson goes on to say that *Lycidas* "is not to be considered as the effusion of real passion; for passion runs not after remote allusions and obscure opinions," we are invited to believe that

> We are whisked out of the world of rhetoric altogether and thrust into quite another critical atmosphere. Sophistication suddenly yields to what must strike us as an almost unbelievable naïveté. For now Johnson attacks on the premise that a poem ought to embody the actual personal emotion of its contriver, presumably—and this is always an embarrassment to theories of self-expression—at the exact moment when the composition was begun."[38]

In reading Johnson's sentence, we experience, I think, no aesthetic shock, no sudden flight from one to another standard of judgment, and I frankly detect no unbelievable naiveté in the comment. What Johnson assumes is that the nature and the ends of elegiac compositons are peculiarly determined by the occasions on which they are written, regardless of whether they are instigated by a real or imagined event. The poet is obliged to express something that the reader can credit as natural to the occasion and to the implied or defined relation of the speaker and the dead person; we can reasonably expect the writer, for example, to focus on the worth of the person who has died and the effect that his death has upon the speaker and perhaps the larger world of which the person was a part, the whole exciting grief (for the speaker's and our common loss) and a desire to honor and emulate his virtues. If we are to be moved, we must be offered something that we can credit.

When we have reason to believe that the poem is occasioned by a "real" event, motivated by genuine personal loss, we naturally expect the poet to express *his* feelings and thoughts. Within the boundaries defined by the occasion and the relationship, the poet has a maximum of latitude. As long as in the process of composition the poet does not obscure the worth he is obliged to illuminate and hence preclude our recognition of the appropriateness of his grief, he is free to give particular immediacy and significance to the occasion and the relation by noting whatever specific reflections and personal details are provoked by the event of death. Thus each friend of King could distinguish his composition by recording those minute particularities by which, to him, the relationship was defined and the merits of his friend established, effective (and affective) communication being contingent upon the general reader's ability to recognize the individuated expression as possible or probable to human life under the specified conditions.

Milton's poem is not designed to satisfy Johnson's requirements or to gratify his expectations, but those requirements and expectations are founded on principles that arise primarily, not from an examination of literary practice, but from a prior consideration of the special occasion of the elegy, the common nature of man, and the general conditions of pleasure. There is undoubtedly something peculiarly Johnsonian in these expectations, but in asserting that there is no effusion of real passion in *Lycidas* Johnson is not being either naive or unsophisticated. Without embarrassment, Johnson demands expression adequate to our nature and experience, under the assumption that the basis of all excellence and all durable pleasure is truth; what we cannot credit cannot move us—except to boredom or indifference. And Johnson does not expect Milton to express the ineffable but to find language capable of transmitting rational praise and natural lamentation. Moreover, to Johnson, it is reasonable to assume that in writing an elegy provoked by the death of a real friend a writer would indeed be moved even as he wrote (*because* of what he was writing, of what he was actually thinking and expressing; how could it be otherwise?). But as far as I can tell, Johnson does not confound emoting with writing poetry, or feeling with its verbal expression; nor does he suggest that the poet emotes poetically. To express and excite emotion in an elegy, the poet must find, within linguistic conventions, the verbal means to the general ends of elegiac compositions.

The advantage that the poet actually moved by a real death has over the poet who must imagine what his condition would be if he were to lose a valued friend, is his immediate access to genuine grief; he has the first qualification of an elegiac writer, direct painful familiarity with natural human emotion, and since he, like the rest of us, can always feel more than he can imagine, artful fiction can give way to truth.[39] But his emotion is poetically valueless unless he can communicate it; if he cannot, then the poet who only imagines the condition may write the better elegy (assuming, of course, force of expression equal to strength of imagination). In truth, all Johnson demands is that Milton be faithful to the natural operations of the mind and express what can be credited as genuine praise and lamentation. From Johnson's point of view, in *Lycidas* truth gives way to fiction, and Milton imagines not only more than he feels, but something other than would naturally be felt on the occasion. If Milton had reflected on the state of man and not on the state of pastoral tradition, he would have avoided Johnson's animadversions, assuming, of course, that he imagined a condition commensurate with our nature and successfully embodied in verse what he had happily supposed. In short, it is important to recognize that a conception of human nature underlies Johnson's comments and that his principal reference is to the poem, not to Milton; the turn to Milton's condition is "reflexive," occasioned by the peculiar

"preconstructional," accidental cause of the poem, namely, the
death of a man whom Milton really knew. Johnson's judgment of
the poem would have been exactly the same had *Lycidas* been
written in the absence of any "historical" motivation. By Johnsonian standards, however, *Lycidas* is not an effective elegy, since
it contains too much that must "be rejected from a species of
composition in which . . . mere nature is to be regarded" (*Rambler*
37). In this section of the critique Johnson merely adjusts general
critical principles to the case at hand, and for "unbelievable
naïveté," we should substitute, I think, "uncommon common
sense."

To Fussell, however, the critical focus has dramatically shifted
without warning, and Johnson, in the next sentence, "goes on . . .
to talk not about the effect of the work on the apprehender but
about a totally different subject, the authenticity of the 'passion'
which, we are led to assume with Johnson, gave rise to the poetic
artifact in the first place: 'Passion plucks no berries from the
myrtle and ivy, nor calls upon Arethuse and Mincius, nor tells of
rough satyrs and fauns with cloven heel.' " Johnson, in fact, is
discussing what he said (or implied) he would discuss in the second
sentence, namely, images and sentiment, specifically the imagery
that expresses or illustrates the sentiment. Johnson is still concerned with speaker and audience, and the nature of human emotion is the mediating link between the two; it is from nature that the
poet derives his material, and it is according to the adequacy of his
representation of nature that the audience is pleased, pleasure
being contingent upon the recognition, in this case, of the congruence between what is said and what might possibly or probably be
said under the circumstances or what can be understood as falling
within the range of expression constituted by the occasion and the
personal relationship. As far as the effect of the work on the
apprehender is concerned, we should recognize that the effect,
though presupposed, is central, and that Johnson is reasoning from
the lack of proper effect to the cause of that lack in the sequence of
images and sentiments presented. The "passion" is not so much
"inauthentic" as "unnatural," because it is not consonant with the
motions and operations of the human mind. Milton's expression is
referred to a type conception of emotional possibilities, one that
does not specifically delineate what belongs within its legitimate

jurisdiction but that nevertheless allows immediate identification
of what cannot properly be tolerated by the conception. It is impossible to predict what will be said by any particular man in a moving
and forceful elegy, but we know immediately when the expression
is improbable and unnatural (i.e., not coextensive with rational
human existence), and we know, of course, by the effect that the
expression has upon us.

The primary evidence for the self-expressive pole of Johnson's
sensibility is in these lines on passion, and Fussell sums up their
significance by affirming that

> what Johnson assumes here—and in a way which he would be
> quick to reprehend when in his rhetorical mood—is that actual
> passion was actually felt by the maker of the poem, and that this
> undeniable passion has leaked away or been invalidated by
> having been encoded injudiciously. Assuming that actual grief
> ought really to be present in the writer—that is, the man and the
> poet are identical—he goes on to assert: "Where there is leisure
> for fiction there is little grief."[40]

It is important to understand that Johnson quite sensibly neglects
to distinguish between poet and man in the case of *Lycidas,* and
that it is not a question of passion's leaking away or being encoded
injudiciously, but of its not being expressed by the writer or excited
in the audience. Johnson's appeal is not finally to the materials of
Milton's psyche (the effectiveness of the poem is not relative to the
fidelity with which Milton has recorded his state of mind), but to the
adequacy of his expression to what can be legitimately credited in a
composition naturally limited as the elegy is to a fairly well-defined
range of concern. More important, Johnson has not switched in the
review of *Lycidas* to a self-expressive theory of literature; he is
applying to the case at hand the distinctive critical principles on
which he regularly relies, which spring from a coherent set of
assumptions about literature. As I shall explain in detail later,
Johnson enunciates in the review of *Lycidas* the general, constitutive purposes of the elegy when he says: "He who thus grieves
will excite no sympathy; he who thus praises will confer no
honour." In the best elegy the various parts should contribute to
the realization of these ends, each aspect of the work regulated by
and functional in relation to them. In short, Johnson expects, as he

says in reference to another pastoral elegy (Virgil's "Fifth"),
"rational praise" and "natural lamentation," both of which are to
him conspicuously absent from *Lycidas* as a result of Milton's
handling of images and sentiment.

Fussell fancies that Johnson is asking Milton to become the
"poetic" equivalent of the "method actor." After referring to the
familiar passage in Boswell's *Life* where Johnson informs Kemble
that "if Garrick really believed himself to be that monster Richard
the Third, he deserved to be hanged every time he performed it,"
Fussell says: "But what Johnson demands of *Lycidas* is very like
what he condemns in theatrical 'enthusiasts'; he really expects
Milton on this occasion to have behaved like a Method actor, to
have felt real grief and to have embodied it in some presumably
non-literary code."[41] Johnson, of course, is convinced that actors
are in their senses when they act; otherwise, they would not only
deserve to be hanged for their heinous "theatrical" crimes, but also
be unable to perform their roles at all, for what would induce an
actor suffering from the megalomaniacal delusion of absolute
identification with dramatic character to appear on cue, to speak
when and what he was supposed to speak, to leave at the right
moment, and to perform the prescribed actions? But what is all this
to *Lycidas?* We have no reason to assume that Johnson expected
grief to find incarnation in some nonliterary code (whatever that
might be). Johnson expected Milton to satisfy the natural demands
of the elegy, to lament and praise in such a manner that the reader
would not put down the poem in a state of frigid indifference.

Johnson, we are assured, regularly resorts to his "legal" sensibility whenever he wishes to denigrate the assumptions "underlying theories of literary 'sincerity,' " and to reinforce the point
Fussell takes the "Preface to Shakespeare" as his text: "The truth
is that the spectators are always in their senses, and know, from the
first act to the last, that the stage is only a stage, and that the
players are only players. They come to hear a certain number of
lines recited with just gesture and elegant modulation." The poles
of Johnson's sensibility engage repeatedly in internecine warfare.
When the passage from the "Preface" is juxtaposed to the critique
of *Lycidas,* it is clear to Fussell that "what [Johnson] requires of
Lycidas is that it cease being a poem, that is, a confessed theater of
artifice, and become instead an actual utterance of instinctive

grief, like a cry or a sob."[42] To my knowledge, Johnson never encouraged poetry of any kind to emulate the condition of a cry or a sob, and enough has already been said, I think, to persuade even the most ardent supporter of our critic's views that Johnson did not expect *Lycidas* to cease being a poem; he expected it to meet the special demands of an elegy.

By Fussell's report, Johnson obviously makes an odd demand of *Lycidas*, but "in his other mood, he knows, of course, much better than this: when, for example, he wants to lament the death of Dr. Robert Levet, he betakes himself to the artificial mechanisms of stanza form and poetic diction, and he uses a meter deriving from previous poems rather than from the impulses of his heart."[43] What this means apparently is that—whatever we may have previously thought—Johnson cannot be accused of expressing personal thoughts or feelings in this poem (or that the poem cannot be discussed in terms of self-expression) *because* Johnson relied on the *artificial mechanisms* of stanza and poetic diction and used a nonphysiologically grounded meter. To have been faithful to his self-expressive pole in his poetic practice, Johnson would have had to have wept nonstanzaically in, presumably, a noncoded physiological diction while employing at the same time a diastolic-systolic meter. That we are moved by Johnson's rational praise and natural lamentation is nothing to the point, for by his conventional meter shall you know his legal mood.[44]

What is exhibited here, it seems to me, is the radical inability of Fussell's dialectical critical machinery to deal with the diversity of Johnson's critical and literary activity. "On the Death of Dr. Robert Levet" is a poem of Johnson's legal mood, we are asked to believe, because Johnson uses stanzaic form, poetic diction, and, for the most part, an iambic tetrameter meter. What Johnson remembers when he discusses Shakespeare's plays and writes on the death of Levet, he forgets when he confronts *Lycidas*. That is, "He chooses to forget that the reader of a poem, very like the spectator in the theater, comes to the poem to be given 'a certain number of lines' contrived 'with just gesture and elegant modulation.' " Surely the *reader* of a poem who expects to be given a certain number of lines contrived with *just gesture* and *elegant modulation* is making unreasonable demands of the poet, especially the poet, alas, no longer alive. The word *contrived* is designed to save the analogy, but by what means does the *reader* discover and validate the gestures that he construes to be appropriate to the poem or confirm the positive correlation between what he construes and what the poet contrived, and how does the poet manage to contrive his gestures (assuming, of course, that he gestures as he writes) in such a way as to make them accessible to the reader? Johnson, of course, is talking specifically about the *delivery of lines by actors;* he definitely does not think the *reader* of a play expects to be given a certain number of lines with just gesture and elegant modulation of voice.

More important, Fussell, in focusing on the remarks relating to delivery of lines and in extrapolating general poetic significance from them, *forgets* (by choice or methodological necessity) that Johnson expected more from plays (and from elegiac poems, for that matter) than a certain number of lines . . . ; he expected to be pleased, and he knew that nothing pleases many and pleases long but just representations of general nature; he expected to be moved and, like other men, he was moved whenever what was presented could be credited "as a just picture of a real original," as an accurate depiction of events, dilemmas, thoughts, or feelings, naturally incident to our state of life. What is left out of Fussell's account is Johnson's emphasis on psychological cause and effect and the ground of "nature" mediating between the two.

Not only does Johnson leap erratically from one pole to the other in the review of *Lycidas,* according to Fussell, but he also manages, on one occasion at least, to perch on both poles at the same time, namely, when he says that "In this poem, there is no nature, for there is no truth." It seems that

> this means two things at once: it means that considered as an act of self-expression the poem is too grossly a lie because we know that the grief it pretends to register was not felt by the author; and at the same time it means that the poem, considered as a piece of rhetoric, employs a code which strikes the reader as too "remote" from the artistically familiar to stimulate a conventional, and thus literary or even "stock" response.[46]

Moreover, although "Johnson's statement means these two things at once, . . . the simultaneousness of the meanings does not make them any more compatible." Now there simply are no incompatible meanings inherent in Johnson's comment; he simply reaffirms, with more force and concision, what he has just said, here bringing the bulk of the preceding paragraph to forceful conclusion. The images are not too *remote* from the *artistically familiar* (one of his points being that they are too tiresomely familiar), but from what can be easily associated with the natural tendencies of the mind in a state of distress; there is no truth because the imagery and sentiments are not proportioned to the operations of our intellectual, emotional nature. Also, what Johnson says here is perfectly consistent with his remark that the "inherent improbability" of the poem "forces dissatisfaction on the mind," which Fussell offers as an instance of Johnson's return to the self-expressive pole. The two meanings that Fussell finds are, finally, nothing more than implications of his governing categories, called univocally into service here to elucidate this remark rather than the one dealing with "inherent improbability," which, by Fussell's mode of inference, is equally vulnerable to categorical divisiveness.

Johnson's statement is certainly complex, but it is not self-contradictory, grounded in mutually exclusive demands, radically ambiguous, or significant relative to two conflicting referents. Fussell's two meanings derive from the terminology in terms of which the statement is examined (as do, of course, the "singular" meanings attached to other isolated remarks), and by this mode of derivation we can always have the meanings we desire, without encumbering ourselves with established canons of demonstration and without being required to supply a rationale for the necessity or appropriateness of any remark in its particular context.

Operating from antithetic subsumptive categories, we can proceed to locate isolated statements that, under categorical coercion, can be interpreted as participating more or less fully in one or the other "discriminatory" class, identifying the isolated remarks as instances of one or the other category as we think at the moment of local and immediate reasons for the identification. Since "this"— in one if its aspects, from one perspective, or under a certain construction—is *very like* (it is Fussell's persistent phrase) "this"—in one of its aspects, from one perspective, or under a certain construction—then we are fully justified in concluding that "this" is really "this." Moreover, since we have previously decided upon our antithetical categories and since all events are marvel-

ously tolerant of the ways in which we happen to interpret them
(just as "reality"—whatever exactly that is—is, as Whitehead once
said, enormously tolerant of the interpretations we impose on "it"),
we may, as Fussell repeatedly does, go about predicating categorical value of whatever remarks we happen to light upon, without
considering whether any particular statement is a subordinate but
necessary part of some larger statement (meaningful, in fact, only
as subservient to that larger statement) or, minimally, whether it
has determinate meaning relative to what immediately precedes
and follows it. Finally, since isolated remarks (like material events,
natural phenomena) are extraordinarily complaisant in the face of
our interpretive propensities and since we are not obliged to
explain what might *cause* any particular statement (considered
independently of our a priori categorical assumptions) to be where
and as it is in a particular work, there is no reason why we cannot
have any remark mean two different things at the same time. By
fiat and by analogy, we arrive at "proofs."[47]

The dreadful psychomachia in which Johnson is engaged, mar-
shaling his forces now behind the one, now behind the other
adversary, is finally resolved, with "rhetoric" gaining the laurel
wreath.

> After another paragraph devoted to condemning "mythological
> imagery, such as a college easily supplies," Johnson discloses
> what has been troubling him all along: the poem, taken either as
> "expression" or artifact,[48] can easily embolden impiety because
> it mingles pagan with Christian myth as if they were of equal
> efficacy: This poem has yet a grosser fault. With these trifling
> fictions [that is, "the puerilities of obsolete mythology"] are
> mingled the most awful and sacred truths, such as ought never to
> be polluted with such irreverent combinations. The shepherd
> . . . is now a feeder of sheep, and afterwards an ecclesiastical
> pastor, a superintendent of a Christian flock. Such equivoca-
> tions are always unskillful; but here they are indecent, and at
> least approach to impiety, of which, however, I believe the
> writer not to have been conscious.

From these comments "we see . . . that it is Johnson's sense of the
subtle moral and theological damage *Lycidas* may do *to the reader*
that provides the spring for the whole critique." Thus it is that, "in
perceiving that his care is ultimately for the reader, we may say that

what finally *wins out* is his sense that literature is primarily rhetoric. But this sense *wins out* only after a very dubious battle with a contrary conception of what writing is."[49] I see absolutely no reason to assume—and Fussell supplies no justification for the assertion—that this passage on the mingling of mythological and sacred truths provides the "spring for the whole critique." All the antecedent critical objections to the poem are not so many implications of the principle of judgment enunciated here, are not enfolded within this objection to a *grosser* fault as potentialities of expression.

To Johnson, the poem has an *additional* fault, one *grosser* than any faults previously noted in the diction, rhyme, numbers, or in the natural probability of expression and illustration, namely, a "religious" fault; from natural, *psychological* truth, Johnson moves to *religious* truth, and he finds in the poem sentiments "which neither passion nor reason could have dictated, since the change which religion [i.e., the Christian religion] has made in the whole system of the world" (*Rambler* 37). The essential point is that this poem, when assessed in relation to *two quite distinct orders of truth* (natural and supernatural), simply cannot be credited. Moreover, the commingling is offensive both *because* it is theologically "improper" and *because* neither passion nor reason could have prompted its expression; the mixture violates psychological and religious truth at one and the same time. And the fact is that the poem would have failed to please, even if Milton had not *mingled* trifling fictions with sacred truths. Johnson, at the end, switches to another—nonpoetic—frame of reference without undermining, invalidating, or contradicting his other principled objections to the poem. That what he mentions last may have disturbed him first we may—without being able to know—suppose, but we can know with certainty that the "theological" judgment is both different from and compatible with the "literary" judgment, that the "literary" judgment is perfectly consistent with Johnson's general principles of judgment, and that logically the last mentioned is not related to the antecedent remarks as cause (i.e., "spring") is to effect.[50]

What happens, of course, when the "religious" remarks are made the "spring" of the whole critique is that the primary critical motivation is ascribed or transferred to Johnson's sensibility, in this case his peculiar religious sensibility, the whole critique exemplifying the emotionally charged, spontaneous outpourings of an untidy, orthodox mind and becoming little more than a "religious" reflex action. Once again attention is directed away from principles of judgment and toward "character" (indeed, eccentricity of character).[51]

Fussell imagines a victor in the critique only because he has imagined a fight, although in fact there is nothing in the nature of his dialectic, as presented, that demands ultimate conquest of disputed territory by one or the other category. Since Johnson is represented as switching erratically from one pole to the other throughout, Fussell could simply maintain that the last leap in the irregular series is to the legal-rhetorical pole without violating the logic upon which the case is built. As it stands, Fussell's dramatic contest lacks probability and necessity; the end is aesthetically displeasing—in spite of his emphasis on "spring"—because it does not emerge as a necessary consequence of the antecedent parts; its own "inherent improbability forces dissatisfaction on the mind."

In summation we are assured that "any lingering superstition [suspicion?] that Johnson can be meaningfully described as, in some way, a 'neo-classic' critic . . . will be evaporated by close scrutiny of his remarks on *Lycidas*, a poem in which 'there is no art, for there is nothing new.' It is precisely the neo-classic element that disgusts him."[52] Now this is puzzling. We have just been informed that in the review of *Lycidas* Johnson's sense that literature is *primarily rhetoric* won out, and in an earlier section Fussell had claimed that the "no art-nothing new" comment indicated that Johnson had "stepped wholly back into the world of rhetorical analysis." It would seem to me that *neoclassic* attaches itself naturally to that side of Fussell's dialectical universe which includes "rhetoric" and "legal mood;" and if this is the case, then, to be fair to Fussell, we would have to say that Johnson can definitely be described as in some way (it is, after all, one of his two critical ways) a neoclassical critic. Fussell's whole "argument" collapses if we take one half of his duality away in the eleventh hour.

Following up on this new assertion, Fussell says that "To turn to the *Life of Prior* is to see clearly that Johnson is not a neo-classicist but an empiricist." When we do make that turn, we again "experience his oscillations between the poles established by the rhetorical and the self-expressive conceptions of writing." Since *rhetoric* has previously been identified with the world of artistic conventions and inherited devices, I cannot reasonably link it now with empiricism (at least, I have not been given any reason to relate empiricism to rhetoric). And since I can discover no grounds for believing that the oscillation between contradictory poles is characteristic of empiricism, I am inclined (invited, I think) to conclude that *neoclassicism* is to the rhetorical as *empiricism* is to the self-expressive conception of writing; the prevailing logic of Fussell's piece encourages me to join the items of one duality to the items of another duality. (Of course, the by-now traditional habit of discussing neoclassicism in terms of rhetorical categories and priorities—for an example of which we have to look no further than the chapter under discussion—induces me to ascribe rhetorical significance to neoclassicism here.) At any rate, Fussell has not previously established any connection between empiricism and oscillation.

Moreover, if implicated in Fussell's assertion is the idea that Johnson's oscillation is true to human nature and thus grounded in empirical reality, we would still be forced to conclude that neither Johnsonian approach is peculiarly or necessarily empirical, and that, conjoined, the two approaches do not amount to a recognizable form of empirical inquiry; to my knowledge, empiricism has never been construed as originating in a contradiction between a social and a religious sense of things, or as being characterized by an alternating commitment to two mutually exclusive conceptions of things. Johnson may behave like a man (allowing inconsistency, for the sake of argument, to be an essential characteristic of man) without being as a writer or critic an empiricist *by virtue* of his inconsistency. Any particular form of empiricism (and the term has been applied to a diversity of approaches, not all of which are intellectually compatible with one another), conceived of as a coherent critical method informed by a stable body of assumptions and principles, could be enlisted to explain Johnson's behavior in its terms, but nothing but confusion is served by identifying what is explained with the hypothesis by which it is explained; empiricism may explain inconsistency, but inconsistency is not empiricism.

The issue of inconsistency is raised, in part, because early in the chapter, Fussell—appearing to be on the verge of discovering a

single, comprehensive, subsuming criterion of critical judgment—
informs us that "Johnson was always hospitable to inconsistencies
so long as they constituted an honest registration of empirical
actuality."[53] But as he proceeds, Fussell concentrates, as we have
seen, on Johnson's inconsistent *behavior,* not on any intellectual
principle that would make "inconsistency" intelligible and meaningful. As soon as we make the registration of empirical actuality
the court of final appeal, we establish a radical principle of judgment, in relation to which Johnson's various critical remarks
should stand as natural consequences and to which particular
works, expressions, and events should be referred for evaluation or
description. But Fussell neither states nor implies that the legal
mood and the self-expressive mood are governed by a fundamental
demand for an honest registration of empirical actuality. In his
self-expressive mood, Johnson is naive and hopelessly unsophisticated, whereas in his legal mood he requests not truth, but mere
rhetorical artifice; in neither mood is the value and effectiveness of
literature determined, according to Fussell, by reference to empirical reality or to the real operations of the human mind. To Fussell,
the two demands are contradictory, radically inconsonant, contentious, and he attempts not to illuminate the principle by which, for
example, Johnson might justify artistic behavior unacceptable to
some critics and to some critical standards, on the grounds that
"there is always an appeal open from criticism to nature" ("Preface
to Shakespeare"), but to record, to document Johnson's inconsistent behavior, deriving his inconsistencies from an a priori
conception of Johnson's bifurcated sensibility (ultimately, of
course, from his conception of literature as compounded of individual talent and preexisting form.)[54]

This review of Fussell's evidence and "argument" can be con-
cluded with a few animadversions on his remarks concerning a
section of the *Life of Prior,* in which the antithetical demands are
again discovered at work. Johnson, we are informed, "begins the
critical part of the *Life of Prior* by stressing Prior's skill in rhetoric,
his willingness to exercise himself in a variety of known styles, not
all of which, obviously, can 'naturally' be his 'own,' in the sense
that a person is conceived to have one style in which he expresses

himself most 'sincerely.' "[55] The logic here is that Johnson is in his rhetorical mood *because* he talks about a variety of styles, and that Prior is insincere *because* he does not write in his one best, most sincere style. All this is deduced from: "Prior has written with great variety, and his variety has made him popular. He has tried all styles, from the grotesque to the solemn, and has not so failed in any as to incur derision or disgrace." Between Johnson's remarks and Fussell's interpretation of them there is a wealth of negative and a paucity of positive correspondence. To the breakdown of faculties according to the special requirements of particular employments postulated (or suggested) earlier, Fussell now supplies a further refinement, a natural propensity in each poet for a particular literary style (with *style* here conceived in the most general, imprecise sense). Johnson certainly never gave support to any such myth, which leads ultimately to a hierarchy of writers based on a hierarchy of styles, and he certainly does not do so in the *Prior* passage to which Fussell directs us. Johnson is praising (or commenting favorably on) Prior's stylistic versatility and stylistic copiousness, not chiding him for failing to hit upon his one "natural" style.

When, according to Fussell, Johnson looks at Prior from the "self-expressive" pole, he "astonishes us" by saying: "In his amorous effusions he is less happy [than in his *Tales*]; for they are not dictated by nature or by passion, and have neither gallantry nor tenderness." Once again Johnson directs us to the universal subjects of poetry, nature and passion, and informs us that Prior's love verses, as selective arrangements of images and sentiments purposively directed, express neither gallantry nor tenderness (two possible objects of expression in love verses, two natural aims that may govern the poet's handling of the verbal signs of nature and passion, gallantry and tenderness being to love verses as rational praise and natural lamentation are to elegies, gallantry and tenderness being at least two qualities naturally expected from love verses) because Prior has consulted not the condition of man, but the resources of his library. Underlying Johnson's criticism is a functional conception of the natural operations of our intellectual, emotional nature, to which an appeal can regularly be made whenever we (Johnson and others) wish to know why, after the experience of dissatisfaction, a particular poem, confined to a relatively determinate range of concern, fails to please.

When Johnson goes on to say that "even when [Prior] tries to *act the lover* without the help of gods or goddesses, his thoughts are unaffecting and remote," we are, according to Fussell, "to deduce that the thoughts are unaffecting and remote because they issue from a *convention* rather than a *unique, genuine personal occasion.*"[56] The simple truth, as Johnson clearly states, is that even when Prior attempts *to act the lover* (without the help of mythological machinery), "He talks not 'like a man of this world' " (*Lives* 2:202). To credit his expression, we must be able to consider it, after the fact of expression, as possible or probable to human life under the specified or implied conditions. In the end Prior's verses display Prior's learning, but they fail to satisfy the conditions upon which the peculiar pleasures of love verses are or can be based. Whether Prior is actually in love or not, he (or his "speaker") must at least speak *as if* he were actually in love in order to please, since our pleasure is determined, finally, not by his actual emotional state, but by the adequacy of his expression to what we can accept as proportionate to the imagined or actual state.[57] Characteristically, Johnson calls not so much for self-expression as for adequate expression.

As a critic, Johnson's primary focus is not on the poet's state of mind, but on the poetic bases of pleasure, on the congruence between what is expressed and what we can legitimately credit, truth to nature being the essential standard to which works dealing with human life are referred; nature is the source from which the poet should draw his material and the standard against which his achievement is measured. Where there is leisure for fiction, there is neither love nor grief. A love poem is not an elegy, but in evaluating both kinds Johnson draws on a stable body of assumptions and a coherent set of critical principles.

I have now exhausted the evidence and the "arguments" by which Fussell has decided to expose what literature seemed to be to Johnson. The end of Fussell's analysis, as he suggests early in the piece, is to enable us to approach Johnson's writings with clear-sightedness, a condition that can be realized only when we refuse to filter the writings through the distorting lenses of Boswell and Macaulay and recognize the fundamental polarity of his critical sensibility. The *spring* of the whole piece is a cognitively inadequate hypothesis relating to the facts of writing, which creates the conditions for a discussion of Johnson's sensibility in terms of antithetical forces of attraction (though, as presented, Johnson's polar "senses" keep apart what the sponsoring hypothesis conceives of as joined), which leads, in turn, to the inevitable conclusion (inevitable because the antithetical senses are not displayed as tending toward or tolerating synthesis) that in Johnson we have a literary sensibility that "for all its appearance of judiciousness, is really madly irrational, unsystematic, impulsive, and untidy." In the end, then, we are offered by Fussell's account what amounts to a "psychical" analogue or counterpart to that "physical" Johnson whom Boswell or Langton might happen upon in the garret, the disordered, disheveled, rumpled Johnson shuffling convulsively about an accumulated rubble, an unsightly assortment of papers, books, and orange peels, with all the reckless abandon of a man at his unbuttoned, unbuckled, periwig-at-a-jaunty-angle ease. Here are the real outward and visible signs of the true intellectual condition; here are the material and tangible vestments of Johnson's mind, the true sacramental significance of which Fussell, as orthodox exegete, has finally made intelligible to us in his authoritative, "infallible" conclusion. Fussell, I submit, out-Macaulays Macaulay; in whole and in part, his account is simply incredible (and there's an end on't).

3

The Limitations of Dialectical
Approaches to Johnson's Criticism

For all the direct attention paid to the views of Sigworth and Fussell in the preceding chapters, I have throughout been less interested in excoriating particular critics than in exposing the shortcomings of the principles of reasoning and the theoretical assumptions upon which their works are founded, in suggesting alternative ways of discussing critical history and Johnson's place in it, and in relating a variety of Johnson's particular critical pronouncements to what I take to be the radical terms, distinctions, assumptions, and principles determining their significance and meaning. And although I may at times have succumbed to the impulse to mingle a little horseplay with my raillery, these occasional indulgences in whimsy should not obscure the fact that the focus, in general, has been on the cognitive inadequacies of the interpretations offered by Sigworth and Fussell. The real end of the detailed examination to which I have subjected these particular essays is (at least it has been my constant intention) to enable readers to resist the disarming charm of critical arguments—of which there has been a regrettable abundance in recent years—founded on dialectical principles, abstract terms, mystical entities. I should like to look upon the preceding "analysis" as an "enabling act." But whether it is or not, the fact remains that our knowledge of Johnson's critical thought cannot be much advanced by means of the principles and methods of argumentation adopted by Fussell and Sigworth. Both critics are noteworthy to the extent that they participate in a kind of critical reasoning that is becoming, once again, alarmingly frequent in Johnsonian studies.

In addition, both critics have singled out for special attention Johnson's critique of *Lycidas,* which is—whatever else it may be—a sort of acid test for any hypothesis affirming the essential coherence and integrity of Johnson's critical thought. It is after all the critical review that even the warmest of Johnson's supporters have tolerated rather than embraced, regarding it usually, in Hagstrum's phrase, as Johnson's "greatest critical faux pas"[1] or, in Bate's terms, as "one of his quaint misfires."[2] Thus these essays provide an opportunity to reexamine the "bases" of Johnson's critical thought and to determine whether the critique, in relation to a determinate body of principles and assumptions, is anomalous.

For all their manifold differences in specific aim, subject matter, and terminology, a large number of recent essays on Johnson share with the two works examined in this book a common confidence in a dialectical method of reasoning from a priori, ruling hypotheses, a common tendency to begin critical reasoning, not from some empirically distinguishable event or effect that it is then the task of criticism to "explain" in all its particularity in terms of necessary and sufficient conditions, but from some basic proposition or truth concerning poetry, criticism, Johnson's thought, or the like, through which particular works or events are then filtered in order to "show" in them the inherence of the terms (variously modified, extended, or ramified) of the proposition or truth, so that in the end what is explained is at least in large part an aspect or an implication of the explanatory hypothesis. A comprehensive survey of writings of this sort would take us well beyond the scope of this book, but some reasonably adequate sense of the general tendencies of these writings can be obtained from a brief examination of two additional studies that exhibit class affinities with the efforts of Sigworth and Fussell.

In 1967 Arieh Sachs's *Passionate Intelligence: Imagination and Reason in the Work of Samuel Johnson* appeared,[3] a book in which the rich complexity of Johnson's thought is discussed in relation to two "faculties," reason and imagination, the essential features of Johnson's thought being determined by an a priori conception of what the nature, function, and relation of those faculties were to Johnson. Since the nature of Sachs's argument has already been discussed in print, I shall treat his work briefly, enlisting the aid of the reviewer who dealt specifically with Sachs's principles of reasoning and system of inference. Speaking of Sachs's general procedure and of its inherent shortcomings, Donald Greene says:

it begins with the dogmatic assertion of a prefabricated formulation of Johnson's "thought," and then selects passages here and there in a handful of his writings that seem to support it, intertwining them with much incidental commentary, often only dubiously relevant, on Swift, Pope, and Donne, and citation of modern monographs by Boas, Lovejoy, and others. Johnson appears only in bits and pieces, *disjecta membra* which may be reassembled at the will of the author into almost any pattern. This game can be played indefinitely by any number of players, and has unfortunately been played only too often with Johnson.

Sachs's dichotomous perspective leads inevitably to oversimplification, as Greene notes: ". . . the major theses of the book rest on vast oversimplifications of Johnson's complex thinking and the vocabulary in which he expressed it." In support of this claim Greene goes on to say:

[The book] begins with the assertion, "Johnson's observations on many subjects have in common the basic notion of a polarity of faculties: Reason and Imagination." Reason is the good pole and Imagination the bad. "I shall argue," Sachs begins his chapter, "that Johnson's satire on man (especially in *Rasselas*) springs from the view that in human nature reason and passion [passion being construed, apparently by means of analogical extension, as exclusively an effect of Imagination], the angelic and the bestial, are intermixed. . . ." Any attentive reader of Johnson's writings will immediately think of a dozen passages which cast doubt on the existence of any such simple "polarity" in his thinking [and, of course, on the adequacy of Sachs's characterization of the faculties].[4]

Once the critical machinery is set in motion and the meaning-values of the primary categories of differentiation are unleashed on selected bits of Johnsonian material, we are frequently able to recognize that just the reverse of what we had long believed is true; indeed, with our categorical lenses firmly in place, we can for the first time clearly see that Johnson advocates what we had formerly —and naively—thought he had absolutely rejected. For example, once we realize that to Johnson reason "is the faculty in man which keeps him in contact with his true state, whereas Imagination, contradistinctly, is the great 'overreacher,' " we can understand that, in spite of his unremitting and persistent vilification of the concept, Johnson really believes in the Great Chain of Being. On precisely this matter, Greene comments:

> Mr. Sachs arrives at his conclusion by an exercise of the naive *petitio principii* common in treatises of this kind, which the late Ronald Crane made a point of detecting and denouncing. Johnson condemns those who affirm the existence of the great scale of being for their "presumption in attempting to answer questions beyond the power of man's mind"; that is to say (according to Sachs), in attempting to "break through human limitations and so become something that is above him in the great scale"; therefore Johnson believed in the existence of the great scale.[5]

In other words, since reason is the faculty that enables a man to define what is within the compass of his powers, it follows, curiously enough, that when he exercises his reason in denying—after due deliberation—to mere man the intellectual capacity to determine, by ratiocination, the existence or necessity of a great chain, he thereby *affirms*, in the *act of denunciation*, man's place in a scale of being. (Since from the perspective of the inside the outside is the inside—in the sense that "it" is what you go "into"—it necessarily follows that when I say that I am going outside I mean that I am going inside.) "Argumentation of this kind," Greene rightly says, "makes the head swim."[6]

A recent article that forms a natural alliance with the works by Sigworth and Fussell is Murray Krieger's "Fiction, Nature, and Literary Kinds in Johnson's Criticism of Shakespeare."[7] As the title partially indicates, Krieger's primary text is the "Preface to Shakespeare." According to Krieger, there is at the heart of the "preface" a central contradiction, a polarity of views respecting the nature of reality, which must be recognized if we hope finally to understand what exactly Johnson is up to in his commentary on Shakespeare. To Johnson the world of experience alternately reflects *causality* and *casualty*, one or the other being stressed as Johnson changes his ontological and, of course, epistemological hats. On the one hand, we have—on the side of causality—the mirror-universe of universals:

> In the mirror-universe of universals, like recognizes like, so that the universal subject reflects the universal object. The general nature outside us, then, is the natural object of the general

human nature in us which responds to it. And as is true even of so rigorous an empiricist as Hume, there is for Johnson no questioning of the rationalist assumption that is smuggled in, the assumption that there surely *is*, beneath the infinite variety of individuated nature and of the individual human responses to it, a general nature and a general core of human nature.[8]

When he is in his causal mood, Johnson praises Shakespeare for representing characters who "act and speak by the influence of those general passions and principles by which all minds are agitated, and the whole system of life is continued in motion" ("Preface"). What Johnson seems to be saying in such remarks is that the "poet, . . . in the service of the universal system, rather than the particular *aberration*, is to neglect the *casual* [i.e., all those 'distinctions superinduced and adventitious'] for the *causal*."[9]

On the other hand, when Johnson comes to the defense of Shakespeare's mingling of the tragic and the comic, he refers to nature as a "chaos of mingled purposes and casualties" ("Preface"). In his doing so, we should note "how radically the notion of nature as [the] object of imitation has shifted! Now the causal has been forsaken for the casual. Far from being overlooked, the casual is, however maddening, to be cherished as *all there is*."[10] From this ontological base, Johnson is saying that down here we are stuck with "the real state of sublunary nature, which partakes of good and evil, joy and sorrow, mingled with endless variety of proportion and innumerable modes of combination; and expressing the course of the world, in which the loss of one is the gain of another; in which, at the same time, the reveller is hasting to his wine, and the mourner burying his friend; in which the malignity of one is sometimes defeated by the frolick of another; and many mischiefs and many benefits are done and hindered without design" ("Preface").

Putting special emphasis on the closing words of this passage, Krieger exclaims: "Precisely—without design." It is important to recognize at the outset that Krieger *gives* cosmic significance to Johnson's mundane "without design," interpreting the phrase in an absolute, metaphysical sense, not in the sense intended by Johnson: in real, everyday life it sometimes happens that our plans are thwarted or advanced by accidental events or circumstances— a visitor may interrupt our work; an unexpected fissure in a rock may facilitate our release from the Happy Valley; or a slanderous attack may bring not obloquy, but fame or unexpected aid and comfort. Krieger himself underscores the metaphysical implications: "Professor Robert C. Elliott has properly pointed out that my argument seems to require that 'without design' refers to cosmic purposelessness when the context of Johnson's passage limits the phrase to the betrayals of private human intention. In defense I would claim only that Johnson's usage—trapped as it is in a passage that emphasizes chaos and the casual—can be seen to treat the futility of human purpose as a microcosmic reflection of the gap between cause and effect that precludes order in our entire 'sublunary nature.' "[11] Cosmic purposelessness precluding order in our entire sublunary nature! Not even Johnson's severest critics have been willing to attribute such heretical notions to him.

It seems clear that it is Krieger, not Johnson, who traps the passage in chaos. Krieger's argument depends upon removing the passage from its context and supplying it with the sort of significance it might possibly have if it were context- and person-free. More exactly, to have his way Krieger must remove not only the passage from its context, but "without design" from the rest of the passage, since, considered independently of Krieger's cosmological imperative, the passage would allow Krieger's reading only if Johnson had suggested, for example, that upon the death of a friend a man joyfully hastened to his wine cellar, while a reveler unacquainted with the departed sat down disconsolately to compose a funeral oration. Under these conditions we might have something in the world inclining toward Krieger's universal purposelessness. But Johnson is not speaking to metaphysical conditions in the phrase *without design*. Moreover, there is no necessary metaphysical conflict implicated in the simultaneous existence of accident and a system of order. The presence and unpredictability of accident in human affairs in no way contravenes those principles by which all minds are agitated and the whole system of life is continued in motion; the influence of the passions, as Johnson says in *Adventurer* 95, "is uniform, and their effects nearly the same in every human breast." In allowing for accident Johnson does not preclude system. There certainly can be no science of the accidental in the sense of a reduction of accident to rules, laws, and principles allowing prediction. But the *conse-*

quences of accident are knowable and predictable (in the sense that they can be embodied in general concepts), and they follow naturally, regularly and of "necessity," from the relationship between the nature of the accident and the nature of the object, event, or person affected. Crudely, a fragile glass accidentally dropped from a great height onto a hard surface will always break; a piece of broken glass accidentally puncturing a human finger will invariably cause pain, bleeding, and some degree of dismay. Accident does not abrogate order; it sets it in motion.[12]

The same event does not affect us all in the same way, but when we know, for example, something about the relation between a person and an event (i.e., how any particular man of determinate ethical character relates to or construes an event), we can determine whether his specific response to the event is or is not humanly appropriate. It is unreasonable to expect the friend and the rival to be similarly affected by the misfortune of a man, but their different responses—governed by different kinds of "self-interested" relations to the man—argue for, not against the essential uniformity of human nature. An infinite number of tunes can be derived from a single system of harmonics (an infinite number of sentences can be generated from the stable, regular, knowable "grammatical rules" of a language), or innumerable modes of combination can trigger the uniform operations of our intellectual and emotional natures. If this were not the case, all responses would be not only possible but appropriate, and hence no particular response would be more probable or more appropriate than another. Unless we understand that an event and the response occasioned by it are in some determinate sense type-bound, we are totally unable to exclude any specific responses to the event on the grounds of class inappropriateness.

To be pleased by his friend's misfortune, a man must construe it, say, as a circumstance likely to promote or contribute to his eventual well-being; if the rival were to construe the misfortune in this manner, he would, of course, be depressed by his rival's bad luck. As the circumstances and the relations become more complex, so too will the responses, but it is only because uniform principles of the mind underlie the manifest diversity of response that Johnson —and we—can legitimately judge represented (or, for that matter, "real") action to be "improbable" or "inappropriate."[13] The "without design" passage signalizes not Johnson's abandonment of "causality," but his awareness of complexity, an awareness that does not in the least commit him to the recognition of cosmic purposelessness in the world.

The sense of the passage notwithstanding, Krieger will have the casual mood.

> In this mood he continually calls for endless variety or diversity, apparently *forgetting* about the unity which is the central quality of the causally controlled system he called for earlier. A world "without design," a chaos in which all is casual, is obviously resistant to any attempt to impose a causal system which must rest on universal models of possible relations among its seeming particulars (only *seeming* particulars because in such a system there are no true particulars insisting on their particularity).[14] But in the chaos of casualties, without design, there can be only the resistant particulars, the "endless variety" and "innumerable modes"[15] precluding the gathering together of particulars into universals that could constitute a system. The poet who before was praised for overlooking the casual for the essential is now praised for cultivating the casual since there is no essential.[16]

I think it is important to recognize that many of the shortcomings of Krieger's analysis stem from his refusal to recognize that the "Preface" is divided into distinct parts, each containing its own special problems and each providing partial answers to related but separate questions. Working from a dialectical base and focusing on isolated statements—divorced from the contexts of which they are a part and from the particular questions to which they are partial answers—Krieger makes conversant sections of the "Preface" that are not on immediate speaking terms. Only when they are isolated and juxtaposed can the passages to which Krieger refers *appear* to carry cosmological significance. In brief, Krieger is interested in tracking down the "potentialities" of his hypothesis in the text—considered in the light of that hypothesis—not in testing that hypothesis against the details of the text—considered independently of that hypothesis. For example, with regard to "without design," it is useful to keep in mind that Johnson simply says that in the affairs of life mischiefs and benefits do not always imply either malice or benefice aforethought in some agent; he does *not* *say* that the *world* is without design.

Krieger arrives at his central contradiction by first isolating remarks from one another and then heaping upon particular terms and phrases within the isolated passages all the metaphysical weight that they can, independently considered, bear. From a certain distance or perspective, "real" life may certainly appear to be chaotic, but as soon as we focus on any specific event or sequence of events we detect the peculiarly individuated expression of uniform principles of life (whatever "reality" may "really" be like, our apprehension of "it" is orderly and regular, and our survival depends upon the "similarity" in our ways of construing "it").

For purposes of illustration let us take an example of the "particularized general" from Johnson's *Rasselas*. When Pekuah is abducted suddenly by the Arab rover—who appears "fortuitously" and thus without warning or preparation—we turn our attention immediately, not to the purpose of the abduction or to the manner in which Pekuah is treated by the Arab, but to the effects of the abduction on those who remain behind. And although the event provokes general distress, the individual responses are both various and peculiarly appropriate. Nekayah, for example, sinks down into hopeless dejection and inconsolable grief, whereas each of her remaining servants tempers grief with the hope that she at least will succeed to Pekuah's place in Nekayah's esteem and affection. Here is variety and natural probability. In what immediately follows we concentrate on the progress of Nekayah's grief and see in particular exemplification the validity of Imlac's assertion that time acts upon the mind as distance acts upon the sight. Nekayah's sorrow, uncomplicated by guilt and peculiarly conditioned by her relationship to Pekuah, takes the course of general sorrow along a particularly individuated path. For Johnson, art is moving to the extent that what it represents can be recognized as congruent with the "concrete universals" of human experience.[17]

If Johnson believed that there were no regularly operative system of human nature to which reference could be made, then he could not say, among other things, that the inherent improbability of *Lycidas* brings dissatisfaction to the mind, improbability being essentially an *exclusion* judgment, which depends upon the recognition—experienced as dissatisfaction—that the boundary of legitimate expression, delimited by the specific occasion and situation, has been passed or neglected. Krieger's paradox dissolves, I think, when, following Johnson, we refuse to treat the general and the particular as ontological competitors, or, more simply, when we restore the isolated terms and phrases to their context within a discussion of tragicomedy and read on: "That the mingled drama may convey all the instruction of tragedy or comedy cannot be denied, because it includes both in its alternations of exhibition, and approaches nearer than either to the appearance of life, by shewing how great machinations and slender designs may promote or obviate one another, and the high and the low *co-operate in the general system by unavoidable concatenation*" ("Preface"; emphasis added).

It would be impossible here to examine Krieger's "argument" in detail without deviating too far from the track, but we must look briefly at some of the striking consequences of his intellectual method. Having defined the ontological values of the antithetical poles, Krieger can proceed to catch Johnson in the throes of vacillating commitment and to note passages, in and out of the Johnsonian canon, of parallel significance. When Johnson—governed by the sense of experiential reality as a chaos without design—affirms that Shakespeare "caught his ideas from the living world, and exhibited only what he saw before him," we have "a preview of the spirit of Wordsworth and of his words that speak of keeping his eye on the object."[18] That by this method and this standard Johnson could just as easily be linked to Pope, Dryden, Ben Jonson, Horace, Aristotle, or Gerard Manley Hopkins as to Wordsworth is nothing to the point, for we are interested in paralleling Johnsonian terms and doctrines—isolated from the particular problems, assumptions, and purposes determining their meaning and significance—with Wordsworthian terms and doctrines. The anticipations of Wordsworth are indeed remarkable once we endow the local with special and decisive importance:

Perhaps even more obviously Wordsworthian is Johnson's praise for Shakespeare's language, which "is pursued with so much ease and simplicity" that it seems "to have been gleaned by diligent selection out of common conversation and common occurrences." This is consistent with Johnson's later (also Wordsworthian) definition of an ideal style in a nation's language as that which is "to be sought in the common intercourse of life,

among those who speak only to be understood, without ambition
or elegance." On these grounds and others, Johnson's criticism
of Milton as artificial and bookish seems preparatory to Wordsworth's criticism of Thomas Gray [and of Johnson himself?].[19]

To all this I could add a plethora of specific remarks that from the
perspective of a priori determination have a Wordsworthian ring to
them, including, for example, the statement that "all true poetry
requires that the sentiments be natural" (*Idler* 77). But, of course,
this is the sort of association game that Johnson can be made to play
with virtually any earlier or later critic. When statements materi-
ally similar in some respects are made contiguous, they do not
necessarily become consanguineous. The kind of analogical reasoning employed by Krieger here can bring things together, but it
cannot prove or demonstrate that between what is conjoined there
subsists any necessary relation or fundamental similarity. The
point is that even if Wordsworth and Johnson did in fact agree on
the issue of poetic style—which we have no reason to believe and
good reasons to disbelieve—we simply could not establish that
agreement by Krieger's methodological procedure.

The bulk of the article is given over to illustrations of the fundamental ontological contradictions in the "Preface," with the
passage containing "mingled chaos—without design" serving as
the constant, steady, and singular referent of the "casual" pole.
When Johnson notes that Shakespeare is "so much more careful to
please than to instruct," he seems, according to Krieger, "to be
complaining precisely about what he has been praising Shakespeare for doing. For the moral order he now wishes to see operating in the plays could operate only if the casual, disorderly realities
were forsaken for a rational, universal system of possible relations.
Fact would have to be forsaken for a fiction in the service of a
higher Truth."[20] These assertions reflect the operations of dialectical necessity, not the implicit possible meanings of Johnson's
thought. For Johnson, "moral" relation is not contingent upon
abandoning fact for a pleasantly delusive fiction, which exhibits
what one would wish rather than what actually obtains in the world.
From Shakespeare's writing "a system of social duty may be
selected, for he that thinks reasonably must think morally" ("Preface"). Johnson's essential point—deriving from basic convictions

about the best ends of art—is that where there is room for choice, where the poet—as the one responsible for the selection, arrangement, and emphasis of material—can choose between possibilities of contrary moral value, *without violating natural probability*, the best moral choice should be made.

Nevertheless, the dialectical machine whirs on:

> How different a sort of universe and how different a function of poetry this call for poetic justice [in Johnson's, Shakespeare "makes no distribution of good and evil, nor is always careful to shew in the virtuous a disapprobation of the wicked"][21]assumes, if we recall his description of the real state of sublunary nature earlier. Johnson can say here, rather stiffly, "It is always a writer's duty to make the world better, and justice is a virtue independent of time or place."[22]

As a critic, Johnson is for Krieger stuck with a metaphysical dilemma:

> Either there is an objective structure or there is not; the role of particulars, as well as the existence of universals, must follow accordingly. Consequently, the poet must either bypass the peculiar properties of the particular in order to imitate its universality or he must dwell on its peculiarities since there is no going beyond them.[23]

Failing to recognize the either/or nature of his "realities," Johnson persists confusedly in demanding both the casual and the causal. Thus when he insists on justifying the combining of tragic with comic elements by asking only that they 'cooperate in the general system by unavoidable concatenation,' " he seems to "forget" (again?) that "the major initial thrust of his argument for mixing genres rested on a denial of any general system, rested rather on the need for poetry to reproduce the sublunary state that is without design."[24]

Fortunately, Johnson's condition is not entirely hopeless, for if we look closely at the "Preface," paying particular attention to an "aesthetic" wrinkle in the metaphysical fabric, we notice, on the one hand, that "chaos . . . without design" is the preeminent reality (the really real) and, on the other, that the critical confusion results from Johnson's habit of subordinating nature to art when he

is in his "universal" mood and art to nature when in his "particular" mood: "The all or none polarity in . . . these contradictory
impulses is reflected in the theoretical extremes that see the poem
either as partaking wholly of the order of art [order, we are being
not very subtly informed, is not so much a feature of reality as a
fiction of art], of total system, or as forsaking all system for a
living reality seen as 'without design.' " Hence "In the first case
nature (like the poem imitating it) is *made into the order of the
artful;* in the second the poem (as *art escaping from its own nature*)
is *made into the disorder of* 'sublunary nature,' nature in its raw,
un-neoclassical, anesthetic naturalness."[25] In switching to the
"aesthetic" dimension, however, Krieger has more than slightly—
and less than inadvertently—altered the either/or nature of the
metaphysical problem, for he now offers us two different, non-
competitive kinds of reality (i.e., an art reality and a "real" reality)
which, while markedly different, are capable of coexistence, since
the possibility of one no longer means the impossibility of the other.
In short, absolute, mutual contradiction has been transcended or
bypassed. We, of course, have no more reason to accept this
redefinition than the earlier definition of the "problem," since
both are products of Krieger's a priori determinations, not "real,"
identifiable "events" of Johnson's text, Krieger's "aesthetic" turn
here being simply a necessary mediating link between the initial
dichotomy and a happy conclusion.

Krieger's redefinition of the problem is a necessary stage in the
process of restoring Johnson's critical respectability. For Krieger,
Johnson's muddleheadedness can be redeemed if, prior to looking
at the discussion of the "unities" in the "Preface," we accept the
idea that sometimes Johnson makes nature into the order of art and
at others, art into the disorder of sublunary nature. Once we
recognize that Johnson's real are only apparent inconsistencies, we
will also see that the "unities" discussion brings Johnson home
free. Krieger notes that in that discussion Johnson stresses the
necessity of unified action and the delight that proceeds from our
consciousness of fiction. (What is particularly insidious here, of
course, is the implicit dependency of one upon the other, the
suggestion that unity of action is the fiction of which we are chiefly
conscious. In Johnson's discussion consciousness of fiction has no
special relationship with unity of action; consciousness of fiction

extends to the parts—thoughts, speeches, local actions—no less than to the whole; conversely, the whole, no less than the part, brings realities to the mind.) What we have in this discussion, in effect, is a new mood: "All this is, clearly, Johnson's consciousness of 'our consciousness of fiction,' such as we have not seen in him earlier."[26] Johnson now clearly sees that while the "poem may be—nay, must be—*like* reality, . . . the imitation is not to be confused with its object; nor is the mimetic process [on which Johnson comments not at all in the "unities" section], as the making of art, to be underestimated." And "Thus it is that, in this [new] mood, Johnson, while willing to forgo the unities of time and place, insists on the unity of action. Nothing else may be 'essential to the fable,' but this unity is."[27]

Now what this all means is that "we are back to a 'general system' after all." Note, however, how different this general system is from the one with which we (i.e., Krieger) began:

> Johnson may not have been able to rest in the unrestricted variety implied by the realism of his most anti-bookish, anti-systematic moments, but neither is his only alternative the general system with which we began. It is now the system created by the poet as his fictional unity of the endless variety found in 'the real state of sublunary nature,' a unity free of all artifice but that required to be 'a just picture of a real original.' If the first claims of Johnson we considered, all-universalizing as they were, seemed exclusively dedicated to an existentially blind unity; if the second, in their particularization, seemed anarchically dedicated to variety; these third seem to point ahead to the organicist's call for unity in variety, for a *discordia concors*."[28]

Here, then, is thesis, antithesis, and synthesis; in the end, Johnson's "Preface," when filtered through the screen of Krieger's terms and system of inference, is a kind of "progress" piece. Johnson, beginning with a naively innocent conception of universal (i.e., metaphysical) system, falls into the world of the existentially real (i.e., into the metaphysics of chaos without design), wavers uncertainly and inconsistently for a while (attracted by two mutually exclusive ontologies), and then achieves a higher innocence, in true apocalyptic fashion, by means of a marriage agreement, Experiential Diversity consenting to live—at least part time—in

the Beulah Land of Fiction with Artistic Unity. This is a pretty story
(and a neat one), but it is no adequate account, I submit, of
Johnson's "Preface"; the text yields to the exigencies of Krieger's
hypothesis, but the hypothesis makes no adjustments to the exigencies of the "Preface". The whole procedure of accountability is
reversed: the hypothesis is not accountable to the text, to the
problems that Johnson actually confronted and attempted to
resolve, but, rather, the text is accountable to the hypothesis; what
is disclosed is not the "internal" necessities of Johnson's commentary, but the "logical" necessities of an argument founded on
opposing ontologies.

Our consciousness of fiction prevents us from mistaking what is
represented for a real event; what is represented, however, pleases
and moves as it brings realities to mind. But how can the representation "gratify every mind by recalling its conceptions," if it represents in its full extent that which cannot really obtain in the real
world, to which we must make reference if we are to be moved at
all? Are we to understand that our delight in fiction is such that we
consent to be pleased by what we cannot possibly credit? What
exactly are we to understand by Krieger's enigmatic statement that
the fictional unity is "a unity freed of all artifice but that required to
be 'a just picture of a real original' "? To be a just picture of a real
original, the fiction would have to free itself first from its unity. In
truth, Krieger only appears to have freed himself from the dilemma
implicated in his self-imposed paradox. Starting from an a priori
base of metaphysical contradiction and recognizing that there cannot be both universal order and disorder in the "real" world,
Krieger chooses to invest disorder with ontological supremacy,
thereby creating the occasion—the dialectical need—for an artistic bridge, in unity, by which Johnson can have both his artifact and
his cosmic purposelessness.

The compelling "neatness" of Krieger's essay notwithstanding,
it is absolutely essential to recognize that Johnson's remarks on the
unity of dramatic action *in the fable* do not resolve any ontological
problem raised earlier in the "Preface." Art is not life; art brings
realities to mind, and the realities our minds entertain while the
fiction lasts move because they are congruent with "real" realities
and because the operations of our intellectual nature are regular
and uniform. Even if a particular work did not achieve unity of

action *in the fable*, its various parts would still be capable of provoking pleasurable response if their local representations of action and passion could be accepted as agreeable to nature. However important unity of action may be (unity of action insures that "the general system makes gradual advances, and the end of the play is the end of expectation"), it is not in Johnson's scheme a first-order criterion of artistic excellence; unity is subordinated to the general conditions of pleasure, which presuppose a uniformity in human nature. Where there is no unity of action, the system of creditable probabilities is likely to break down and hence our pleasure to be disrupted; where one event is not concatenated with another, the conclusion will not follow by easy consequence, and an "improbable" conclusion forces dissatisfaction on the mind. Unity of action is subordinated to the principles of the mind on which that unity makes its impact. Unity of action *in the fable* may be a necessary condition of artistic success, but it is not a sufficient one (if only because—by virtue of inept handling or staleness— what is unified may attract no interest and excite no pleasure).

What Krieger ultimately derives from his analysis of the metaphysics of the "Preface" is a better understanding than we have previously had of Johnson's proper relation to critical history, for in spite of his many anticipations of the Wordsworthian spirit, Johnson has really managed, however fitfully, to shadow forth what will be made strikingly vivid in the time to come by that other critical Samuel, namely, Coleridge. In the "Preface" we have something that is "not quite fulfillment, nor yet quite prophecy, but somehow something of both."

> If nature's universal structure has become questionable in the heavy drag of "the real state of sublunary nature," man need not surrender to the imitation of experiential chaos. Through an organizing act of the mind, man can impose his own system, thus opening the prospect of unity in variety. Here lies the romantic imagination and with it Coleridge. But if Coleridge looked as I have here, he may have found how much of his path had been cleared by a few casual master strokes by that arch-neoclassicist himself, Samuel Johnson.[29]

Like Sigworth, then, Krieger will have us believe that because *we can read compatible doctrinal significance into* selected pas-

sages from the writings of two critics, we have established sufficient grounds for asserting that at least on one fundamental issue
Johnson and Coleridge are in substantial agreement. In fact, by
this method we can indicate only that two doctrines appear, on the
surface, to be similar. For substantial similarity to obtain, both
doctrines would have to derive their significance and meaning from
the same set of primary assumptions and premises and be elicited
in response to essentially the same question, since between two
doctrines there can be neither fundamental consonance nor genuine contradiction unless the subsistence of both is relative to the
same determining conceptual context, the same system of reference. In short, doctrines are not discrete intellectual units; they
are units whose meanings are relative to the larger conceptual
framework from which they emerge and on which they depend for
their determinate meaning.

Why the retention of unity of action *in the fable* brings Johnson
into theoretical alignment with the Coleridge who focuses on the
esemplastic power of the secondary imagination, I am unable to
guess. Indeed, even by Krieger's account Coleridge is, in relation
to Johnson, a soft-headed revisionist, who refuses to make the
"Divine Creator" the agent of cosmic purposelessness; it is Coleridge, after all, who conceives of the primary imagination as the
principal "agent of all human perception" and hence as responsible for the "repetition in the finite mind of the eternal act of
creation in the infinite I am," and who understands poetic creativity—the working of the secondary imagination upon the materials
of the primary imagination—to be analogous "in the kind of its
agency" and "in the mode of its operation" to divine creativity.
(*Biographia Literaria*, chap. 13) Now, nothing in Krieger's account
suggests that we have in the "activity" of Johnson's playwright an
analogue to God's—the infinite I am's—creative activity (of course,
there is not even a hint of such a suggestion in Johnson's text);
instead, we have the writer doing unto his materials what God has
neglected to do unto His (at least unto his sublunary materials). The
delight we take in considering the happy colligation, the felicitous
compatibility of 1 and 2 Samuel tends to overwhelm the fact that
Krieger has not provided us with any secure intellectual basis,
finally, for accepting the legitimacy of what he has brought
together. Upon close inspection of the "similarities," Krieger's

thesis would seem to be the only *casualty* resulting from the accidental collision of Johnsonian and Coleridgean doctrine.

Instead of illuminating a relation, Krieger succeeds only in confusing and misrepresenting the distinctive critical achievements of both Johnson and Coleridge. Krieger, as Greene notes of Sachs, is involved in the sort of intellectual game that any number can play, with the results varying as the a priori determinations of the players vary. Although both Johnson and Coleridge talk about "unity," the salient and essential fact is that whereas Johnson's focus is on psychological effects, Coleridge's focus is on analogous creative processes. As soon as we recognize that Johnson and Coleridge have, in fact, different subject matters and are addressing radically different problems, we effectively destroy the grounds of theoretical correspondence or critical similarity.

In all the writings that I have selected for particular examination—selected in large measure because they are, I think, representative of an increasingly common form of critical procedure with Johnson's works (and with those of many other writers as well)—"analysis" begins with the postulation of an essential contradiction, of a striking inconsistency in Johnson's thought, or of two basic antithetical terms, to one or the other of which all expressions of thought or opinion significantly or characteristically Johnsonian can be reduced (in the sense that the antithetical terms or distinctions determine the kinds of meanings that can inhere in local expressions). Generally, once the ruling hypothesis has been selected (presumably because it is self-evidently true of thought, discourse, the nature of mind, the act of writing, the eighteenth-century mentality, Johnson's dichotomous vision, etc.), the next effort of mind is to demonstrate that wherever we look the special inconsistency or the distinguishing antithesis is on display. For purposes of demonstration, it is necessary only to extract a few passages or expressions from a text or a variety of texts and then to read them as isolated in terms of the distinctions that governed the choice of items in the first place. What has been predicated of one passage can be predicated of another passage similar to the first in some terminological or doctrinal respect, because the meanings of the passages are relative to the possibilities of meaning implicated in the ruling hypothesis, the agency of double predication (not relative to any particular question, problem, context, or any coherent set of premises, only on the assumption of which could we account for the full particularity of the piece of which the selected passage is a necessary, functional part).

Reasoning is from like to like, like to unlike, unlike to unlike ("likeness" being determined, in general, by the persistence of analogous terms or by the persistence of categorical habits of interpretation, even in the absence of "like" terms), not from effect to cause or from some empirically identifiable result or feature of the text to the necessary and sufficient conditions of its existence. Reasoning, in short, proceeds by means of "logical" equation and disjunction within the limits established by the differentiating categories. Argument thus is essentially paratactic (or perhaps anaphoric), closure being achieved by reasserting, following the citation of a number of exemplary passages, as a conclusion the hypothesis with which "analysis" began, by claiming on the basis generally of some quantitative standard that either the "good" or the "bad"—the high or the low, the natural or the supernatural, the rational or the imaginational—pole is ultimately more highly esteemed, or by altering, just when opposition seems most obdurate, the terms of the conflict slightly so that the antagonists can be translated into mutually dependent constituents of a final integrative hypothesis, which insists that the contradiction has been only apparent, not real, all along. In the end the procedure achieves neither explanation—since nothing "external" to the hypothesis can really be explained by a hypothesis accountable, finally, only to itself—nor description—since the "facts" have no status as precisely those facts independently of categorical coercion. From first to last the procedure is an exercise in saving the hypothesis, not the facts.

If the project is ambitious some attempt will usually be made by critics employing this mode of reasoning to place Johnson within some particular critical or intellectual tradition, to define his relation to his critical forebears or successors. In general, Johnson is understood to be on the cusp of two distinct critical movements, neoclassicism and romanticism, both of which are usually treated as though they were self-intelligible, self-defining "ism" classes, as though, at any rate, they were distinguished by a discrete set of specific doctrines to which all participating members of the class wholeheartedly subscribed. Occupying a peculiar critical twilight zone, living at a time when one "ism" was dying and the other struggling to be born, Johnson can, as the predilections of the critics vary, serve as the bell-ringer for what is passing, the herald of what is to come, or as one interested in preserving the old and welcoming the new. The critical method under discussion can choose to exalt any of these Johnsons simply by focusing on terms and doctrines that, when considered in isolation, appear clearly to signalize his association with an "ism" class and by then finding in antecedent or subsequent critical documents passages that, divorced from the conceptual frameworks informing them with specific significance, appear to run parallel to or exhibit some positive correlation with those extracted from Johnson's writings.

Nothing, I suppose, surfeits like success, and nothing pleases more than plausible novelty, especially a novel interpretation that allows us to believe that something is exactly what we had formerly believed it could never be. The neoclassic Johnson has pretty much run his course, and the time is ripe—once again—for his friends, who do not much like neoclassicism, to put the "romantic" (or "modern") Johnson on the track, since he at least runs ahead with his gaze fixed on the goal, not on the field behind him. Johnson, the assumption seems to be, will be worthy of esteem to the extent that he can be shown to be a spokesman, however haltingly, for the romanticism that succeeds rather than the neoclassicism that precedes him. Find Wordsworth and Coleridge in Johnson and you gain access to a Johnson who can be respected. What we lose in the process, I think, is Johnson's specific contribution to literary criticism, the specific intellectual integrity of a kind of criticism that is permanently useful to readers who are interested in the sorts of questions and problems with which Johnson was concerned and with which his assumptions and principles of reasoning were peculiarly equipped to deal. However, as long as critics are determined to locate the quintessential Johnson in one or both of two critical houses and to ascertain his whereabouts by juxtaposing passages of "similar" doctrinal significance, he will continue to live restlessly, taking up his successive residences at the command of succeeding categorical instructions.[30]

From the above I would not have the reader conclude that Johnson's criticism cannot be discussed in relation to historical currents of critical thought or that romanticism and neoclassicism are totally useless abstractions or pleasing fictions reified for the sake of making complex relationships amenable to summary treatment. Although the assiduous scholar may discover as many varieties of neoclassicism as Lovejoy identified kinds of romanticism, and although he may be unable to find anything approaching pure, unadulterated neoclassicism (however defined) in the complete writings of any single English critic, it is still possible to say, for example, that among the distinguishing characteristics of at least one of the most prominent kinds of criticism that we call *neoclassical* is a tendency (indeed, an obligation) to measure all particular works against standards recognized as permanently established for the various species of literary art, to subordinate both work and artist to the art itself, with its accumulated precepts for success in the various genres being derived from the "great" achievements of the past and with excellence being in large measure a function of the positive correlation between the discrete traits of a particular work and the traits—of character, thought, fable, diction, rhyme, verse, and so on—specified as necessary to a work of its "kind."

In this criticism the general ends of art are the practical ends of delight and instruction, the means to those ends in any given "kind" of work being previously determined by an examination of the nature, number, and kind of discrete parts in the "best" works of that "kind." Similarly, the best audience is the one capable of judging each performance in relation to the "technical" standards (i.e., characters of a certain kind speaking on certain kinds of occasions, in prose or verse of a certain "quality" or elevation, etc.) accepted as "natural" to the genre. Thus in this criticism the audience, although the target of writing and the final arbiter of value and success, is also subordinated to the art, in the sense that its judgments and reactions are more or less valuable as they are more or less informed by a prior knowledge of the technical requirements, of the "rules" for artistic achievement in the various genres, refinement of taste being largely a matter of the extent of personal concurrence with informed opinion or of the exquisiteness with which the special properties of each of the necessary parts are distinguished and discussed.

Early and late in the eighteenth century we find no perfect or even regular adherence to the assumptions and premises of this

criticism, in part perhaps because it is a period of great intellectual
and philosophical ferment. It is, among other things, a great age of
intellectual experimentation and testing, of formulating varieties of
philosophical and critical questions that necessarily highlighted
aspects of art not amenable to treatment in terms of the distinctions
and premises of the sort of "neoclassical" criticism outlined above,
questions that are radically different in kind from those implicated
in a critical approach designed primarily to deal with the specific
technical prerequisites to beauty and excellence, with the specific
means to delight and instruction, in the various discrete genres.
Throughout the period critics, often the same ones who in other
contexts were preoccupied with the technical details of artistic
construction in the particular genres, were writing essays and
books in which the first principles of critical reasoning were
founded on an interest, not in literary species, but in genius, in the
psychological bases of emotion, in the nature and sources of terror
and pity, pain and pleasure, in the universal affective properties of
language and external objects, and so forth. Consequently, questions of genre, if they appeared at all, were subordinated to more
comprehensive issues relating, for example to the general causes
of human pleasure, to the general qualities in nature and mind
responsible for astonishment, surprise, calm delight, and the like,
to the natural or acquired qualities in the artist or to the kinds of
tropes necessary to the production of great art.

   Taken together, the writers who turned to the universal qualities
of nature or mind for their first-order principles shared, for all their
manifold differences, a conspicuous lack of interest in refined
generic distinctions, since to them the qualities on which artistic
excellence depended were universal and hence indifferent to
peculiarities of genre. Some sense of the diversity of critical
approaches comprehended under the general class of "qualitative" criticism can be obtained by considering the following partial
list of writers (and writings): Addison ("Pleasures of the Imagination" papers). Hutcheson, Hume ("Of Taste," "Of Tragedy"),
Burke, Akenside, Kames, Harris, Johnson, Reynolds, Gerard,
Webb, Twining. Criticism of this sort has, of course, both a history
and a future; and, to name only one critic on each side of the great
eighteenth-century divide, both Longinus and Coleridge should be
enrolled as charter members. That at this level of abstraction

Johnson and Coleridge can, indeed, be placed within the same general intellectual category should not obscure the fact that their individual critical approaches (instigated by fundamentally different questions and directed to fundamentally different ends) are in no significant respects similar.[31] To know whether two critics are in essential agreement with one another, we must first determine whether they are asking similar or compatible questions, dealing with the same subject matter (subject matter being only so much of the "subject" as can be dealt with by the linguistic and logical framework of the discourse by which the subject is constituted), and using similar critical methods to substantiate hypotheses informed by the same or compatible intellectual assumptions.

As a critic Johnson can conveniently be grouped with many critics of the late and mid-eighteenth century who were interested in defining and distinguishing those general qualities in language, art, nature, artist, audience upon which artistic success and value, in any genre, depended, but his particular relation to any other critic in this large group is a matter that can be settled only by examining in detail the intellectual bases and specific purposes of particular critical writings, not by juxtaposing passages containing ostensible doctrinal similarities (juxtaposition of passages is warranted only after a prior analysis of specific essays).[32] Johnson has both a place in critical history and a critical distinctiveness, but the establishment of the former has as its necessary precondition the determination of the latter.

What is particularly disturbing about the views of critics examined in this book is that in a radical sense they are neither confirmable nor falsifiable; they exist by authorial fiat, and they are grounded in the "take-this-for-granted." What passes for confirmation is merely a form of guilt by association, a form of variation on a theme, in which the substantive "redundancy" of meaning in a few select passages is a presumption of a ruling hypothesis. The sponsoring hypothesis "mediates" between the selected instances without establishing between the instances compared any necessary relation. Reasoning in this manner enables us to "know" anything and to "prove" nothing. Of course, even when the hypothesis advanced is actually "confirmed" by the details of, say, Johnson's writings (in the sense that the material dealt with can be read in such a way as to disclose meanings congruent with the meanings stated or implied in the hypothesis), we cannot treat the hypothesis as cognitively adequate on the basis of this sort of "confirmation," for the value and sufficiency of any hypothesis is not determined by whether or by how much of the "objective" other can be enlisted to support it (confirmation is the easiest part of hypothesis testing), but by, among other things, how well it competes with alternative hypotheses or ways of construing the same material or by how well it stands up against recalcitrant evidence, evidence, that is, that cannot be assimilated by it or that tends to falsify or invalidate it.

In an important sense the critical essays with which I have been concerned cannot be falsified, because the facts with which they deal are accessible only as previously interpreted; that is, the facts "supporting" the hypothesis are facts *of* the hypotheses. Although it is perhaps true that no facts could be confronted as facts independently of an interpretation—that, as many linguists tell us, for example, we could not understand the early part of a sentence without some conception of the type of meaning to which the part belonged, "meaning" thus anteceding both writing and understanding—we can (and should) make value distinctions among kinds of interpretation. Thinking in broad terms, we can distinguish, for example, between the kind of hypothesis that respects the facts to be interpreted and the kind that respects the interpretation to be factualized.

There is a vast difference between (1) an interpretation that, starting from a coherent conception of realized effect, suggests that *Othello* would be less effective and moving than it is if Desdemona had in fact been unfaithful and then proceeds to reason to the artistic "rightness" of the choices (choices relating to selection, arrangement, and emphasis of the materials of action, character, thought, diction, etc.) that Shakespeare actually made, *or* (2) one that asserts that when a writer refers or alludes in a work of fiction to a historical event that could not easily or readily be predicted or anticipated, it is reasonable to *assume*—at least tentatively—that the work was composed after the event, *and* (3) an interpretation that declares that the differentiating characteristic of all tragedy is a conflict of good versus good (or, more specifically, a conflict between the "good" of society and the "good" of the individual) and then proceeds to track down in the "thought" of any particular play the successive articulations of the two "goods."

Both of the former views make reference to details that in a fundamental sense antedate any explanation, whereas the latter view
makes reference to details that "logically" postdate the explanation, even though the "explanation" undoubtedly emerged from a
response to actual textual details (once the "explanation" is formulated and generalized, successive responses to texts are really
forms of awareness, not of textual details, but of the controlling
statement in which the details can be said or are understood to
participate as consequential terms).

Although these "model" explanations differ from one another in
a great many more respects than I have chosen to identify, it is
important to recognize that the difference under discussion is not
of nugatory significance and that this difference is immediately
relevant to the issue of hypothesis testing and falsification. The
first two are falsified, invalidated, or rendered inadequate by a
change in the facts for which they purport to provide an account.
Revision or abandonment of hypothesis would be forced by the
emergence of new, incontrovertible facts or by awareness of
unassimilable but previously unacknowledged facts: by the
appearance, for example, of a text or an argument conclusively
establishing Desdemona's infidelity or, in the other case, by the
appearance of evidence or a compelling argument demonstrating a
date of composition prior to the historical event. On the other hand,
no "independent" facts could force the dismissal of the last explanation, since it deals with no independent facts, facts, that is, that
are not consequences of the categories in terms of which the
material under discussion is construed. No "facts" could be
brought forward to invalidate, for example, the assertion that in
Othello we witness the tragic conflict of two mutually exclusive but
ontologically equal goods, love and reason—or whatever—or that
in *Antigone* one good, the authority of the state—or whatever—is
represented in vivid opposition to another good, the automony of
the individual—or whatever.[33]

Thus the first kind of interpretation, since it is accountable to the
"facts" and must adjust to them, is always vulnerable to attack
from the "outside"; it is immersed in the "tentative," the "highly
probable," and its acceptability and sufficiency are always
dependent upon and relative to the state of our knowledge concerning the subject matter. On the other hand, the second kind, in

which the "facts" are accountable to a priori determinations, is not in general vulnerable to any such attack; hypotheses of the second kind are not heuristic or working hypotheses, subject to dismissal as new or previously unrecognized information erupts into daylight. Also, if the adequacy and power of explanatory hypotheses are functions of their *range*—roughly speaking, the "amount" of subject matter accounted for—and their *precision*—roughly speaking, the exactness with which everything within the subject matter is accounted for—then hypotheses of the second kind fall short of adequacy on the side of precision, inasmuch as generally they account for much—all tragedy, for example—without accounting for anything very precisely (why such and such traits of character, for example, are necessary to Cassio, Emilia, etc.).

What is at issue here, of course, is the fundamental difference between explanations that are designed to satisfy minimum demands of demonstration and proof in particular matters of fact and those which are not. All of the approaches to Johnson's thought examined above, though failing to satisfy rigorous standards of substantiation, provide for a kind of "confirmation," in that they all "demonstrate" that "real" details in Johnson's works can be read in such a way as to participate in the kinds of meanings compatible with their a priori determinations. (As I have shown, double predication and analogy are the devices by which the many and diverse participate in the subsuming categories.) Also, the approaches considered—though inadequate—cannot be falsified, since every time the selected "facts" of Johnson's writings are examined in the light of the sponsoring hypotheses, they will be capable of bearing the significances attached to them by the hypotheses. "Confirmable" and nonfalsifiable though they may be, the several views cannot meet the tests of adequacy, if only because they cannot account with any precision for the specific deployment of any particular material at any particular time in relation to any particular larger or smaller context. In short, they cannot explain, except in the most perfunctory manner, why what is said should be said as it is said at any particular moment, or explain what are the necessary and sufficient conditions, internal and external, of any particular exemplification in a specific text of their preferred terms. We are given by these critics "explanations" that have their theological counterpart in the view that things are as they are

because God in His inscrutable wisdom made them so, or—
parallels come easily to mind—their mundane counterpart,
perhaps, in the view that a garret is evidently a habitation favorable
to composition because the muses chose to live in the garrets of
nature—mountains. (Thus an urban writer in a "low" land should
bring his person to some conspicuous height before attempting to
elevate his prose to poetry.)

Between the terms of the views we have been considering and
the particular works "illuminated" by the terms there are assumed
and analogical relations, but no necessary or probable mediating
relations; the terms of the hypotheses supply no necessary or
sufficient conditions of the material examined. And we are under
no obligation to grant that the *possibility* of reading material in the
ways determined by a hypothesis establishes sufficient grounds for
believing that the material should or must be read in such ways.
Such a large grant of confidence is less hesitantly made as views
approach sufficiency of explanation, understanding *sufficiency* in
the following terms:

> The ideal is for the [interpreter] to be able to say of any hypoth-
> esis he settles on, not merely that it makes sense of the facts . . .
> but that *only* if it is true could the facts, in their totality, be what
> they are. And he knows that to be able to say this, with even
> moderate confidence, of any hypothesis, he cannot allow him-
> self to be guided by this hypothesis alone. For he knows that
> proof in matters of particular fact is always a comparative
> matter, and that he cannot safely commit himself to a given
> hypothesis until, with a mind as free as possible from doctrinal
> prepossessions, he has weighed its probability against the prob-
> abilities of all other relevent hypotheses that he can think of.
> Only thus can the confirmation of a hypothesis of fact be prop-
> erly independent of theoretical or other general reasons that may
> have suggested it, and the a priori element [in criticism] be
> reduced to a minimum.[34]

This ideal—the proper aim of scholar, critic, scientist—is neither
met nor honored by our critics, who, as we have seen, maximize the
importance of the a priori element, and who assume that a hypothesis is sufficiently corroborated if a text, in some select few of its
particulars, can be shown to be consonant with what is stated or
implied in the preferred hypothesis.

With regard to Johnson's criticism, an adequate, tentative hypothesis would be one that with maximal precision and economy enabled us to account for the specific choices that Johnson made on specific occasions in the process of dealing with specific issues or problems; the hypothesis would allow us both to know that Johnson's practical decisions follow of necessity from or are compatible with a determinate set of principles and assumptions and to show that the textual matter would be as it is only on the supposition of that set of principles and assumptions. In other words, the hypothesis would lose none of its precision as it extended its range, though, of course, in dealing with particular texts the number of traits synthesized and the nature and number of the relations involved would vary. Such a hypothesis would focus, not on the persistence of terms and doctrines (though it would attempt to deal with and account for any significant terminological and doctrinal redundancy), but on the regular and flexible adaptation of basic principles and criteria of value to the demands of specific problems, the adequacy of the explanatory hypothesis being continuously tested against the material examined and against as many alternative conceptions of the material as could be entertained. If there were no coherent body of assumptions and principles underlying and informing Johnson's various judgments, then local instances of criticism would convict, by their recalcitrance, the explantory hypothesis of *cognitive vagueness* ("an inability to come to close quarters with" particular facts). To the extent that the hypothesis dealt effectively only with some texts or some parts of several texts, it would be inadequate on the side of scope or range, inadequacy of this type informing us either that there is no underlying coherence to Johnson's critical thought or that the constitutive principles of that coherence had not been discovered.[35]

PART II

Johnson's Criticism: Theory and Practice

The Intellectual Integrity of Johnson's Principles of Criticism

Throughout this book, in addition to outlining the general cognitive inadequacies of some recent Johnson criticism, I have assumed—what our critics are generally unwilling to grant and often ready to deny—that there is a stable intellectual basis to Johnson's criticism. What is particularly disturbing about the views of these recent critics—"confirmable," nonfalsifiable, but nevertheless inadequate—is that individually and collectively they bring back into prominence the Johnson of sensibility, the view of Johnson as a kind of critical barnstormer, flying through the clouds of controversy by the seat of his pants, the erratic critical marksman who, by always shooting from the hip, delights as much by his misses as by his hits, the Johnson whose criticism impresses us not so much by its intellectual integrity and validity as by the force and authority of its expression, or whose thought derives its value from its occasional prescience, from its anticipations of later critical or psychological doctrines, the Johnson, in short, whom scholars and critics from the late nineteen forties through the early sixties undertook to remove from center stage by sedulously inquiring after the principles underlying his critical and scholarly practice and by then carefully defining the bases of his judgments, without oversimplifying the rich diversity of his pronouncements or disregarding the many and various occasions that prompted them.

Our critics, then, not only have failed to build on the solid accomplishments of their immediate predecessors but have brought back into prominence and use the intellectual machinery that precludes the extension or advancement of those accomplishments. They have made current and restored to circulation precisely those terms, distinctions, and methods of reasoning which it was the business of those who advanced our understanding of the systematic operations of Johnson's critical intelligence to discard and dismiss as positively deleterious to inquiry, knowledge, and proof. This recent criticism is a reversion to the kinds of approaches to Johnson's thought that were shown to be woefully inadequate by, among others, Keast, Hagstrum, Wimsatt, Abrams, Hilles, Crane, Greene—by all those, in fact, who in abandoning the way of the a priori and in delineating the coherent body of principles and assumptions informing his practical pronouncements, gave us something answerable to the richness and complexity of Johnson's critical thought and to our experience.

When we examine our critics from the perspective, say, of Hagstrum's "Preface" to *Samuel Johnson's Literary Criticism* or Keast's opening remarks in "The Theoretical Foundations of Johnson's Criticism," we immediately realize that the formerly routed dialectical forces have regrouped and resumed their hostilities. At the outset of his study Hagstrum notes:

> Few writers have been so often quoted out of context as has Dr. Johnson, with the result that many students, acquainted with only a limited amount of evidence but nevertheless unable to refrain from forming a theory, have constructed a framework upon isolated passages and have imagined that they have understood the critic's system. Even the careful student of Johnson is handicapped by the fact that, in literary criticism as well as in other areas of human concernment about which he spoke and wrote, he was not a theorist: he pursued no lengthy systematic analyses; he wrote no "Enquiry into ————." This of course does not prove that he was unsystematic or inconsistent, but it does mean that the inquirer must labor to make explicit what is implicit and to deduce theory from practice. . . .
>   . . . Most of the nineteenth-century ghosts about Johnson the critic have fortunately been laid, and it would now be work of sheerest supererogation to demonstrate that he was no arid neoclassicist. But in the process of historical revision many of the shibboleths of the last century have been retained only to be reversed in their application. If Johnson was not in actuality the insensitive rationalist and literalist Wordsworth and Coleridge felt him to be, perhaps he was the opposite. Thus some have been impressed with the "romanticism" of the Great Cham: he did actually love outside nature; he was capable of wonder and even terror; he was a friend of the Wartons and praised Chatterton. But to attempt to determine the ingredients in the John-

sonian mixture of the classical and the romantic is, it seems to
me, an impossible task, chiefly because the terms have not been
and perhaps can never be satisfactorily defined and because no
great writer of the Age of Reason can be pressed into those
molds.

For the same reasons, attempts to affirm or deny that Johnson
was predominantly a humanist, an authoritarian, a tradi-
tionalist, a skeptic are necessarily obfuscating. The terms used
are either too vague or too intimately a part of our own intellectual battles. Johnson was all of these or none depending on
the particular meanings attached to those indeterminate
expressions.[1]

After quoting Lionel Trilling's praise of Leavis as a critic who, like
Johnson, requires "no formulated first principles for his judgment
but only the sensibility that it is the whole response of his whole
being,"[2] and C. B. Tinker's opinion that "Johnson's criticism is
not a *system*, every detail of which must be consistent with certain
principles from which all casual expressions are supposed to
derive,"[3] W. R. Keast says that "the common denominator of
these modern estimates of Johnson's distinctive quality and value
is the conviction evident in them that Johnson has or needs no
principles, theory, or systematic view of literature and the belief
that his absence of principles and theory from the conduct of
practical criticism is a positive virtue."[4]

Held in abeyance for years by compelling evidence and sound
argument, the dialectical powers have again assembled to reassert
the legitimate primacy of a Johnson whose many observations can
be seen as reflecting his notions of a basic polarity of faculties
(reason and imagination); who, by recognizing the need for unity of
action in the fable, anticipated Coleridge; who abandoned received
apodictic criteria for the standards of the heart; and who wavered
between conceptions of literature as quasi-legal argument and as a
vehicle for self-expression, each and every one of these critics
believing perhaps that time works upon sound arguments as wind
and tide work upon castles of sand, or that former judgments would
not be invoked when old appeals were presented in new briefs. To
whatever cause we attribute this resurgence of inadequate views,
the disturbing fact is that such views are likely to be influential, for
there is operative in the field of criticism something analogous to
Gresham's economic law, namely, a tendency for later articles and

books to drive earlier ones out of circulation (and hence out of mind). Additionally, there is a tendency in students to assume—on the basis, I suppose, of some suppressed analogy to developments in the physical sciences—that the latest in print is the least suscep- tible to factual or logical impeachment, that the latest on the market is both "new" and improved."

To undermine the authority and influence of these recent views of Johnson, we can, first, examine their inadequacies as explana- tions of the material they address and, second, bring back into currency (here using the critical counterpart of Gresham's Law to advantage) those alternative conceptions of Johnson's thought and the opertions of his mind which proved so negotiable in the past (assuming that no less than in the eighteenth century, readers today need more often to be reminded than informed) and which, to the present writer at least, seem most nearly consonant with one's experience in the face of Johnson's writing. I should like to think that the first task has been accomplished in Section 1 and that the second is handled expeditiously below.

In the interest of brevity, I shall call attention to one salient feature of many earlier discussions, namely, the idea, informed by experience, that although Johnson distrusted theorizing and abstract speculation, wrote no general theory of literature or aesthetics, and was not a systematizer, he had nevertheless a complex and systematic mind. Throughout these earlier discus- sions there persists the conviction that it is possible to deduce from the diversity of Johnson's practice the coherent body of principles underlying it, the sense that the multifarious utterances of Johnson are anchored in the bedrock of a principle. For example, taking a close look at Johnson's method as a lexicographer, W. K. Wimsatt does not detect a sensibility "madly irrational, unsystematic, impulsive, and untidy."[5] Rather, he sees Johnson's procedure as a "signal instance of that sanity, perspective, balance, and sense of proportion for which [his] whole career is so notable."[6] Similarly, in his perceptive essay on the critical "lenses through which [John- son] gazed" at literature, M. H. Abrams calls our attention, not to any central contradiction, polarity, or inconsistency, but to the dependence of Johnson's critical skill on a peculiarly felicitous collocation of "precept and habit," on, that is, the happy cooperation of an intricate, relatively stable set of "conscious principles and established responses."[7]

Recognizing that Johnson was neither unsystematic nor inconsistent, Hagstrum announces early in his trenchant study that he has attempted "to do somewhat more systematically and thoroughly what every reader [he assumes] tends to do for himself, often inadequately and impatiently: to get behind the particular critical occasion to the underlying principle."[8] And R. S. Crane, taking a broad view and highlighting the general foundations of Johnson's criticism, notes that it is a criticism "in which principles for judging poems are derived not from a specific consideration of the internal nature of poetic products but from a general analysis of the psychological factors which condition the responses of audiences to them."[9]

However differently some of these critics may define or construe the essential integrity of Johnson's thought, they all, in one way or another, unlike our dialectical critics, insist on the fact of integrity, recognizing one and all that, as far as the manor of principles is concerned, Johnson came early and stayed late. Betraying no insensitivity to manifest contradictions or inconsistencies in Johnson's thought, they in general recognized that central significance could not be attached to instances of Johnson's disagreeing with himself and that an adequate understanding of characteristic or distinctive tendencies of mind could not be derived from any preoccupation with doctrinal self-contradiction in Johnson's writings. Moreover, they understood that divergent statements could sometimes issue from a single principle and that while one statement could be shown to deviate substantively from another, Johnson could rarely be shown to deviate from the bases of his judgment.

I have long suspected, without wishing (or perhaps being able) to prove, that critics are drawn so irresistibly to instances of inconsistency in Johnson because, oddly enough, he is for the most part so remarkably consistent. (There are, perhaps, few of us who, having looked in vain one way, do not hope, at last, for "eminence from the heresies of paradox."[10]) Whenever inconsistency is discovered, the critic, exalted by his own percipience and acuity, runs the risk of elevating the anomalous to the level of the characteristic or of founding a massive thesis on what may possibly be implicated in the incongruity when considered abstractly and independently. However, anyone with even a modest acquaintance with Johnson's early and late work knows from experience how frequently Johnson agrees with himself, how often he finds occasions to enforce the same or similar points, and how regularly he recurs, unconsciously and unpremeditatedly, it seems, to the same or companionable language in the expression of those points. Not only are there many *Rambler* papers embedded in *Rasselas* and the *Lives of the Poets,* but there are in the later works innumerable repetitions or echoes of early phrasing. On the level of doctrine, Johnson is extraordinarily consistent. Even in his casual-serious conversation, as recorded by Boswell and others, Johnson manages to extemporize in the manner and often in the terms that he had employed many years earlier in deliberate compositions.

Over and over again we witness Johnson's particularized anticipation of himself. Writing on the false wit admired by ladies in the ironic, playful-serious *Rambler* 141, Johnson, through the voice of a "correspondent," says:

> A wit, Mr. Rambler, in the dialect of ladies, is not always a man, who by the action of a vigorous fancy upon comprehensive knowledge, brings distant ideas unexpectedly together, who by some peculiar acuteness discovers resemblances in objects dissimilar to common eyes, or by mixing heterogeneous notions dazzles the attention with sudden scintillations of conceit.

Six months later, Johnson, presumably without consulting his earlier paper, writes through another "correspondent":

> Wit, you know, is the unexpected copulation of ideas, the discovery of some occult relation between images in appearance remote from each other; an effusion of wit therefore presupposes an accumulation of knowledge; a memory stored with notions, which the imagination may cull out to compose new assemblages. Whatever may be the native vigor of the mind, she can never form any combinations from few ideas, as many changes can never be rung upon a few bells. Accident may indeed, sometimes produce a lucky parallel or a striking contrast; but these gifts of chance are not frequent, and he that has nothing of his own, and yet condemns himself to needless expenses, must live upon loans or theft. (*Rambler* 194)

From here the passage is easy to the discussion of metaphysical wit in the Life of Cowley, written approximately twenty-six years after *Rambler* 194:

> Wit, abstracted from its effects upon the hearer, may be more rigorously and philosophically considered as a kind of *discordia concors;* a combination of dissimilar images, or discovery of occult resemblances in things apparently unlike. Of wit, thus defined, they have more than enough. The most heterogeneous ideas are yoked by violence together; nature and art are ransacked for illustrations, comparisons, and allusions; their learning instructs and their subtlety surprises. . . .
> . . . if their conceits were far-fetched, they were often worth the carriage. To write on their plan it was at least necessary to read and think. No man could be born a metaphysical poet, nor assume the dignity of a writer by descriptions copied from descriptions, by imitations borrowed from imitations, by traditional imagery and hereditary similes, by readiness of rhymes and volubility of syllables. (*Lives,* 1:20—21)

With uncommon regularity Johnson manages to illustrate and aggrandize consanguineous ideas by means of a distinct kinship-group of images. In differentiating Shakespeare's works from those of "correct" writers (Addison most immediately), Johnson writes:

> The work of a correct and regular writer is a garden accurately formed and diligently planted, varied with shades, and scented with flowers; the composition of *Shakespeare* is a forest, in which oaks extend their branches, and pines tower in the air, interspersed sometimes with weeds and brambles, and sometimes giving shelter to myrtles and roses; filling the eye with awful pomp, and gratifying the mind with endless diversity. ("Preface to Shakespeare.")

Exemplifying a correlative distinction and adjusting the topography slightly to suit the principals, Johnson, in the *Life of Pope,* notes that "Dryden's page is a natural field, rising into inequalities and diversified by the varied exuberance of abundant vegetation; Pope's is a velvet lawn, shaven by the scythe and levelled by the roller." On another occasion, with a peremptory finality perhaps animated by national pride, Johnson gave the basic point the concision of a maxim, while maintaining the horticultural vehicle:

"Corneille is to Shakespeare as a clipped hedge is to a forest."[11] From the rich development of concepts from a radical metaphor in the first passage to the pithy abruptness of illustration in the last, we witness the perdurable congeniality of idea and image. Examples of this sort of doctrinal and imagistic persistence could, of course, be accumulated indefinitely, but, in all likelihood, no congregated testimony to consistency would disabuse some critics of the notion that weighty significance should be assigned to the irrefragable discordancies that they had detected and upon which they had founded elaborate theses.

Our dialectical critics put great stress on inconsistency in the writings and on "forgetfulness" in the writer, forgetfulness serving as the convenient psychological bridge between instances of supposed conflict ("forgetfulness" is a pleasing fiction that preserves the "inconsistency" by "explaining" it). According to Sigworth, for instance, "Johnson as a critic makes trouble because there are few statements in his criticism which some other statement does not seem to refute."[12] If presented in a somewhat more moderate form, Sigworth's assertion would perhaps be rejected by few readers, since few would feel that a charge of credulity could be leveled at them for simply acknowledging the plain truth of what many critical guides had noticed or of what they had directly observed themselves.

Like Boswell (who makes a good deal less of inconsistency than our critics), we all take some (mean) pleasure, I suppose, in catching Johnson in the act of disagreeing with himself (and our pleasure, it seems to me, is directly proportionate to the uncommonness of the doctrinal discrepancies; if Johnson were regularly and obviously self-contradictory, we would derive no satisfaction whatsoever from our detections. On what would we found our elation, our ephemeral sense of superior perspicacity, if Johnson's intellectual "gaffes" were common and immediately identifiable by the quick and slow alike?). Nevertheless, any "inconsistency" hunter with one eye for the job should return from "Johnsoniana" with a bag full of game. Indeed, most of the "self-evidential" blunders are now common property.

For example, Johnson insisted time and time again that if the biographer were interested in writing a life and not a panegyric, he should tell the whole truth about his subject, recording the faults as well as the strengths, the vices (the excessive drinking of Addison and Parnell, for example) as well as the virtues, for "If we owe regard to the memory of the dead, there is more respect to be paid to knowledge, to virtue, and to truth" (*Rambler* 60). Nevertheless, in his own *Life of Addison,* Johnson informs us that he is approaching the time when it will be "proper rather to say 'nothing that is false, than all that is true' " (*Lives,* 2:116).

Again, on the relative merits of generality and particularity, a selection of passages would seem to indicate that Johnson was not only inconstant, but capriciously inconstant. In chapter 10 of *Rasselas* alone, we are informed that the poet must "be conversant with all that is awfully vast or elegantly little" and, only three paragraphs later, that "the business of the poet is to examine, not the individual, but the species; to remark general properties and large appearances: he does not number the streaks of the tulip. . . ." In *Rambler* 36 we find:

> Poetry cannot dwell upon the minuter distinctions, by which one species differs from another, without departing from that simplicity of grandeur which fills the imagination; nor dissect the latent qualities of things, without losing its general power of gratifying every mind by recalling its conceptions.

However, in the *Life of Rowe,* particularity is called for:

> I know not that there can be found in his plays any deep search into nature, any accurate discriminations of kindred qualities, or nice display of passion in its progress; all is general and undefined. (*Lives,* 2:76)

Yet, in *Idler* 66 Johnson says: "The most useful truths are always universal, and unconnected with accidents and customs." Yet again, he notes that in *Comus* "the invitations to pleasure are so general that they excite no distinct images of corrupt enjoyment, and take no dangerous hold on the fancy" (*Life of Milton).* Finally, recall his praise of Thomson:

> He thinks in a peculiar train, and he thinks always as a man of genius; he looks round on Nature and on Life with the eye which Nature bestows only on a poet [are we now to suppose, despite all Johnson has elsewhere said about genius being a mind of

large general powers accidentally determined, that the poet is a man endowed by nature with special faculties or general faculties in a special degree], the eye that distinguishes in everything presented to its view whatever there is on which imagination can delight to be detained, and with a mind that at once comprehends the vast, and attends to the minute. (*Lives*, 3:298−99)

Johnson would appear to be a hard critic to please or to agree with.

Perhaps no "inconsistency" is more frequently cited than that relating to poetic justice. In his "Notes" to *King Lear*, Johnson writes:

A play in which the wicked prosper, and the virtuous miscarry, may doubtless be good because it is a just representation of the common events of human life; but since all reasonable beings naturally love justice, I cannot easily be persuaded, that the observation of justice makes a play worse; or, that if other excellencies are equal, the audience will not always rise better pleased from the final triumph of persecuted virtue.

However, in the *Life of Addison*, he writes on the "same" subject in the following terms:

Whatever pleasure there may be in seeing crimes punished and virtue rewarded, yet, since wickedness often prospers in real life, the poet is certainly at liberty to give it prosperity on the stage. For if poetry has an imitation of reality, how are its laws broken by exhibiting the world in its true form? The stage may sometimes gratify our wishes; but if it be truly the *mirror of life*, it ought to shew us sometimes what we are to expect. (*Lives*, 2:135)

To conclude this array of items involving apparent doctrinal disagreement, let us look briefly at two comments in the "Preface to Shakespeare." Concluding a section of praise, Johnson writes: "a poet overlooks the casual distinction of country and condition, as a painter, satisfied with the figure, neglects the drapery." A few pages later, discussing faults, he chides Shakespeare for being a writer who "had no regard to distinction of time and place, but gives to one age or nation, without scruple, the customs, institutions, and opinions of another, at the expence not only of likelihood, but of possibility."

This list could, of course, be greatly extended (indeed, the Johnsonian scholar knows that this enumeration amounts to little more than the very tip of the exposed part of the iceberg), but what should not be overlooked is that in most of these—and in most other—examples, we are dealing with—and the word demands stress—*apparent* contradiction or inconsistency. What needs to be emphasized in Sigworth's assertion is the phrase *seem to;* there are many statements in Johnson's criticism that other statements *seem to* refute. What these examples in fact tell us is that when two passages are lifted from their contexts and placed together, they may *appear to* contradict one another or be out of register. Moreover, even if the doctrinal conflict were real rather than apparent, we would have no immediate or necessary reason to believe that the conflict extended to the level of principle.

Several of the examples cited involve, in fact, no contradiction of any kind. When the last two items, for example, are restored to their rightful places within the "Preface," we immediately recognize that Johnson is not praising and blaming Shakespeare for the same thing. In the first instance, Johnson is praising Shakespeare's superiority to those "false" notions of propriety of character which would prohibit bringing a fool to the Roman senate or inebriety to a king of Denmark, whereas in the second, he is rebuking Shakespeare for introducing unnecessary and palpable historical absurdity, for, among other things, anachronism. The distinction is between characterization commensurate with life and experience and real factual confusion, between the happy neglect of "accidental" rules of propriety of character and real confusion among "historical" particulars, in which inaccuracy or misrepresentation adds nothing to general or "dramatic" truth and calls attention to awkwardness or anachronism (Hector quoting Aristotle, for example).

And when the several passages on generality and particularity are examined together within their contexts, it will be found, I think, that Johnson nowhere expresses any absolute preference for either one or the other. In very few of the passages is the immediate subject matter (the object of direct interest) generality or particularity; and although the terms persist, the referents of those terms do not remain constant. Where Johnson does stress one or the other, he is generally incited to do so because of real deficiencies on the side of generality or particularity in the specific material that he is immediately discussing. Early and late, Johnson calls for both generality *and* particularity, for the new *and* the familiar, and especially for the union of the two, for those minute discriminations peculiarly appropriate to character or scene and yet resonating with general significance or reflecting the general operations of nature and passion. In brief, there are fewer doctrinal contradictions in Johnson's writing than a collection of ostensibly disjunct passages would seem to indicate, and even though Johnson may on occasion be found to have changed his mind on a topic, he will rarely be found to have also changed his principles or the bases of his judgment.

The critical imperatives implicated in the preceding accounts of "consistency" and "inconsistency" are few and relatively clear. When two or more passages, extracted from different works or contexts, appear to conflict, the following should be among the next actions of critical intelligence:

(1) to look closely at the passages within their contexts, trying to determine whether or not the recurrent statements or terms have the same referents, whether or not the subject matter under discussion is similar, whether or not there is difference rather than contradiction (the latter being possible only when the passages are functional within the same system of intellectual reference).

(2) to examine the passages in terms of the degree of emphasis they receive in their respective contexts (although coequal in strength when juxtaposed, one may be incidental to the argument from which it is taken and thereby less qualified for competition with its supposed antagonist).

(3) to consider whether there is not something *exceptional* in the circumstance of one of the passages to justify a deviation from an established or long-standing conviction. B follows from A except when circumstance C occurs; there is no reason to assume, for example, that Johnson abrogates any settled biographical principle when he hesitates to tell all that he knows about *some* poets for fear that, by "unseasonable detection," "a pang [might] be given to a widow, a daughter, a brother, or a friend." The point is that special circumstances may either destroy the contradiction or diminish its significance.

(4) to ascertain whether the meanings of two ostensibly incongruous passages are not relative to and compatible with a single principle; whether the general nature of the principle does not allow different or alternative judgments.

(5) to determine (when the tendency is to look upon the perceived contradiction as constituting an aspect of a characteristic polarity in Johnson's thought) whether the conflicting units are, on balance, endorsed with equal force and regularity throughout the corpus; whether one unit of the pair is not, in fact, anomalous or infrequently expressed and thus, though undeniably present, insufficiently resonant or recurrent to unsettle the ongoing integrity of the larger system of relations by which the dominant unit is subsumed; whether, in short, when the suffrages of the two are balanced, one unit is not more persistent and resonant than the other and more nearly consonant with clearly established assumptions. The issue here concerns how much incongruity can be tolerated before established principles are utterly subverted. For example, substantive correspondences in several remarks made by Johnson on occasions when he was talking for victory would not necessarily undermine principles or criteria of value articulated on serious occasions in deliberate compositions, even though those conversational remarks were directly antithetical to the established views.

When Johnson's remarks are examined in the light of the preceding sorts of questions, we discover, I think, that Johnson is not thoroughly, but generally consistent. However, as long as emphasis is placed on ostensible doctrinal conflict, as long as critical reasoning proceeds from a consideration of what is implicated in the terms of conflict abstractly considered, Johnson will appear to be erratic, inconsistent, a critic of sensibility, notable for variety and diversity of statement, sometimes anticipating the future and sometimes giving cogent expression to what are taken to be moribund standards. With Johnson, as with any other critic, very little can be learned about the nature and springs of judgment when attention is focused on doctrines, not on particular problems, choices, and principles of reasoning. Although C. B. Tinker is undoubtedly right when he says that Johnson's criticism is not comprised of principles from which *every* statement deliberate or casual may be said to derive, the fact remains that Johnson would not be—as he so clearly is—a man ready for all critical occasions, if he did not bring to the exigencies of the moment certain fundamental convictions about the nature, value, and ends of art, if he had to find his intellectual base of operation, his generative principles of judgment with each new occasion. And we would clearly have nothing approaching the subtlety and complexity of Johnson's judgments if his decisions were simply the automatic consequences or reflexes of a polar conception of literature or life.

What distinguishes our critics from their immediate predecessors is not an ability to find discordancy or inconsistency, but rather a willingness to swell what is detected to a giant's bulk and to endow the occasional, incidental, or adventitious with the authority of the essential or characteristic. Moreover, it is precisely because they proceed from doctrine to doctrine and leave the conduct of their cases to the hands of analogical insinuation that they cannot explain, in any precise way, why Johnson writes as he does on any specific occasion.[13]

Johnson is, as T. S. Eliot once said, a dangerous man to disagree with,[14] and that is so, I think, because his various views are well grounded, because he carries to his work a determinate and useful set of critical tools,[15] because, in general, he avoids "arbitrary decision and general exclamation . . . by asserting nothing without a reason, and establishing all [his] principles of judgment on [what he understood to be] unalterable and evident truth" (*Rambler* 208).

It is not the business of every critic, before settling down to deal with his immediate task, to outline the intellectual bases of Johnson's thought, but without some reasonably adequate working conception of the first-order critical priorities and assumptions governing Johnson's reasoning or some general sense of the essential coherence of his thought, every critic is likely to give undue emphasis to doctrinal correspondences or dissonances and to discuss them, in turn, in relation to a priori assumptions about the nature of literature, writing, history, neoclassicism, romanticism, psychology, the eighteenth century, or whatever. On the other hand, with such a working conception or understanding, no critic, in all likelihood, will polarize Johnson's thought or leap to any conclusions, say, about a late conversion to "romantic" standards, on the basis of some presumed affinity between context-free passages.

In practical terms, what I am suggesting is that the modern critic should approach Johnson's writings with the understanding that the meanings of particular remarks, however striking and interesting considered independently of or in relation to statements elsewhere, are most immediately relative to the specific questions and problems with which Johnson is concerned and to the critical framework within which he habitually works. His persistent interest in certain questions and problems reflects the durability of certain primary assumptions about the nature, ends, and value of art. Thus, the critique of *Lycidas,* for example, takes off from specific considerations that are generated by the immediate task, a comparative analysis of Milton's poetic achievement, and by the details of the poem as construed in relation to certain determinate critical values and priorities, which determine the kinds of things that can be said about the poem, and which are based on a prior analysis of the general subject matter of poetry and the pleasurable ends of literature. Johnson's engagement with the poem is of the sort that is possible to his assumptions and principles.

In an effort to bring the principal points of this essay to bear on the critique, I shall approach Johnson's particular judgment of Milton's poem by way, in this chapter, of his underlying critical principles and, later, of their more specialized reflection in his discussions of the pastoral and the elegy.

What we most need to know about the principled coherence of Johnson's criticism has been articulated at various lengths, by many Johnsonians, especially, of course, by Crane, Hagstrum, and Keast. Indeed, the purposes of this book could be realized only by drawing on their findings. To get at the underlying principles, I have decided, in the interests of expedition, to take Keast's crucial article, "The Theoretical Foundations of Johnson's Criticism,"[16] as my primary text of reference, because it contains nothing of substance that Crane and Hagstrum would hesitate to endorse (or would reject outright); because it provides quick and convenient access to the essential features of Johnson's criticism; and because nothing has appeared since its publication to diminish confidence in its explanatory power or cognitive adequacy.

Although Johnson is primarily a practical critic, writing to the demands of immediate practical occasions, his "papers on criticism and the rules of art in the *Rambler* (Nos. 37, 125, 156, and 158) and [his] discussions of tragicomedy and the unities in the 'Preface to Shakespeare' offer an especially advantageous point of departure" for those interested in defining the theoretical framework within which Johnson works, "for here not only does he address himself at some length and in considerable detail to large questions of critical theory, but he seems to be engaged in an attempt to summarize and evaluate an entire critical tradition and to define the alternative with which he would supplant it."[17] In these writings the established rules that Johnson opposes "have a uniform characteristic: each specifies, for the genre to which it applies, a peculiar limitation of literary means—language, character, subject, manner of representation, and the like—which alone can be regarded, in the opinion of the critics, as the proper or artistic way in which to achieve the effect aimed at."[18] From Johnson's point of view the desired effects in the various genres could just as easily be realized by means different from those specified by the critics, and he finds the restriction of means prescribed by critical legislation to be "arbitrary and partial" for *three* principal reasons.

In the *first* place, the prescribed restrictions are partial and hence inadequate, because they have been founded, not on reason or the nature of things—life, passion, pleasure, and so forth—but on the practice of particular, especially ancient poets. To Johnson, "Poets, exercising their essential faculty of choice, have selected such subjects, diction, modes of organization, and the like as fitted their peculiar interests, abilities, and circumstances; these choices, if made by early or honored poets have been identified with the *art itself* rather than with the special causes which produced them."[19] However, if we disregard the edicts of critical legislators and consider poetry in terms of the choices available to the writer, it is clear that the imagination has virtually limitless possibilities open to it and hence that choices other than those which were actually made could have been elected.[20] A precept founded on special or accidental causes cannot be erected into a rule of art.

In the *second* place, the specific generic limitations defined by critics are arbitrary and partial because the subject matter of poetry, the object of the poet's activity, is nature, principally human nature. If the imagination of the poet is "licentious and vagrant, unsusceptible of limitations and impatient of restraint" (*Rambler* 125), the subject matter to which the poet directs his attention is similarly immense and inexhaustible. In the world before him, the poet sees, in Johnson's phrase, the "boundless ocean of possibility." To Johnson nature presents limitless choices to the artist. And those critics who restrict, say, comedy to representations of "mean or bad men" or to the depiction of "trivial actions" fall into absurdity because "the various modes of exhilarating [the] audience, not being limited by nature, cannot be comprised in precept" (*Rambler* 125). As Keast notes, "That some poets, like the ancient writers of comedy and tragedy, have elected to restrict themselves to a part of the diversified whole cannot warrant the critics in imposing a similar restriction on others."[21] To Johnson, critics, in arriving at their rules, have consulted too often literary works of the past and too seldom the nature of life and passion, and such critics "have generally no other merit than that [of] having read the works of great authors with attention . . ." (*Rambler* 158). From Johnson's point of view, critical rules are too frequently drawn from precedents rather than reason, and hence "practice has introduced rules, rather than rules have directed practice" (*Rambler* 158).

In the *third* place, the restrictive precepts are unsatisfactory because they are not founded on the recognition that literature has as its end the satisfaction of the general conditions of pleasure. When dealing with the readers of literature, the "rules" critics have assumed or argued that the demands of readers are for specific pleasures arising from specifically distinct types or "kinds" of works. On the other hand, "Johnson, having examined the tastes of the common reader with some care, is convinced that this is not so, that, instead, readers demand the more general pleasures of recognition and novelty."[22]

The essential point is that "Whichever of these three bases Johnson uses to ground his case against earlier critics, . . . he is endeavoring to replace what he considers narrow principles with principles more commodious," an effort that regularly leads him "to forsake the view of art as manifesting itself in distinct species . . . for the ampler domain of nature, in which, as he conceives of it, distinctions and definitions hitherto thought inviolable and 'natural' can be shown to be rigidities, arbitrary constrictions, or, at best, ideal manifestoes."[23]

What in large measure distinguishes Johnson from his critical predecessors is his tendency to regard literature as a natural process, "set in the context of other natural processes such as social behavior, and thus amenable to treatment *in relation to its psychological causes and effects*, its *natural materials*, and its *circumstantial determinants*."[24] For Johnson, then, literary works are to be considered not as fixed classes of works, "embodying more or less perfectly an ideal form, but as human acts to be judged in relation to the agency of their production and appreciation." And since from this perspective the nature and traits of literary works, whatever the species, are the unpredictable consequences of the activity of the poet upon the diverse materials of nature, art itself (as the more or less perfect realization of objects having determinate characteristics) cannot supply the principles for its own evaluation. Consequently, Johnson, in an effort to find a stable basis for judgment, switches the foundation of the principles for the assessment of literature from art to nature.

In relocating the foundation of the principles, however, Johnson is beset by difficulties of his own, since in his view the infinite complexity and diversity of nature prevent the mind of man from enclosing it completely or from determining its direction with perfect accuracy. (Indeed, it is the complexity and variety of nature that account, in large part, for Johnson's disdain for abstract speculation and the importance in his criticism of the "test of time" as one of the arbiters of merit.) But whatever difficulties are entailed in the attempt to locate natural principles that will enable the critic to account for literary excellence, Johnson is sustained in the undertaking by the conviction that the general and common features of nature are identifiable and by the fact that men, the producers and appreciators of art, are essentially the same in all times and places. Moreover, experience informs us that the general conditions of pleasure are simple and fixed: "all men take pleasure in the recognition of truth—the consonance of what is done or said to 'the general sense or experience of mankind'—and in the surprise of novelty or variety." It is, of course, impossible to predict the means by which these conditions may be satisfied, for Johnson will not, "like many hasty philosophers, search after the cause till . . . certain of the effect" [*Rambler* 61]; "but the stability of the grounds on which literary effects may be produced affords a principle from which the critic can reason to their causes and hence from which he can argue questions of literary merit." It is on the basis "of these assumptions concerning the nature of literature and the task of criticism [that] Johnson develops the scheme of analysis which underlies his discussions of technical problems, works and genres, and individual authors."[25]

With regard to the four elements in the literary process—author, work, nature, and audience—Johnson considers the author and the audience to be primary; it is in relation to these that the other two are defined. To Johnson literature is an activity designed to please and instruct the general or common reader. Thus it follows that *works* are successful or not depending upon the extent to which they embody or present truth and novelty, the general bases of pleasure. "Nature, being both regular and inexhaustibly varied, provides subject matter for art and, being external, a measure for judging it." The extent to which works embody truth and novelty (or variety) depends "on the power of the author to discover these in nature, to select or invent matter which will embody them, and to represent it in words." The general conditions of pleasure, "discovered by experience and guaranteed by the essential identity of men, provide the first principle of critical reasoning."[26]

This first principle identifies end, purpose, or effect, but to Johnson criticism must go further, since critical reasoning is concerned with the causes of literary pleasure (the critic's task being essentially "to distinguish those means of pleasing which depend upon known causes and rational deduction from the nameless and inexplicable elegancies which appeal wholly to the fancy").[27] Now, to Johnson the chief cause of literary pleasure is the *author*, not only because he initiates the process, but also because the features of the *works*, the extent to which they reflect *nature*, and their capacity to provoke pleasure in the *audience* are all based on his selective activity and peculiar abilities and skills. To understand the preeminence of the author in Johnson's scheme of analysis, it is necessary to recognize the relations that he stresses among the four elements in the literary process. *Works* "are treated as perform-ances manifesting the powers of the *author*, as compositions of materials which resemble—in themselves and in their conjunc-tion—the traits of *nature* [as they can be conveyed by or inferred from words], and as the sources of recognition or surprise in the *audience*."[28] Works, then, are taken to be relative to the other three, and the terms in which works are discussed are founded on "a prior consideration of authors, nature, and readers." Moreover, *nature* is also a relative element in Johnson's scheme, since it "is the link between author and reader—the common elements that guarantee truth and the accidental variations that produce variety being the basis of selection by the one and for comparison and judgment by the other."[29]

Essentially, nature is a psychological, not an ontological concept in Johnson's criticism; that is, nature is considered primarily in terms of its power to produce specific responses in men. (Pleasur-able response is the natural emotive consequence of expressions or representations agreeable to nature.) Thus both truth and variety—when the focus is on the principal subjects of poetry, human nature and passion—"arise from the constant linkage between human passions and their effects: the regularity with which the same passions produce effects of the same kind permits recognition and hence truth; the infinite accidental modifications in the actual manner in which the passions do their uniform work afford novelty and variety."[30] (When the poetic focus is on "physical nature," the depiction is similarly valuable and valued to the extent that the general conditions of pleasure are satisfied; the depiction is validated in pleasurable response to truth and novelty or variety.)

Johnson's way with works leads to the elimination or the reduc-tion in significance of traditional distinctions founded on the special characteristics of works and genres, and his psychological conception of nature fosters a generalized procedure for dealing with the subject of poetry. To Johnson poetry "has a universal subject—nature and passion—but particular works have as their matter more or less specific subjects selected or dictated by choice, convention, [occasion], or accident from the wide realm in which the imagination is free to rove." But such particular subjects "always raise for Johnson the question of how far they approximate the universal subject of poetry, i.e., of the degree to which they are capable of satisfying the general conditions of pleasure—truth and novelty. This alone is the test applied to poetic subjects."[31]

When we turn to an examination of the audience, we find that the "importance of the reader in Johnson's scheme . . . lies not merely in the fact that literature has a pleasurable end, for such an end has been stated by critics in whose work the reader plays a relatively unimportant role, but in the fact that Johnson is seeking a stable basis in nature on which to rest critical inquiry and judgment: the audience is the only fixed element in the process; for while nature has invariable features, they can be identified only through general recognition, and while poets may excel in the power to discover and represent nature, we become aware of this capacity only through its effect upon us." And to Johnson "the demands which readers make of literature are not confined to literature but are, indeed, the general causes of pleasure, operative in the affairs of life as well." The proper reader is the "common reader, the reasonable man, no other traits being involved than rationality and common experience of the world."[32]

Nevertheless, although "the audience supplies . . . the basis for critical inference," Johnson, "in his search for causes explanatory of the effects of literary works and hence permitting judgment of praise and blame, . . . addresses himself primarily to the author." The central importance of the poet for Johnson "arises from the fact that it is the poet's activity which imparts to literature its peculiarly tentative and experimental character and from the fact that the power of the author is the ultimate ground on which rests the capacity of works to evoke pleasure." Johnson's emphasis on the poet reflects "the fundamental orientation of his theory to the natural conditions of artistic activity, and it displays the tendency

we have noticed in his treatment of works, subjects, and readers to
avoid derivation of his basic terms from an analysis of the peculiar
traits of art."

The focus on the author leads inevitably to comparative analyses
of genius. To Johnson "Genius is merely the sum of all the powers
of the mind operating with maximum effect," and he finds a "comparative criterion for the measurement of genius or power in his
concept of the 'general and collective ability of man' " *(Preface to
Shakespeare)*. The general level at which men may operate, however, "cannot be determined precisely and finally because a new
genius may always appear to break through the levels previously
established and force a revision of our conception of what human
nature may accomplish." Johnson's notion of the general and
collective ability of man is consequently "a concept of the limit of
human capacity, not deduced from a consideration of the ends or
objects or forms of poetry, but derived empirically, 'discovered in a
long succession of endeavors' " (and hence subject to revision as
new powers are disclosed in new achievements). Johnson, in short,
grounds his inferences concerning genius on "an induction from
past performances rather than on an absolute scheme of values";
the measure against which genius is tested is thus both open-ended
and relatively stable.[33]

Such, then, in broad outline is what can be accepted, I think, as
a cognitively adequate account of the theoretical foundations of
Johnson's criticism; it is sufficiently comprehensive to cover Johnson's critical diversity and sufficiently precise to come to close
quarters with the details of the individual texts within that diversity.[34] Finally, it is an account that enables us to reason from
generative principles and assumptions to particular critical pronouncements, without getting entangled along the way in the
possibilities that a consideration of isolated doctrinal similarities
and dissimilarities might suggest to ingenuity.

Pastoral Defined

The specialized reflection of the principles outlined in the preceding chapter can be clearly seen in Johnson's effort to arrive at a
"distinct and exact idea" of pastoral writing. When in *Rambler* 37,
Johnson examines the received notions of pastoral—as promul-
gated by critics and supported by poetic practice—he finds that
men have "entangled themselves with unnecessary difficulties, by
advancing principles, which, having no foundation in the nature of
things, are wholly to be rejected from a species of composition in
which, above all others, mere nature is to be regarded." To arrive
at principles having a foundation in the nature of things, Johnson
begins by inquiring after the proper subject matter of pastoral
poetry, on the assumption presumably that whatever limitations
may legitimately be imposed on the selectivity of the poet who
chooses to write in the pastoral mode must derive initially from the
nature of the life to be depicted or represented. And in fact, all
subsequent distinctions and restrictions emerge from a primary
consideration of the nature of human life (nature and passion being
the universally satisfying subjects of poetry) as peculiarly modified
or qualified by the special conditions of rural existence. Thus "If
we search . . . for the true definition of a pastoral, it will be found
'a poem in which any action or passion is represented by its effects
upon a country life' " (*Rambler* 37).

From this base Johnson proceeds to necessary or natural consequences, defining in the process criteria of inclusion and
exclusion. For example, by considering pastoral in general (within
its special subject-matter restrictions), Johnson discovers no
grounds for prohibiting the exhibition of the "ideas and sentiments
of those, whoever they are, to whom the country affords pleasure or
employment" (or, in other words, no grounds for restricting

pastoral—as was the common critical practice—to "a dialogue, or narrative of men actually tending sheep") (*Rambler* 37). By Johnsonian definition "Pastoral admits all ranks of persons, because persons of all ranks inhabit the country." Thus "It exludes not, . . . on account of the characters necessary to be introduced, any elevation or delicacy of sentiment [the speakers need not be uncouth, nor the speech coarse]; those ideas only are improper, which, not owing their original to rural objects, are not pastoral." And from the restriction to rural existence in, of course, rural locations, it follows that the imagery characterizing poetry in this mode must also be rural: "Pastoral being the 'representation of an action or passion, by its effects upon a country life,' has nothing peculiar but its confinement to rural imagery, without which it ceases to be pastoral. This is its true characteristic, and this it cannot lose by any dignity of sentiment or beauty of diction" (*Rambler* 37).

Johnson's conception of the limiting requirements of the genre is completed when a codicil is added to the subject-matter item. If representation is to be restricted to the effects of action and passion upon rural existence, then "it would seem necessary, to the perfection of this [kind of] poem, that the occasion which is supposed to produce it, be at least not inconsistent with a country life, or less likely to interest those who have retired into places of solitude and quiet, than the more busy part of mankind" (*Rambler* 37). Conceived thus broadly, the pastoral is a form that clearly admits a rich diversity of poetic embodiments.

Nevertheless, it should be recognized that, the broadness of his conception of genre notwithstanding, Johnson has carefully and precisely defined the area of human concern in which the poet's imagination may move and hence the conditions on which the pleasures that we derive from this kind of poetry depend. On the latter point, it is clear that our pleasure increases in proportion to the extent that we can credit the representation of life, as qualified by the special conditions of rural existence and by the particular occasion presumably motivating expression. Our pleasure depends, in other words, on our recognition of the consonance between what is said or done and what we can credit as possible or probable to rural life operating under the demands of the immediate occasion. What cannot be credited cannot please, and the pleasure excited by this kind of poetry is, by definition, dependent upon our recognition of the congruity between representation and human experience.

To Johnson's mind those critics and writers who operate from narrower conceptions of the genre fall into absurdity, inconsistency, or improbability. There is no reason in the nature of things, for example, why pastoral poets should be restricted to a representation of the manners of the "golden age." The only reason that Johnson has found for this rule is that "according to the customs of modern life, it is improbable that shepherds should be capable of harmonious numbers, or delicate sentiments; and therefore the reader must exalt his ideas of the pastoral character, by carrying his thoughts back to the age in which the care of herds and flocks was the employment of the wisest and greatest men" (*Rambler* 37). To justify the numbers and sentiments, the critics are obliged to suppose a condition of life that never obtained and to reason to conclusions from false notions of probability, notions, that is, of the sort that encourage some students, responding appropriately to the complexity of Shakespeare's representation of human experience, to ask whether people in Shakespeare's time really spoke to one another so sensibly and in blank verse. The problems for which the critics attempt to provide solutions can, in Johnson's terms, be easily avoided by not restricting pastoral speech to those who actually tend sheep. Once the restriction is dropped, poets save themselves the bother of creating a language rich in obsolete terms and "rustic" vocabulary, of creating "a mingled dialect which no human being could have spoken."

However, although pastoral speakers in Johnson's scheme are not restricted to a particular time (real or mythical) or social condition, they are nevertheless obliged to speak on those occasions and to those subjects which can readily be supposed to be compatible with the conditions of country life. Thus while Johnson broadens the base of representation, refusing to limit the pastoral to a specific subject matter, speaker, style, or effect, he also excludes, on grounds of probability, many of the topics and sentiments that

successive generations of writers had been willing to load onto
pastoral, so that it came in time to be accepted as the natural beast
of burden for all manner of improper didactic and satiric baggage.

> It is improper . . . to give the title of a pastoral to verses, in
> which the speakers, after the slight mention of their flocks, fall
> to complaints of errors in the church, and corruptions in the
> government, or to lamentations of the death of some illustrious
> person, whom when once the poet has called a shepherd, he has
> no longer any labour upon his hands, but can make the clouds
> weep, and lilies wither, and the sheep hang their heads, without
> art or learning, genius or study. (*Rambler* 37)

In sum, it is important to recognize that the effect of Johnson's
criticism of the received analyses of pastoral is "not to eliminate
the concept of the genre, but to reduce its value and importance as
a principle of criticism by stripping it of most of its peculiarities,
and to throw the emphasis in criticism away from the analysis of
genre and toward the more general causes on which, in common
with other forms of poetry, it depends."[2] Here, as elsewhere, the
specification of the peculiarities of the form depends upon a prior
analysis of poetic activity, nature, and the general bases of pleasurable response.

In Johnson's analysis the imagination of the poet, while free to
exercise on a long tether, must adjust nevertheless to the range of
experience naturally implicated in the conditions of country life,
poetic success being contingent upon the capacity of the author's
selection, arrangement, and expression of material to produce a
pleasurable response in the general audience (the response being
the natural consequence of the opinion—the basis of response—
that the representation is creditable as a "just picture of a real
original"; the representation, if it is successful, brings "realities to
mind" ("Preface to Shakespeare").

But the facility of treating actions or events in the pastoral mode
(when the writing is based on inadequate principles and the examples of predecessors),

> has incited many writers from whom more judgment might have
> been expected, to put the sorrow or the joy which the occasion
> required into the mouth of Daphne or Thyrsis, and as one
> absurdity must naturally be expected to make way for another,

they have written with an utter disregard of both life and nature,
and filled their productions with mythological allusions, with
incredible fictions, and with sentiments which neither passion
nor reason could have dictated, since the change which religion
has made in the whole system of the world. (*Rambler* 37)

Starting with a common occasion—one "naturally incident to our
state of life"—and hence calling for a representation that runs level
with common life, these writers rummage about in the warehouse
of shopworn poetic commonplaces only to produce at last characters and sentiments that would be commensurate with the occasion
and hence naturally affecting, only if we were, as beings, other
than we are, living other than we do; or only if, to carry the
illustration to the center of Johnson's concluding remark, we could
suppose, at this point in human history, that pagan consolations
could soothe Christian distress, that that lamentation is creditable
which has recourse to pagan eschatology; only if Milton and King
had been shepherds battening their flocks and listening to the grey
fly wind its sultry horn long before the change that religion has
made in the whole system of the world.

Although following it in order of time, *Rambler* 37 is, in order of
logic, prior to *Rambler* 36, since the principles from which number
36 proceeds are either articulated directly in or inferrable
immediately from number 37. In *Rambler* 37 Johnson defines
generally the natural scope of pastoral representation and the
"special" imagery by which scene is described and action or passion illustrated, whereas in *Rambler* 36 he discusses the grounds of
the pleasure activited by the pastoral—making explicit what is
implicit in the more "theoretical" paper—and the natural limitations of the form, which follow of necessity from the scenes and
occasions to which it is restricted.

On the first matter it is clear to Johnson that pastoral poetry
pleases because it gratifies "every mind by recalling its conceptions." From Johnson's point of view "It is generally pleasing,
because it entertains the mind with representations of scenes
familiar to almost every imagination and of which all men can
equally judge whether they are well described"(*Rambler* 36). Johnson legitimately assumes in the general audience a common familiarity with the natural scenes of the pastoral and hence a common

ability to recognize the consonance between the depiction and life; the pleasure is widely diffused because the pastoral exhibits a world to which we all bring from our experience something answerable.

Also pastoral pleases, in part, because of what its scenes force upon our minds by strong impulses of nature and strong habits of association. Immediate pleasure derives from our recognition of the positive correlation between the representation and life, but our pleasure is augmented considerably by ancillary reflections, by the reflex movement of our minds to what we are inclined to associate with rural scenes:

> The images of true pastoral have always the power of exciting delight, because the works of nature, from which they are drawn, have always the same order and beauty, and continue to force themselves upon our thoughts, being at once obvious to the most careless regard, and more than adequate to the strongest reason, and severest contemplation. Our inclination to stillness and tranquillity [which we associate with pastoral existence] is seldom much lessened by long knowledge of the busy and tumultuary part of the world. In childhood we turn our thoughts to the country, as to the region of pleasure, we recur to it in old age as a port of rest, and perhaps with that secondary and adventitious gladness, which every man feels on reviewing those places, or recollecting those occurences, that contributed to his youthful enjoyments, and bring him back to the prime of life, when the world was gay with the bloom of novelty, when mirth wantoned at his side, and hope sparkled before him. (*Rambler* 36)

From this delineation of the peculiar ancillary pleasures attending the reading of pastoral poetry (the associative effects of rural imagery), we can, I think, anticipate what will constitute for Johnson the special weaknesses and limitations of the form. The pastoral is pleasant enough, but it makes a rather thin soup; it is perhaps sufficient to take the edge off the hunger of the imagination, but it is not "a dinner to ask a man to." The pastoral encourages us "in any hour of indolence and relaxation," to abstract our minds from perplexity awhile and to consider that haven of gaiety, mirth, and hope from which we departed or that port of stillness and tranquillity to which we long to return. However, between the pastoral and the poetry that Johnson truly admires, there is, topographically speaking, the distance separating the Midlands from Fleet Street and, in terms of human history, that separating childhood from adult experience. Although pastoral poetry is capable of making life more endurable and more enjoyable, it does so generally by fostering delusive—albeit harmless—reverie. By its very nature— since on the level of human action and passion, as well as of imagery, it is restricted to rural existence—pastoral poetry cannot do much to enlarge our comprehension, elevate our fancy,[3] or increase our virtue, inasmuch as it portrays little that speaks to our adult experience or that can be applied to the circumstances of our real sublunary nature, "which partakes of good and evil, joy and sorrow, mingled with endless variety of proportion and innumerable modes of combination."[4]

When we are moved by pastoral poetry, it is undoubtedly because the persons speak "by the influence of those general passions and principles by which all minds are agitated, and the whole system of life is continued in motion" ("Preface to Shakespeare"), but the fact is that "the state of man confined to the employments and pleasures of the country, is so little diversified, and exposed to so few of those accidents which produce perplexities, terrors and surprises, in more complicated transactions, that he can be shewn but seldom in such circumstances as attract curiosity" (*Rambler* 36). To Johnson it is in the more complicated transactions of life that we discern "those parallel circumstances, and kindred images, to which we readily conform our minds" (*Rambler* 6). To the extent that pastoral poetry offers a just representation of general nature (to the extent, that is, that pastoral poetry exhibits the operation of general principles in variously individuated circumstances), it pleases immediately, not secondarily or reflexively, but since both the range of its concern and the store of its images are naturally limited, it soon exhausts the various possibilities by which it might please. And it is on the imagery and the conditions of life to which pastoral writing is restricted (according to Johnson's differentiation of the form in *Rambler* 37) that Johnson chiefly concentrates in *Rambler* 36.

Johnson is convinced that rural imagery does not admit much variety of description, and the common stock of its imagery is but slowly augmented:

The range of pastoral is indeed narrow, for though nature itself, philosophically considered, be inexhaustible, yet its general effects on the eye and on the ear are uniform, and incapable of much variety in description. . . . However, as new plants or modes of culture are introduced, and by little and little become common, pastoral might receive, from time to time, small augmentations, and exhibit once in a century a scene somewhat varied. (*Rambler* 36)

As it is with the imagery, so it is with the occasions to which the imagery is applied:

Not only the images of rural life, but the occasions on which they can be properly produced, are few and general. The state of man confined to the employments and pleasures of the country, is so little diversified . . . that he can be shewn but seldom in such circumstances as attract curiosity. His ambition is without policy, and his love without intrigue. He has no complaints to make of his rival, but that he is richer than himself; nor any disasters to lament, but a cruel mistress, or a bad harvest. (*Rambler* 36)

The pleasure excited by pastoral poetry is genuine and has its basis in our recognition of truth, but the general paucity of the material of which it is necessarily constructed leads to predictable consequences: pastoral writers are successful

after the manner of other imitators; [they transmit] the same images in the same combination from one to another, till he that reads the title of a poem, may guess at the whole series of the composition; nor will a man, after the perusal of thousands of these performances, find his knowledge enlarged with a single view of nature not produced before, or his imagination amused with any new application of those views to moral purposes. (*Rambler* 36)

In transferring the location from the country to the shore, Sannazaro, in his *Eglogae Piscatoriae,* could not overcome the natural limitations of the form in its imagery and occasions, though he is not, according to Johnson, to be censured—as he was by some prescriptive critics—for failing to show the sea as an object of terror (in the nature of things, as the soldier is not always a blunt, gruff man, so the sea is not always in a storm, and to Johnson only false notions of propriety could abrogate the poet's right to select such characteristics for representation as suited his purpose; the poet is "no more obliged to shew the sea in a storm, than the land under an inundation; but may display all the pleasures, and conceal the dangers of the water, as he may lay his shepherd under a shady beech, without giving him an ague, or letting a wild beast loose upon him"). Indeed, the piscatory eclogue is even more restricted in its range of imagery than the rural pastoral, and it cannot extend the number of occasions calling for illustration. The "natural" defects (i.e., defects in the material substance of the poetry) of the picatory eclogue are precisely those which are intrinsic to rural pastoral:

> There are . . . two defects in the piscatory eclogue which perhaps cannot be suppled. The sea . . . has . . . much less variety than the land, and therefore will be sooner exhausted by a descriptive writer. When he has once shewn the sun rising or setting upon it, curled its water with the vernal breeze, rolled waves in gentle succession to the shore, and enumerated the fish sporting in the shallows, he has nothing remaining but what is common to all other poetry [limited to the representation of life in its less complicated transactions], the complaint of a nymph for a drowned lover, or the indignation of a fisher that his oysters are refused and Mycon's accepted. (*Rambler* 36)

Additionally, the piscatory eclogue, unlike the pastoral, is severely limited in both its immediate and its associative appeal, since the general audiance, unfamiliar in large measure with the scenes and conditions of shore existence, is unable to play the description against its own experience.[5] However faithful the depiction of scene and manners to life, such poetry cannot please many, because it cannot gratify every mind by recalling its conceptions:

> Another obstacle to the general reception of this kind of poetry, is the ignorance of maritime pleasures, in which the greater part of mankind must always live. To all the inland inhabitants of every region, the sea is only known as an immense diffusion of waters, over which men pass from one country to another, and in which life is frequently lost. They have, therefore, no opportunity of tracing, in their own thoughts, the descriptions of winding shores, and calm bays, nor can look on the poem in which they are mentioned, with other sensastions, than on a sea-chart, or the metrical geography of Dionysius. (*Rambler* 36)

From these two *Rambler* papers we can recover the primary assumptions and the principles of reasoning informing and hence governing Johnson's particular judgments of individual works. In *Rambler* 37, Johnson defines the peculiar distinguishing attributes of the genre, whereas in *Rambler* 36, he focuses attention on the inherent limitations in those two aspects of the poetry by which it is distinguished as a form. *Rambler* 36 refines within the system of inference ordained by Johnson's generalized conception of the genre. When we free our minds from arbitrary restrictions and consider pastoral in the light of those principles which have their foundation in the nature of things, it will be seen, Johnson claims, that pastoral, like any other kind of poetry, pleases to the extent that it satisfies the general conditions of pleasure, which it can do only when what the poet manages to express in words can be credited as probable or possible to human life under certain specified or implied conditions; pastoral is differentiated from other kinds by virtue of the fact that probability and possibility are determined by what the general reader, drawing on his own experience or what is inferrable from that experience, can suppose is consistent with the conditions, circumstances, and interests of those residing in the country, where the scene of action and passion is necessarily set. Where improbability is detected dissatisfaction is forced on the mind, and pleasure is converted to the pain either of confusion or annoyance. The natural defects of the form cannot be overcome except by breaking across the borders delimiting the legitimate range of the pastoral, but as soon as those borders are passed, the conditions on which our pleasure depends cannot be satisfied.

It is reasonable to assume that the diversity that the pastoral form, admitting little variety of description and confined to few and general occasions, is capable of achieving would be realized early, and Johnson finds his pattern of excellence in the performance of Virgil: "their descriptions[6] may indeed differ from those of Virgil, as an English from an Italian summer, and, in some respects, as modern from ancient life; but as nature is in both countries nearly the same, and as poetry has to do rather with the passions of men, which are uniform, than their customs, which are changeable, the varieties, which time or place can furnish, will be inconsiderable. . ." (*Rambler* 36). Johnson's preference for Virgil, it should be recognized, is a derivative of his critical principles and is well grounded; it is not a sign of abject veneration of the ancients or of blind neoclassical prejudice.

In the first place, when Virgil's compositions are examined in the light of what may be determined those "preconstructional" circumstances promoting artistic success, those adventitious benefits contributing to the excellence and facilitating the composition of literary works, it is clear that

> every advantage of nature, and of fortune, concurred to complete his productions; . . . he was born with great accuracy and severity of judgment, enlightened with all the learning of one of the brightest ages, and embellished with the elegance of the Roman court; . . . he employed his powers rather in improving, than inventing, and therefore must have endeavored to recompense the want of novelty by exactness; . . . taking Theocritus for his original, he found pastoral far advanced toward perfection, and . . . having so great a rival, he must have proceeded with uncommon caution. (*Rambler* 37)

Native ability, then, was supported by auspicious circumstances.

Second, from the perspective of Johnson's conception of the pastoral, Virgil would seem to have exhibited the genre in virtually all the modes of description and action that it can properly accommodate, to have played virtually all the changes on the form that it, naturally limited as it is, will allow.

Third, wide familiarity with what has passed under the heading of *pastoral* since the time of Virgil tends to confirm the preceding point, for it would seem that Virgil's successors have been able to do little more than rehearse his accomplishments, introducing from time to time slight modifications but surviving in general by loan or theft. Where divergence from Virgil has been more than superficial, the novelty has been achieved at the expense of "true pastoral"; ingenuity, introducing change, has undermined the bases of the pleasure that the pastoral is fitted to excite. Virgil, a great genius advantageously located in time and place, has carried to excellence what Theocritus had brought a great distance.

As a critic ultimately interested in how highly we may rate our native force, in the limits of our human capacities, Johnson is convinced that Virgil's productions, as signs of human ability, establish what may tentatively be accepted as the outside limit of human achievement in pastoral writing. The measure or standard defined by Virgil's accomplishment is stable, because in the course of time it has not been extended by a long succession of endeavors, and tentative, because in the course of time it is possible that a new poet will emerge who will fly higher and stay longer on the wing than Virgil. Nevertheless, although Virgil's achievement provides us with a standard of excellence, no single poem in the canon can claim any rights of privilege that would exempt it from judgments that follow by hard necessity from critical principles. In other words, nothing in Virgil's practice can serve as a precedent (and hence a justification) for the inclusion of material in pastoral poetry that is not within the limits of toleration implied in a definition of the form agreeable to reason and having its foundation in the nature of things, for unlike many of his critical predecessors, Johnson will have his principles of judgment from reason, not from precedent. By looking briefly at Johnson's praise of and animadversions on some of Virgil's pastorals (as expressed in *Adventurer* 92), we can acquire some refined sense of the practical critical consequences of his conception of the genre and the coherent view of literature underlying that conception.

Although Virgil's "general merit has been universally acknowledged, [Johnson] is far from thinking all the productions of his rural Thalia equally excellent: there is, indeed, in all his pastorals a strain of versification which it is in vain to seek in any other poet; but if we except the first and tenth, they seem liable either wholly or in part to considerable objections" (*Adventurer* 92). Of the second pastoral, for example, Johnson says: "I know not that it contains one affecting sentiment, or pleasing description, or one passage that strikes the imagination or awakens the passions" (*Adventurer* 92).

The fourth, while "filled with images at once splendid and pleasing" and "elevated [by a] grandeur of language worthy of the first of Roman poets," invites us to yield to a possibility that even credulity could not credit, namely, that "the golden age should return because Pollio had a son" (Johnson not being inclined to confound pagan fiction with Christian truth, i.e., to read Christ into so "wild a fiction"). The inherent improbability of the fiction provokes a dissatisfaction that simply cannot be overcome by the congregated forces of versification, imagery, and diction.

Johnson's commentary on the fifth pastoral strikes the chord that will reverberate throughout the critique of *Lycidas;* here we encounter the flower in the seed: "The fifth contains a celebration of Daphnis, which has stood to all succeeding ages as the model of pastoral elegies. . . . yet whoever shall read it with impartiality, will find that most of the images are of the mythological kind, and therefore easily invented; and that there are few sentiments of rational praise, or natural lamentation" (*Adventurer* 92). The poem admits what, by virtue of its occasion, it should reject and neglects what, by virtue of its occasion, it should emphasize. Johnson's primary objections to this poem have their theoretical base (as I hope to show below) not so much in his conception of pastoral as in his conception of elegy; his specific objections here emerge essentially from a prior consideration of the nature of the occasion actually or presumably prompting composition.

In the sixth, Virgil rises again "to the dignity of philosophic sentiment and heroic poetry" (neither of which is inconsistent with the pastoral, as defined by Johnson), but "since the compliment paid to Gallus fixes the transaction to his own time, the fiction of Silenus seems injudicious" (*Adventurer* 92). The shortcomings of this poem are spelled out in greater detail in *Rambler* 36: "The Silenus is of a more disputable kind, because though the scene lies in the country, the song being religious and historical, had been no less adapted to any other audience or place. Neither can it well be defended as a fiction for the introduction of a god seems to imply the golden age, and yet he alludes to many subsequent transactions, and mentions Gallus, the poet's contemporary" (*Adventurer* 92). Its status as a pastoral is disputable because the subject of the poem, although not entirely inconsistent with country life, has no natural association with that life, and the fiction displeases, not because it is fiction, but because a *single* fiction is not sustained. Displeasure, that is, is excited by the coexistence of competing frames of "historical" reference, the objection here being precisely of the sort that underlies Johnson's negative comments on Hector's quoting Aristotle. The suppositions which are activated and encouraged by the poem and upon which probability expectations and demands are founded are, in this poem, incompatible with one another, and the reader can discover in the poem no means of linking the frames of reference; what the poem imparts by way of philosophic sentiment it withdraws by way of internal inconsistency.

The seventh repeats the subject of the third, a musical contest between two shepherds, and thus it cannot be mentioned without some reproach being cast upon Virgil's "inventive power": ". . . of ten pastorals Virgil has written two upon the same plan" (*Adventurer* 92). Although Johnson specifically focuses on the matter of inventiveness, the repetition also offers mute testimony to the narrow range of the pastoral. Moreover, this poem has another shortcoming: its outcome is not probable, and to Johnson the reader can take no delight in a conclusion which does not follow naturally from its antecedents, which he has neither expected nor wished and in which he has no interest. As Johnson says: "One of the shepherds now gains an acknowledged victory, but without any apparent superiority; and the reader, when he sees the prize adjudged, is not able to discover how it was deserved."[7] In the seventh pastoral, Virgil does not excite any interest in the outcome of the contest; the contestants are not discriminated morally, intellectually, or in terms of musical skill, and, consequently, we stand impassive (or worse) before the competition, the equality of the contestants not being sufficiently interesting in itself to activate apparently any wish even for a draw. If such a contest is *very like* life, then it is met with a response which is *very like* that which would attend its actual occurrence. What is represented must at least draw our attention by irresistable attraction. The general conditions of pleasure are truth and novelty (or variety), but the silent injunction in these conditions is that the matter of the representation be intrinsically interesting, that is, capable of engaging our interest by its beauty, value, and human significance, of exciting our emotions by the ethical importance of its action and the moral qualities of its agents.

Johnson dispatches the eighth and ninth pastorals abruptly. The eighth is dismissed because to Johnson "so little [of it] is properly the work of Virgil": "he has no claim to other praise or blame than that of a translator" (*Adventurer* 92). The ninth is dismissed because "it is scarce possible to discover the design or tendency" of it and because "there is nothing [in it] that seems appropriated to any time or place, or of which any other use can be discovered than to fill up the poem" (*Adventurer* 92).

Adventurer 92 concludes with an account of the peculiar merits of the first and tenth pastorals, and it is in this account that the positive merits of Johnson's critical priorities are most clearly revealed. He begins by asserting that "the first and tenth pastorals, whatever may be determined of the rest, are sufficient to place their author above the reach of rivalry." In the tenth "the complaint of Gallus disappointed in his love is full of such sentiments as disappointed love naturally produces; his wishes are wild, his resentment is tender, and his purposes are inconstant." The performance is proportionate to the occasion, and Virgil's expression betrays a "knowledge of those precepts in the mind, those operations of intellectual nature, to which everything that aspires to please must be proportioned and accommodated."[8] Here is the "genuine language of despair," the richly individuated expression of general motions of mind; the details function within the horizon of implication constituted by a distinct type of human emotion, and the reader of common experience immediately recognizes that the details by which the passion is individuated are the legitimate progeny of a distinct type of emotion, are explicit realizations of possibilities implicated in a subsuming emotional category.

The reader approaches all representations of life with a finely tuned system of response "rules," a highly structured response mechanism, which for convenience and for lack of a better term we can call his *experience competence.* Just as we can understand sentences in our native language that we have never heard before and can immediately recognize that certain verbal combinations cannot be "right," cannot be said (e.g., "the the is man hat on"), so we all bring to representations of "new" experiences of determinate kinds an ability to recognize, with exquisite precision, their appropriateness, their legitimacy; Virgil does not say what has been said before; he says what is "right." Milton, on the other hand, says not only what has been said before but what, our *competence* tells us, is "wrong."

Roughly speaking, unacceptable verbal combinations are to our *linguistic competence* as improbabilities are to our *experience competence,* namely, conditions forcing dissatisfaction on our minds. What we can credit is a function of our competence working upon determinate suppositions relating to event, scene, character, and action. In any given instance we cannot know before the fact what disappointed love will say, but we do know after the fact whether the sentiments expressed are of the sort that disappointed love naturally produces. It is by virtue of this competence (a concept that presupposes an essential intellectual and emotional uniformity in all men) that the "new" is recognized as natural, as an explicit fulfillment of possibilities naturally implicated in the "typical" condition. The happiness of the tenth pastoral (as of so much of the poetry that Johnson most admires) is that it enables us to encounter what, without Virgil's particularized expression, we do not know (in precisely this form at least) as an embodiment of our own knowledge. (Of course, competence—linguistic or experience—is longer on recognition than on invention.) The poem gratifies every mind by recalling its conceptions—and here I am talking about conceptions of action, passion, and thought, not of scene, scenery, and so on—in the sense that the general reader of common experience brings to the representation the means by which to interpret or understand its several parts as mutually supportive and distinctly type-bound, as possible traits of a particular type of action, condition, or passion.

If the truth we find at once gives us back the image of our minds (as Pope says in the *Essay on Criticism*),[9] it is so only in the sense that the particular representation falls within the range of implication tolerated by our generalized, relatively content-free—that is, relatively inexplicit—intuition of a subsuming whole of a certain kind. This point is more forcefully expressed by Johnson himself in, for example, his review of Gray's *Elegy in a Country Churchyard:* "The four stanzas beginning 'Yet even these bones' are to me original: I have never seen the notions in any other place; yet he that reads them here *persuades* himself that he has *always felt them*."[10] We *recall* the conceptions that Gray *makes available* to us, recollection here being an immediate awareness of the adequacy of these notions to our nature; Gray's notions are, in short, explicit realizations of latencies enfolded in our working understanding of the nature of man. The sentiments are immediately validated; once expressed, they are immediately recognized as our own (or, alternatively, as views naturally incident to or commensurate with our state of life). What a man may say on the occasion of the death of a friend, we cannot predict, but we immediately know when any given expression does not fit within the borders of the

occasion and the presumed relation of the men, and this is the case
because in the course of time—as we learn to regulate imagination
by experience—we "gain more principles of reasoning and found a
wider basis of analogy" *(Journey to the Western Islands of Scotland).* These fruits of experience are, then, the cognitive constituents of our competence, which enable us to assimilate the
unknown (i.e., the material never before encountered in precisely
this form) to the known, to determine that the "new" is agreeable to
the nature of things and within the generative or constitutive capacities of the "known." The tenth pastoral satisfies the general
conditions of pleasure, as well as the specific conditions of pastoral
composition as delineated in *Rambler* 37. Its occasion is consistent
with rural life, and the effects of genuine despair (despair that is
credited because it is immediately recognized as a richly individuated expression of what is typical of disappointed love) are transmitted by rural "ideas."

What is true of the tenth is likewise true of the first pastoral, to
which Johnson gives the preference, finding it no less "natural"
but more various than the tenth: "But notwithstanding the excellence of the tenth pastoral, I cannot forbear to give the preference
to the first, which is equally natural and more diversified. The
complaint of the shepherd who saw his old companion at ease in the
shade, while himself was driving his little flock he knew not whi-
ther, is such as, with variation of circumstances, misery always
utters at the sight of prosperity" *(Adventurer* 92). Here, then, as in
the tenth, we witness the regular motions of the mind operating
under the influence of particular local conditions; the general
operations of our intellectual-emotional nature are made vivid and
affective by the concrete particulars of scene, character, and
circumstance.

According to Johnson, when we "analyze the mind," we discover
that although "the passions from whence arise all the pleasures
and pains that we see and hear of . . . are very few," those few,
"agitated and combined, as external causes shall happen to operate," are the great "fund, from which those who study mankind
may fill their compositions with an inexhaustible variety of images
and allusions" *(Adventurer* 95). In Johnson's scheme, as Keast has
remarked, both "truth and variety arise from the constant linkage
between human passions and their effects: the regularity with

which the same passions produce effects of the same kind permits recognition and hence truth; the infinite accidental modifications in the actual manner in which the passions do their uniform work afford novelty and variety."[11] In the first pastoral genuine misery—occasioned by a variety of circumstances and provoking a series of reflections consistent with rural life—is naturally expressed: the shepherd's "account of the difficulties of his journey gives a very tender image of pastoral distress. . . ." And "the description of Virgil's happiness in his little farm combines almost all the images of rural pleasure . . ." (*Adventurer* 92). Attesting to the impact of the poem on him, Johnson writes "he . . . that can read it with indifference, has no sense of pastoral poetry." Within the limits of the pastoral form, Virgil has in these two poems found the means to unite truth with variety, thereby securing those pleasurable effects which have their basis in the universal psychological condition of man.

To his account of these two poems Johnson adds a characteristic postscript: "It may be observed, that these two poems were produced by events that really happened; and may, therefore, be of use to prove, that we can feel more than we can imagine, and that the most artful fiction must give way to truth" (*Adventurer* 92). Johnson here specifies what he takes to be one of the "preconstructional" circumstantial determinants or causes of the peculiar force of these two poems: these poems have their originals in lived experience. And what he says here is perfectly consistent with his remarks on Pope's *Epistle of Eloise to Abelard:* "The heart naturally loves truth. The adventures and misfortunes of this illustrious pair are known from undisputed history. . . . So new and so affecting is their story that it supersedes invention, and imagination ranges at full liberty without straggling into scenes of fable."[12] Truth supersedes invention.

Johnson's fondness for biography is partially explained by the principle articulated here; biography deals with real men and real events, and thus "those parallel circumstances, and kindred images to which we readily conform our minds, are, above all other writings, to be found in narratives of the lives of particular persons . . . " (*Rambler* 60). It is also to this principle that Johnson appeals when, in *Idler* 84, he explains, on essentially epistemological grounds, why autobiography may be more trustworthy than biography: "The writer of his own life has at least the first qualification of an historian, the knowledge of the truth." Analogously, the poet who gives expression to lived experience and felt emotion has that advantage over the poet who must, before and during expression, imagine the experience and the feelings excited by it which the autobiographer, in general, has over the biographer, knowledge of the truth (even the most capable biographer, impartial and personally familiar with his subject, always runs the risk, for example, of misreading the natural and conventional signs of emotion and the real motives of observed behavior: "what we collect by conjecture, and by conjecture only can one man judge of another's motives or sentiments, is easily modified by fancy or desire"). "Certainty of knowledge not only excludes mistake but fortifies veracity" (*Idler* 84).

From all this, however, the reader should not assume that Johnson is asserting, as a fundamental critical principle, that all great and valuable literature has its origin in personal experience, that he is demanding from poets autobiographical poetry, cries personal and sincere. Poetry moves when it can be credited as a faithful representation of what is possible or probable to human life under certain specified or implied conditions. The lived experience is useless poetically unless the poet can find the means to give it vivid and powerful expression in language. It is important to recognize that at the end of *Adventurer* 92 Johnson is not describing the poetic bases of our pleasure, which are in the textual details that convey genuine misery, but a "preconstructional," accidental cause of the material which, when successfully presented, provokes pleasure. Virgil has successfully embodied in verse material originating in real events. The external stimulation saves invention some expense, but it does not guarantee the effectiveness of the poetic product.

As less intellectual energy is expended on invention when real experience provides the materials and supplies the object of representation, so more energy can be apportioned to the selection and arrangement of diction, imagery, and so on, in the effort to produce the appropriate response to and the maximum effectiveness of the experience, to produce, in short, a response comparable to the poet's own response, which presumably, since in essential respects men are everywhere the same, is the natural consequence of the event or experience. Johnson is simply giving critical emphasis to that painful knowledge we own, for example, when someone, anxious to mitigate our suffering by linking himself to it, asserts that he knows exactly how we feel. The indissoluble truth is that, in the absence of any clear and accurate expression of our condition or state of mind, the sympathetic friend imagines less than we feel. The poet who begins from a "real" experience has a "preconstructional," accidental advantage over the poet who must imagine that experience because he has ready at hand the material requisite to the task of bringing our imaginations to that condition from which appropriate feeling may proceed, but the advantage expires before inarticulateness or inadequate powers of expression. That we are moved by so much that poets must inevitably imagine demonstrates, of course, that readers and poets alike have the capacity, in greater and lesser degrees, to apprehend and respond to "truth" independently of "real" experience (such capacity being a function of our principles of reasoning and powers of analogy).

Throughout *Adventurer* 92 Johnson applies to Virgil's pastoral compositions those criteria of value which everywhere distinguish his critical judgment and reflect his coherent view of literature. As with other pieces of literature, pastorals are valued when they satisfy the general conditions of pleasure, and Johnson's comments on Virgil's ten pastorals follow naturally from his working definition of the form, which merely insists that the general ends of poetry be realized within the limiting conditions of rural imagery and topics consistent with rural life. In moving from *Ramblers* 36 and 37 to *Adventurer* 92 we move from precept to practice, from principles to those judgments demanded by and implicated in the principles.

That Johnson had more than a passing acquaintance with the history of pastoral composition and the particular pastoral tradition in which Milton wrote, there can be no doubt. When Johnson came to examine *Lycidas* he brought with him a mind well stocked with information on the pastoral accomplishments of Milton's poetic forebears; some sense of the extent of his knowledge can be obtained by recalling his brief history of the form, from Theocritus to Spenser, in the "Life of Ambrose Phillips":

The rustick Poems of Theocritus were so highly valued by the Greeks and Romans that they attracted the imitation of Virgil, whose *Eclogues* seem to have been considered as precluding all attempts of the same kind; for no shepherds were taught to sing by any succeeding poet till Nemesian and Calphurnius ventured their feeble efforts in the lower age of Latin literature.

At the revival of learning in Italy it was soon discovered that a dialogue of imaginary swains might be composed with little difficulty, because the conversation of shepherds excludes profound or refined sentiment; and, for images and descriptions, Satyrs and Fauns, and Naiads and Dryads, were always within call, and woods and meadows, and hills and rivers, supplied variety of matter, which, having a natural power to sooth the mind, did not quickly cloy it.

Petrarch entertained the learned men of his age with the novelty of modern Pastorals in Latin. Being not ignorant of Greek, and finding nothing in the word *Eclogue* of rural meaning, he supposed it to be corrupted by the copiers, and therefore called his own productions *Aeglogues*, by which he meant to express the talk of goatherds, though it will mean only the talk of goats. This new name was adopted by subsequent writers, and amongst others by our Spenser.

More than a century afterwards (1498) Mantuan published his *Bucolicks* with such success that they were soon dignified by Badius with a comment, and, as Scaliger complained, received into schools and taught as classical; his complaint was vain, and the practice, however injudicious, spread far and continued long. Mantuan was read, at least in some of the inferior schools of this kingdom, to the beginning of the present century. The speakers of Mantuan carried their disquisitions beyond the country, to censure the corruptions of the Church; and from him Spenser learned to employ his swains on topicks of controversy.

The Italians soon transferred Pastoral Poetry into their own language: Sannazaro wrote *Arcadia* in prose and verse; Tasso and Guarini wrote *Favole Boscareccie*, or Sylvan Dramas; and all nations of Europe filled volumes with Thyrsis and Damon, and Thestylis and Phyllis.

Philips thinks it "somewhat strange to conceive how, in an age so addicted to the Muses, Pastoral Poetry never comes to be so much as thought upon." His wonder seems very unseasonable; there had never, from the time of Spenser, wanted writers to talk occasionally of Arcadia and Strephon, and half the book in which he first tried his powers consists of dialogues on queen Mary's death, between Tityrus and Corydon or Mopsus and

Menalcas. A series or book of Pastorals, however, I know not that any one had then lately published.

Not long afterwards Pope made the first display of his powers in four *Pastorals,* written in a very different form. Philips had taken Spenser, and Pope took Virgil for his pattern. Philips endeavored to be natural, Pope laboured to be elegant.[13]

This chronicle, richly seasoned with hearty condescension and acidulous asperity, has its substantive base, of course, in that particular conception of "true" pastoral delineated in *Ramblers* 36 and 37.

To Johnson a succession of innovations had deflected pastoral from its true course; the selective activity of some poets has caused the form to deviate from its nature, and in Johnson's estimate no single poet did more damage to the form than Mantuan, who, by introducing speakers who carried their disquisitions beyond the country, effectively removed from the pastoral the chief characteristics by which it could be differentiated from other kinds of poetical compositions. After Mantuan it was no longer necessary to consider pastoral as "a poem in which any passion or action is represented by its effects upon a country life;" its occasion was no longer required to be consistent with country life and, consequently, the imagery by which the action or passion was supported was no longer obliged to be consistently rural. When the poetry deals principally with topics of controversy which, if not entirely and always inconsistent with country life, are at least more likely to interest the "more busy part of mankind than those who have retired into places of solitude and quiet," the suppositions upon which credibility is based (and pleasure depends) cannot properly be maintained,[14] and when such topics are supported by rural imagery (as they frequently were), the reader draws his dissatisfaction from verbal as well as "natural" improbability. To Johnson, Milton could find in the productions of his predecessors precedents for, but no justifications of his practice; the poet, no less than the critic, should derive his principles from reason, not precedent.

This survey of Johnson's views on pastoral poetry and the critical premises underlying those views can be brought to conclusion with a few brief remarks on a statement at the end of the "Life of Ambrose Philips," which some readers might construe as incompatible with Johnson's steady conception of "true" pastoral. Of

Philips's pastorals Johnson writes: "That they exhibit a mode of life which does not exist, nor ever existed, is not to be objected; the supposition of such a state is *allowed* to Pastoral."[15] The key word here, of course, is *allowed*. Johnson *allows* what many critics, operating from narrower principles, postulate as a fundamental condition of composition in the pastoral mode.[16] In *Rambler* 37 Johnson does not prohibit poetic recourse to Arcadia; he simply refuses to restrict composition to the exhibition of a golden age, thereby expanding the scope of pastoral representation and avoiding many of those silly critical disputes over, for example, how much ignorance must be interspersed with learning in order "to support the character of a shepherd."[17]

It is clear, however, that to Johnson the best pastorals (compositions, after all, "in which mere nature is to be regarded") do not depend for their effects upon the supposition of a state that never existed. The fiction adopted by Philips has Johnson's tolerance, if not his warm approbation, and it should be remembered that his "defense" is directed primarily at those who were willing to hang their objections to the writings of "Namby-Pamby" on any peg within easy reach. Moreover, Johnson's preferences notwithstanding, the fiction adopted by Philips—and supported by critical precept—places no insurmountable obstacles in the path of poetic pleasure, for while "poets indeed profess fiction . . . the legitimate end of fiction is the conveyance of truth,"[18] and within the limits of Arcadian fiction, it is possible to incite delight by rural scenes of natural beauty, and by depictions of scenes "of which all can judge whether" they are well described, and to move the general audience with representations of actions and passions that in their nature and motivation can be understood as consonant with what is "naturally incident to our state of life" (*Rambler* 60). Arcadian poetry can, in short, satisfy the general conditions of pleasure without wandering beyond the confines of rural occasions and imagery.

In such poetry our pleasure undoubtedly derives more often from the felicitous descriptions of the generally familiar natural scene—and only secondarily from the pleasant reveries activated by the depiction of that happy condition of existence (impossible to achieve in this our transient and probatory state and hence no proper object of the writer who desires to curtail our vain wishes

and to make life more endurable) in which there is in general
"pleasure without danger and security without restraint"[19] —than
from the general consonance of what is said and done to what we
know from experience of the nature and possibilities of life. Nevertheless, when we are moved by this poetry it is because what is said
or done can, by means of extension or analogy (the cognitive
grounds of our "competence"), be adjusted to fit within the range
of our experience or within the boundaries of what is implicated in
our condition, because what is exhibited is in some degree coordinate with human life and the operations of our intellectual nature.
Where there are few traits in the representation easily adjustable to
our condition, our response is nevertheless the natural emotive
consequence of our awareness of determinate moral quality in the
actions and purposes of the characters. Even when we cannot
credit the representation, we are moved—in ways strictly determined by our natures—by the ethical content of the representation
(undeserved misfortune naturally exciting our pity, selfless
generosity our admiration, for example). Where the *nature* of the
characters does not run level with our own, our pleasure depends
upon the ethical consonance obtaining between the representation
and life; the work brings ethical "realities" to mind and thus runs
level with truth, which we credit by appropriate response. We do
not suspend disbelief in the possibility of a golden age (we are
conscious of fiction, but neither belief nor disbelief is suspended
because the issue of belief never arises in our minds).

For illustration let us consider, not Arcadia, but the world of
Pope's Belinda. We do not suspend disbelief in the existence of
sylphs and gnomes when with Johnson we detest a gnome and love
a sylph; our response follows directly from the nature of their moral
quality and purpose as represented by Pope. Immersed in the
comic and completely inefficacious, this aerial race never seen
before can be credited with having attitudes and motives that can
be assimilated to our own, and we "adopt their interests" because
those interests, if not the incredible beings in which they reside,
are "real"; the strangely located passions act upon us exactly as
they would if they were instead familiarly located in real persons or
in creditable literary characters. As character, scene, and situation
more closely approximate the real possibilities of life and as action
and passion more exactly conform to the operations of our intellect,

so our pleasure from the representation increases proportionately, inasmuch as more "realities" are brought easily to mind when fewer incredibilities adhere to the representation. As there is more of nature in the representation, so there is more truth and hence, in the audience, more pleasure.

In moving from Arcadian pastoral to works such as Virgil's first pastoral, Pope's *Eloisa to Abelard,* or detailed narratives of the lives of particular persons, we move from works that, containing little that correlates with life, please more by novelty[20] and variety than by truth, to works that, exhibiting parallel circumstances and kindred images, "enchain the heart by irresistible interest" and "diffuse instruction to every diversity of condition." In his descriptions of external nature and his expressions of sentiment, the writer of Arcadian pastoral finds his chief opportunities for conveying truth, and while Philips can be allowed his Arcadia, the reader should not expect from works constructed on the Arcadian plan much that will enlarge his comprehension.

From Johnson's point of view the trouble with a good deal of this poetry is that it pleads for more credit than the general reader can reasonably grant. For Johnson it is from those works which run level with life that we derive greatest pleasure, since "nothing pleases many and pleases long but just representations of general nature." Finally, in defending Philips against unjustified criticism, Johnson clearly lends no encouragement to Arcadian pastoral and overturns no settled opinion concerning the bases of excellence in pastoral composition.

According to Johnson there is nothing in the nature of pastoral, radically considered, that prevents it from fulfilling the general ends of poetry, satisfying the general conditions of pleasure (as his analysis of Virgil's pastorals clearly demonstrates). And if the preceding investigation into Johnson's way with the pastoral accomplishes nothing else, it should at least undermine or invalidate the unfortunately persistent notion that Johnson's reaction to *Lycidas* reveals little more than a stock antipathy to pastoral writing. To account adequately for Johnson's repeated attacks against modern pastorals, the reader should turn for his information to Johnson's critical principles and that particular conception of the genre underlying his recurrent judgments, not to any putative, stock—and hence automatically released—antipathy to a *kind* of writing. For the most part the works passing under the rubric of pastoral had, to Johnson, no proper claim to the title, being collectively little more than exasperatingly redundant puerilities, written "with an utter disregard both of life and nature" and requiring for their production neither art nor learning, neither genius nor study; taken together, they were little more than trifling, "mechanick echoes of the Mantuan song."[21] What we hear as we walk down the long, dark, winding corridors of *Lycidas* is not the sound of human voices, but the steady ruffling of pages in the Renaissance songbook. Like so many other works published since the "revival of learning in Italy," *Lycidas* cannot be considered in Johnson's view a true pastoral.

Rational Praise, Natural Lamentation, and the Elegiac Occasion

To understand Johnson's reaction to *Lycidas* fully, it is necessary to consider it in relation to his working conception of the special demands of elegy. What in the critique has most disturbed or embarrassed Johnson's apologists follows naturally from his "elegiac" expectations. Warren Fleischauer has reminded us that Johnson does not exactly say that *Lycidas* is a pastoral; he says instead that "its *form* is that of a pastoral. . . . " *Lycidas* is "an elegy in the pastoral vein. . . . "[1] Of the two terms in the compound *pastoral elegy*, critical priority should be given to the latter term. Whatever distinguishes the poem as a pastoral must subserve the purposes of elegy; the subject matter and the imagery, on the proper handling of which our pleasure depends, are responsible to the elegiac occasion. In short, pastoral is to elegy as integument is to pith. Since death, the common fate of mankind and the principal occasion of elegy, is as consistent with country as with urban life, pastoral can be differentiated from nonpastoral elegy only by its confinement to rural imagery. Pastoral and nonpastoral elegy, having a common occasion, must have a common project, one consistent with the occasion and naturally suggested by it. Whatever is essential to pastoral elegy is also essential to nonpastoral elegy; in both, the nature of the occasion is what principally limits the selectivity of the poet and the expectations of the audience.

Although Johnson wrote no extended essay on the elegy,[2] we can arrive at an adequate understanding of his generalized, working conception of the form by examining his various "practical" statements or definitions (noting, wherever possible, how the "practical" statements either imply or are implied by Johnson's fundamental critical assumptions and coherent view of literature). In the *Dictionary*, Johnson supplies three definitions; an elegy is: (1) a mournful song; (2) a funeral song; (3) a short poem without point or turns. From these three definitions we obtain no very clear and exact idea of the elegy, but enfolded in them are implications that facilitate an adequate specification of the peculiarly limiting requirements of elegiac composition. The elegy is a mournful song because it is generally a funeral poem.[3] Presumably, the writer, whether prompted by a real or an imagined death, is a friend of the deceased. From such an occasion and such a relationship it is reasonable to expect from the poem some account of the character of the deceased and some expression of personal and perhaps general loss. Whatever is said in the poem must be commensurate with the occasion, and an expression is commensurate when it can be credited as a reflection of the natural operations of our intellectual-emotional natures under the special motivating impulse of elegiac composition. Pleasure is the effect of an expression that can be recognized as adequate, under the particular circumstances, to our faculties and "agreeable to nature" (*Rambler* 92). For his primary distinctions Johnson, characteristically, turns, not to any received analyses of the elegy as a species of literature, but to the human occasion and the condition of man; the occasion provides the primary limiting restriction on the selectivity of the poet (and on the expectancy of the audience).

In his remarks on particular elegies Johnson repeatedly calls our attention to the peculiar purposes of such poetry. Of *Lycidas* Johnson says: "He who thus *grieves* will *excite no sympathy;* he who thus *praises* will *confer no honour."* Of Virgil's fifth pastoral: " . . . there are few sentiments of *rational praise* or *natural lamentation."* Of Edmund Smith's "To the Memory of Mr. John Philips": it is "a poem, which justice must place among the best elegies which our language can shew, an elegant mixture of *fondness* and *admiration,* of dignity and softness." Of Dryden's *Elenora:* "the *praise* being therefore . . . general fixes no impression on the reader nor excites any *tendency to love,* nor much *desire of imitation."*[4] What this series of italicized terms and phrases defines in effect is the general range of purpose consistent with the elegiac occasion.

Implicit in these remarks is the idea that the focus of the poem should be on the deceased. Lamentation is justified (and intelligible to the audience) in proportion to the manifest goodness of the subject of the poem. The merit of the subject, the basis presumably of the friendship, provides both the subject and cause of the speaker's sorrow. The sorrow of the speaker is an appropriate object of contemplation only as it is understood to be the natural emotive consequence of reflection on the particular distinguishing merits of the subject, merits that must be defined or described with sufficient precision to allow us to recognize the appropriateness of the sorrow and hence its consonance with genuine human experience. We are moved to the extent that the poet or speaker is able to represent the "character" of the subject as worthy of our interest and our concern, so that in the end fondness, pity, admiration (the grounds of expression), and a desire to emulate virtue are the natural emotive consequences of our full empathetic perception of the exemplary character of a man no longer capable of exercising his virtues in this world. The diversity of elegy, as with that of biography, derives from the character of the subject praised.

Underlying Johnson's call for rational praise and natural lamentation are questions of the following sort: who would naturally write on the occasion, and to what purpose would he write? The obvious answers to these questions are contained within his assessments of particular elegies. From elegy the reader naturally expects and from satisfying elegies always gets "sincere" praise of the deceased; the occasion demands that the poet speak in honor of his real or imagined friend. To speak otherwise is to speak not like a man of this world. Dissatisfaction with the composition is inevitable whenever the poet thinks more on the condition of poetry than on the character of the friend. However happily the poet designs his fictions, however ingeniously he manages to manipulate "traditional" machinery, however wittily he attacks the state of the nation or the church, the reader of the composition, finding no foundation in the nature of things for these matters, cannot avoid being struck by the massive improbability of the whole, and cannot possibly reconcile his mind to the disproportion between the occasion and the sentiments and reflections supposedly triggered by it. Whether the occasion is real or imagined, the poet is obliged to speak like a man of this world upon those matters and in that manner dictated by the mournful event.

To better understand what in general is necessary to the perfection of this kind of writing, we can, I think, legitimately draw on those Johnsonian comments on epitaphs which would seem to apply equally well to elegies. Johnson does not confound the two, but he clearly recognizes that, having a common occasion, they have likewise a common subject matter, and what he says of the subject matter of the epitaph is clearly relevant to the subject matter of the elegy.[5] As is the case with elegies, "those epitaphs are . . . most perfect, which set virtue in the strongest light, and are best adapted to exalt the reader's ideas and rouse his emulation." In writing epitaphs, as in writing elegies, "the difficulty . . . is to give particular and appropriate praise." However, regardless of whether the "character" is drawn for an epitaph, an elegy, or a biography, the praise of character—if it is to be properly effective—"ought not to be general, because the mind is lost in the extent of any indefinite idea and cannot be affected with what it cannot comprehend." In the elegy *Elenora*, Dryden, having no knowledge of the woman he celebrated, had no choice but to praise her in general terms; as a result, the poem "fixes no impression on the reader nor excites any tendency to love, nor much desire of imitation. Knowledge of the subject is to the poet what durable materials are to the architect."[6]

What the common occasion calls for is that particular praise which, in discriminating a specific congeries of qualities and actions, exhibits and distinguishes character. Although particularization may be achieved by a detailed citation of honors acquired, preferments granted, offices held, works published, and so on, the best and most useful "subject for epitaphs [as for elegies] is private virtue; virtue exerted in the same circumstances in which the bulk of mankind are placed and, which, therefore, may admit of many imitators." And in his account of the peculiar, distinguishing aspects of character, the poet, while not free to invent virtues (assuming a poem written in honor of a real person), may neglect to register faults, since memorials for the "dead are not intended to perpetuate the memory of crimes, but to exhibit patterns of virtue." From the "Essay on Epitaphs" we may justly borrow one final detail: it is reasonable to suppose that what may not properly be omitted from an epitaph should be included in an elegy (especially when the occasion is real), namely, the name of the deceased.

Because the writer of elegy is a friend of the deceased, he has from personal experience presumably all the "material" he needs for the purposes of the occasion ready at hand. And because the occasion is serious and the character of the deceased is the matter of his concern, the poet, if the operations of his intellect are coextensive with those of general human nature, will not run after remote allusions, obscure opinions, incredible fictions, or mythological machinery in his efforts to produce pleasurable effects and to satisfy the demands of the occasion. Whatever the poet chooses to say must, if it aspires to please, be proportioned and accommodated to "those operations of intellectual nature" which obtain universally and are coextensive with the race of man; otherwise, the expression will not be credited.

It is a stable conception of the regular and universally operative motions of the mind that underlies and informs the much-noted and oft-lamented demand for "sincerity" in Johnson's criticism, in, for example, his remarks on Hammond's elegies:

> these elegies have neither passion, nature, nor manners. Where there is fiction, there is no passion: he that describes himself as a shepherd, and his Neaera or Delia as a shepherdess, and talks of goats and lambs, feels no passion. He that courts his mistress with Roman imagery deserves to lose her; for she may with good reason suspect his sincerity. Hammond has few sentiments drawn from nature, and few images from modern life. He produces nothing but frigid pedantry;[7]

in his remarks on *Lycidas:*

> It is not to be considered as the effusion of real passion; for passion runs not after remote allusions and obscure opinions. Passion plucks no berries from the myrtle and ivy, nor calls upon Arethuse and Mincius, nor tells of "rough satyrs and fauns with cloven heel." Where there is leisure for fiction, there is little grief;[8]

and, to bring illustration to an end, in his statements on Cowley's elegy on Hervey:

When he wishes to make us weep, he forgets to weep himself,
and diverts his sorrow by imagining how his crown of bays, if he
had it, would *crackle* in the *fire*.[9]

Johnson himself frequently supplies the intellectual framework in
which to read remarks such as these correctly. He does so, for
example, when, just prior to commenting on Hammond's elegies,
he chides the writer of the preface to the poems for valuing in them
precisely what they lack; this writer's praise calls attention ironically to their conspicuous deficiencies: "But of the prefacer,
whoever he was,[10] it may be reasonably suspected that he never
read the poems; for he professes to value them for a very high
species of excellency, and recommends them as the geniune *effusions of the mind,* which expresses a *real passion in the language of
nature.*"[11]

"Sincerity" simply is not, for Johnson, a first-order critical term;
sincerity is a *secondary* reflection necessarily presupposing a prior
and *primary* perception of improbability or inappropriateness *in
the expression* (a perception grounded in a refined, working sense
of the psychological nature of man). Actually, in attributing insincerity to the author (or in implying insincerity in the author),
Johnson is doing nothing more than postulating a logical, hypothetical, "preconstructional" *cause* of a *constructional* defect. Johnson
demands not sincerity so much as appropriate expression. The
charge of insincerity would not be made explicitly or implicitly if
Milton, Hammond, and the others, though insincere to their bones,
had given creditable expression to a condition that, thanks to
genius and acuity of observation, they had only imagined.

As a judgment, insincerity is a reflexive consequence of a prior
judgment upon the incredibility of the poetic representation; in this
charge we see the natural movement of Johnson's mind from an
effect to a cause, in this case from the poetic cause of the dissatisfaction to the probable "biographical" cause of the poetic defect.
Only when there is sufficient reason to believe that the poet is
speaking seriously on a matter or occasion of genuine personal
concern can the critic, upon the recognition of inherent improbability, reason from the details of the text to an insincerity in the
poet. Johnson does not impose any naive standard of sincerity on
literature; rather, by their imaginative failures, writers force the

judgment of insincerity on themselves. Johnson is not unsophisticated; the writers are, from the perspective of Johnson's critical principles, unimaginative; they have failed to imagine what in the nature of things would be their actual case if, in fact, they had to speak like men of this world on the occasion, say, of the death of a friend.

It is essential to recognize that Johnson would bring to elegies not occasioned by real events the same critical standards and principles of judgment that he brings to those "historically" grounded. What is said of *Lycidas* would have been said of the poem if it had been only an "imaginative" elegy. Of sentiments in an "imaginative" elegy that could not be credited as consonant with human experience, Johnson would say: "passion runs not after remote allusions and obscure opinions." However, in the "imaginative" case, he would no more accuse the poet of being insincere than he would Shakespeare upon detecting "unnaturalness" in a speech by, say, Hamlet; the elegiac poet and Shakespeare would be guilty only of not imagining sufficiently well what sort of expression would be appropriate under the specific circumstances. But in failing to make the charge of insincerity in these instances, Johnson would not be abandoning or deviating from any critical principle; the principle of judgment, based on assumptions concerning the nature of man and the grounds of pleasure, remains constant. What accounts for the charge of insincerity is the poet's relation to the subject or the material, not the critic's naiveté. Insincerity is a judgment of imaginative failure, ethically qualified in a certain way; without the ethical qualification we have only a judgment of imaginative failure, and imaginative failure, with or without ethical qualification, is a *preconstructional* cause of a *constructional* defect. It is to the constructional defect that Johnson's critical principles primarily speak.

To Johnson the poet pays insufficient attention to nature—the source, end, and test of art—and fails to meet the conditions upon which our pleasure depends.[12] Insincerity is not the cause of our dissatisfaction; the inherent improbability of the expression (as determined by our "competence") is the cause of our dissatisfaction. If, with Johnson (a critic who regularly refers from human works to human abilities), we ask what is the probable cause *of the cause* of our dissatisfaction, then, like him, we will quite sensibly

suppose in the poet, as the evidence dictates or the probabilities
accumulate, insincerity, imaginative deficiency, inexperience with
life, a tendency to follow the lead of a bad crowd, or worse.

Throughout the "sincerity" section of the critique of *Lycidas*,
Johnson's focus, is clearly, on the way emotions behave, not on the
psychological condition of Milton. Only at the end of the paragraph
("Where there is leisure for fiction, there is little grief") are we
strongly invited to think about Milton, though even here what is
said could just as easily be applied to a "fictional" speaker, to some
sycophantic hypocrite in a drama, for example (the speech serving
as an indication of character),[13] or, for that matter, to a "real"
person (a clergyman required by his office to praise a departed but,
alas, unknown parishioner) as to Milton. Given the occasion, we
have every right to expect Milton to be sincere, but sincere or not,
he should speak like a man of this world, not like an animated
concordance to pastoral elegy, compiled some time after the
revival of learning in Italy.

When Johnson says of Cowley's elegy that "when he wishes to
make us weep, he forgets to weep himself, and diverts his sorrow
by imagining how his crown of bays, if he had it, would *crackle* in
the *fire*," he is not calling for any outpouring of wracking grief, any
linguistic embodiment of uncontrollable sobbing; rather he is
saying that at this point in the elegy Cowley has not found language
capable of sustaining the suppositions upon which the poem is
based, that the reference to the fate of his *imaginary* bays carries
us beyond the limits of credibility implicated in the nature of the
situation we have been invited to accept as the generative base of
the poem—that, in short, Cowley has not found adequate means to
the effect that he wishes to provoke. The standard against which
Cowley's expression is measured is the same standard that would
be invoked had Cowley written an "imaginative" elegy, namely,
the standard of psychological "truth." The expression does not
excite the proper response because it is not consistent with nature
or passion.

To Johnson a man dealing with the fact of the death of a friend
simply does not consider what would be his case if he were not as he
is now, but as he might be—what would happen to the sign of his
national office if he were deprived of a social comfort when he was
to the nation poet laureate. By writing of his "imaginary" bays,

Cowley drives our attention away from the loss of Hervey and toward, at least obliquely, the national neglect of Cowley. Are we invited to suppose how barren and empty earthly honor would be to Cowley if Hervey had postponed his demise until such time as Cowley had obtained the honor? Or are we invited to derive some consolation from the reflection that, by virtue of Hervey's timely departure, Cowley's grief has not been complicated and augmented by the spectacle of a crackling crown of bays? Whatever the reference forces upon our minds cannot be compatible with the occasion or consonant with the natural operations of intellectual-emotional nature, working from the demands of the occasion and of personal relationship to the deceased. The burden on Cowley is not to weep poetically, but to consider the condition of man—his condition—and to find language adequate to the effect he wishes to produce.

Presumably, the man actually moved has from experience what invention would otherwise have to supply. Where material sufficient to the effect is not to be found in actual experience, the poet must suppose the experience and give what he supposes forceful expression. Although we can feel more than we can imagine, we must, in the absence of feeling, imagine what we would feel in the special circumstances, if we hope finally to have our composition credited. Once again what Johnson says of Cowley here would apply if Cowley had written an "imaginative" elegy. The basic assumption underlying Johnson's remark is that the writer who sets out to exhibit "life in its true state, diversified only by accidents that daily happen in the world, and influenced by passions and qualities which are really to be found in conversing with mankind" (*Rambler* 4), should have some extensive familiarity with life as it is lived, so that he will be able to represent the regular motions of passion and intellect as they function within the peculiar, refining conditions of special circumstances or situations. Cowley's task, as it is that of Shakespeare and of any writer principally concerned with the pains and pleasures naturally incident to our state of life, is to keep his writing level with "truth," so that pleasure is the natural emotive consequence of his expression.

Nothing perhaps would more faithfully reproduce Cowley's immediate emotional reaction to the death of Hervey than a tape recording of actual weeping, but such a recording would make a very ineffective and, for the most part, unaffecting poem. In brief, Johnson rebukes Cowley not for failing to weep, but for failing to bring his mind—and, consequently, our minds—to those "realities" which are necessary preconditions of appropriate expression and response. Remarks directed at the metaphysical poets can properly be applied to this section of Cowley's elegy and to *Lycidas* generally:

> they had no regard to that uniformity of sentiment, which enables us to *conceive* and to *excite* the pains and pleasures of other minds: they never enquired what on any occasion they should have said or done, but wrote rather as beholders than partakers of human nature; as beings looking upon good and evil, impassive and at leisure.[14]

The rebuke is grounded in the perfectly sensible belief (as sensible, useful, legitimate, and justifiable now as it was in the eighteenth century and in the fourth century B.C., when Aristotle gave powerful expression to it) that the poet who places himself in the condition that he is to represent "will devise what is appropriate, and be least likely to overlook [or to fall into] incongruities."[15] In referring to his imaginary bays, Cowley falls into incongruity. Cowley, Hammond, and Milton are judged, as it were, on the rebound, inasmuch as the judgment follows necessarily from a prior perception of incommensurateness between the expression and the demands of the occasion. For Johnson an elegy is, finally, "the effusion of a *contemplative* mind, sometimes plaintive, always serious. . . . "[16] It is an effusion that confers honor on the deceased and excites sympathy in the audience in proportion to the skill and "truthfulness" of the poet.

Up to now we have considered the "natural" subject-matter implications, for writer and audience, of Johnson's generalized conception of elegy, roughly speaking the "what" of a mournful song, a funeral song. But to Johnson the nature of the occasion carries with it implications for the manner as well as the subject matter and diction. It is in the third *Dictionary* definition that we find the "how" requirements of the elegy: "A short poem *without point or turns*." Characteristically, and contradistinctly from many of his predecessors, Johnson's limitations on matter and manner are general rather than precise; working from basic assumptions about the nature of man and the general grounds of pleasure, Johnson reasons to the general poetic consequences of the collision of those assumptions with the elegiac occasion. The natural ends of the elegy, to praise, confer honor, express natural lamentation (in order to excite sympathy and encourage emulation of character in the audience) should not, of course, be obstructed by the manner of expression. The trouble with "point" (an expression carrying epigrammatic sting or abounding in conceits) and "turns" (sudden deviations from original intention) is that they presuppose in the writer or speaker an inventive leisureliness not consistent with the occasion and deflect our minds from the deceased and toward the writer or speaker (we reflect on his ingenuity, acuity, subtlety of mind and not on the merits and virtues of the deceased). Of course, the line separating matter and manner is not clear and well-defined; the distinction is primarily a convenience of the abstracting intelligence, for points and turns, while identifiable as shifts in the manner of expression, are objectionable essentially because they interfere with our apprehension of the character of the deceased, because, that is, of their effects on the subject matter, on the proper handling of which our pleasure depends. The "inventive" manner of expression forces upon our minds reflections that cannot properly be accommodated to the occasion and purposes of the poem; the "poetic" devices are bulldozers that push expression into the pit of psychological incongruity. Even though in "content" the points and turns may refer immediately to the deceased, their effect is to focus attention on the speaker or writer, not, however, in his capacity as a man moved by the event, but in his capacity as a wordsmith.

Under the general heading of *manner* I may enroll one final item—ease—which, like the other requirements, has its basis in a consideration of the nature of the occasion and the grounds of pleasure. Assessing Shenstone's elegies in what by now we should recognize as characteristic terms, Johnson writes:

His conception of an elegy he has in his Preface very judiciously and discriminately explained. It is, according to his account, the effusion of a contemplative mind, sometimes plaintive, and always serious, and therefore superior to the glitter of slight ornaments. His compositions suit not ill to this description. His topicks of praise are the domestic virtues, and his thoughts are

pure and simple, but wanting combination they want variety.
. . . That of which the essence is uniformity will be soon
described. His *Elegies* have therefore too much resemblance to
each other.

He then goes on to say:

> The lines are sometimes, *such as elegy requires, smooth and
> easy;* but to this praise his claim is not constant; his diction is
> often harsh, improper, and affected; his words ill-coined or
> ill-chosen, and his phrase unskillfully inverted.[17]

The lines of an elegy should be smooth and easy, not harsh and
difficult (as they frequently are in Shenstone's elegies, and as they
are throughout *Lycidas*). Where harshness has no local warrant
from the nature of the character to be represented or the thought to
be expressed, Johnson's general preference is for "easy" poetry,
that is, that poetry, as Johnson explains in *Idler* 77,

> in which natural thoughts are expressed without violence to the
> language. The discriminating character of ease appears prin-
> cipally [though not exclusively] in the diction; for all true poetry
> suffers by harsh or daring figures, by transposition, by unusual
> acceptations of words, and by any license which would be
> avoided by a writer of prose. Where any artifice appears in the
> construction of the verse, that verse is no longer easy.

To Johnson there is clearly nothing in the nature of the elegiac
occasion to justify harsh diction (or, for that matter, uncertain
rhymes, or unpleasing numbers). Like point and turns (which can
contribute to the roughness and difficulty of poetry), "harshness"
in an elegy carries our attention away from the subject of the poem;
full empathetic perception of character is thwarted by the clamor-
ing "look-at-me" demands of those components of versification
which serve best when they work unobtrusively in support of
imagery and sentiments, the primary causes of our pleasure.

Unlike human offspring, these poetic "children" should be
heard and not seen; they should subserve the ends of conferring
honor or of expressing or exciting sympathy. Harshness is to the
body poetic what insubordination is to the body politic, the
truculent refusal of subalterns to know and to stay in their place. If

rhymes, numbers, and diction do, in fact, usurp the rightful claims of imagery and sentiments on our attention, they should at least be independently beautiful, so that we receive some partial compensation for the loss of that primary pleasure which derives from our recognition of the congruence between representation and life. In *Lycidas,* these conveyors of secondary, ancillary pleasure are in themselves displeasing. Their persons are as unattractive as their effects on our minds are dissatisfying: "the diction is harsh, the rhymes uncertain, and the numbers unpleasing." In the way of sound, music, and diction, Milton offers us what is regularly condemned by Johnson and exactly what, by virtue of the purposes for which the poem is composed, is unsuited to the elegy.

That Johnson attacks the rhymes, numbers, and diction of *Lycidas* should surprise no reader familiar with the conclusion to the *Life of Milton,* in which Milton's characteristic way with diction and versification is discussed at length, or familiar with the series of *Rambler* papers on versification in general and Milton's practice in particular (*Ramblers* 86, 88, 90, 92, 94), in which we find the articulation of the prosodic principles underlying Johnson's later, practical pronouncements (in the *Life of Milton* and, indeed, through the *Lives*). Agreeing with Milton that "rhyme is no necessary adjunct of true poetry," Johnson goes on to say:

But perhaps of poetry *as a mental operation* music or metre is no necessary adjunct; it is however by the musick of metre that poetry has been discriminated in all languages, and *in languages melodiously constructed with a due proportion of long and short syllables* [as, to Johnson, English is not] metre is sufficient. But one language cannot communicate its rules to another; where metre is scanty and imperfect some help is necessary. The *music of the English heroick line strikes the ear so faintly* that it is easily lost, *unless all the syllables of every line cooperate together;* this cooperation can be only obtained by the preservation of every verse unmingled with another as a distinct system of sounds, and *this distinctness is obtained and preserved by the artifice of rhyme.* The variety of pauses, so much boasted by the lovers of blank verse,[18] changes the measures of an English poet to the periods of a declaimer; and there are only a few skilful and happy readers of Milton who enable their audience to perceive where the lines end or begin. 'Blank verse,' said an ingenious critick, 'seems to be verse only to the eye.'[19]

Poetry may often subsist without rhyme, but *English poetry* will not often please; nor can rhyme ever be safely spared *but where the subject is able to support itself.*[20]

In order to preserve the distinctness of sound in every verse by the artifice of rhyme, it is necessary that the rhymes be exhibited according to a regular pattern or scheme; otherwise the function of rhyme is lost, and the "ear," struggling vainly to find a principle to guide expectancy, is repeatedly offended by sounds for which no mental accommodation has or can be made. In *Lycidas* the office of rhyme is not so much neglected as abused, though the distinction is without much of a difference, since negligence and abuse equally contribute to the destruction of a distinct system of sounds. (The vagaries of rhyme in *Lycidas* are adequately illustrated in the first twenty-five lines: abccbbdebdebfbghiijjkllm.) Johnson's objection to the uncertainty of the rhyme is the consequence of prosodic principle and personal experience (experience conditioned by specific prosodic expectations and priorities), not petulance.[21]

Without inquiring into the particular rationale supporting Johnson's prosodic views, we can nevertheless indicate what specific infelicities of versification prompted the general attribution of "unpleasing numbers" to *Lycidas*. In the lines of *Lycidas*, as in those of many of Milton's poems, "the law of metre is very grossly violated by mingling combinations of sound directly opposite to each other . . . and setting one part of the measure at variance with the rest" (*Rambler* 86). Now, although "every poet affords us innumerable instances" of mixed measures, "Milton seldom has two pure lines together, as will appear if any of his paragraphs be read with attention merely to the music" (*Rambler* 86). To Johnson "the detriment which the measure suffers by this inversion of the accents is sometimes less perceptible, when the verses are carried into one another, but is remarkably striking . . . where the vicious verse concludes a period; and is yet more offensive in rhyme, when we regularly attend to the flow of every single line" (*Rambler* 86). In general Milton is "more attentive to his syllables than his accents," but "the great peculiarity of his versification, compared with that of later poets, is the elision of one vowel before another, or the suppression of the last syllable of a word ending with a vowel, when a vowel begins the following word" (*Rambler* 88). The effect of elision is frequently harsh cadence. And although Milton's "elisions are not all equally to be censured . . . , "the abscision of a vowel is undoubtedly vicious when it is strongly sounded, and makes with its associate consonant, a full and audible syllable" (*Rambler* 88). In this practice "Milton . . . seems to have somewhat mistaken the nature of our language, of which the chief defect is ruggedness and asperity, and has left our harsh cadences yet harsher" (*Rambler* 88).

As Warren Fleischauer—commenting on the attribution of metrical deficiency to *Lycidas*—has reminded us, Johnson's response to the versification of Milton's pastoral elegy is the predictable consequence of prosodic principle, not of a querulous sensibility:

> as a critic, Johnson not only condoned, but required a variation of meter to relieve the ear. However, such a variation presumed a pattern the like of which one will look for vainly in *Lycidas*. Johnson, who also reprehended Dryden's *Threnodia Augustalis* for the "irregularity of its meter," might well be expected to condemn *Lycidas*, a poem much more licentious in this respect and according to Johnsonian norms, than Dryden's. Though Mr. Hagstrum assures us that Johnson's metrical system "was essentially that of Edward Bysshe," Johnson is in fact both more tolerant and flexible in his criticism than was Bysshe,[22] and he made his concession historically to seventeenth-century laxity elsewhere than in his critique of *Lycidas*, when he censured Dryden's *Threnodia* for metrical irregularity with the extenuation that it was something "to which the ears of that age . . . were accustomed." And that Johnson, in his strictures on the rhymes and numbers of *Lycidas* was speaking for *his* age, rather than for Milton's or the pre-Romantic day a-dawning, is confirmed for us by the comment, thirty years before the publication of the *Lives*, in a 1748 letter from William Shenstone to Richard Jago: "The censure you have passed upon Milton's *Lycidas*, so far as it regards the metre which he has chosen, is unexceptionably just; and one would imagine, if that argument concerning the distance of the rhymes were pressed home in a public essay, it should be sufficient to extirpate that kind of verse forever."[23]

Whatever may be the modern estimate of the diction of *Lycidas*, to Johnson it could be distinguished by no more appropriate epithet than *harsh*. To appreciate the appropriateness of the adjectival judgment it is first necessary to understand what *harsh* meant to

Johnson and what varieties of "crimes" came within the range of its jurisdiction. For the elucidation of the term, our first and chief debt is to Joseph Epes Brown. As Fleischauer has noted,

> Brown made clear that Johnson most often used "harsh" to indicate not merely what is offensive to the ear, but what is grating to the whole aesthetic sense, a usage found everywhere in Johnson's criticism, confined not only to lines of verse lacking "music" [i.e., harsh cadences], but extended to figures of speech, tangled syntax, words in unusual significations, even to Warburtonian emendations and explications of Shakespeare text, to anything unduly labored or strained, either stylistically or intellectually.[24]

In documenting his reading of *harsh* as a term denoting some "awkwardness or obscurity" in the writer's style or some "departure from the normal," some "affectation of the antique or exotic," Brown draws his illustrations from the *Lives of the Poets:*

> the diction of Collins is "often harsh, unskilfully labored, and injudiciously selected. He affected the obsolete" (*Lives*, III. 341); Akenside "rarely either recalls old phrases or twists his metre into harsh inversions" (*Lives*, III. 418); Gray's "language [in *The Bard* and *The Progress of Poesy*] is laboured into harshness. The mind of the writer seems to work with unnatural violence" (*Lives*, III. 440); Shenstone's diction is "often harsh, improper, and affected; his words are ill-coined or ill-chosen, and his phrase unskilfully inverted." (*Lives*, III. 355)[25]

In these remarks we see the practical exemplification of Johnson's view that *harshness* has its antithesis in *ease*. Here are those "daring figures," "transpositions," "unusual acceptations of words," and "licenses" by which Johnson differentiated harsh from easy poetry in *Idler* 77.

With regard to Milton's compositions, harshness is a regular trait of language; it is no anomalous feature of his poetry erupting suddenly in *Lycidas* to disfigure the otherwise unblemished surface of an easy style: there *prevails* in Milton's works "an uniform peculiarity of *Diction*, a mode and cast of expression which bears little resemblance to that of any former writer, and which is so far removed from common use that an unlearned reader when he first

opens his book finds himself surprised by a new language."
Johnson goes on:

> This novelty has been, by those who can find nothing wrong in
> Milton, imputed to his laborious endeavors after words suitable
> to the grandeur of his ideas. "Our language," says Addison,
> "sunk under him."[26] But the truth is, that both in prose and
> verse, he had formed his style on a perverse and pedantic
> principle. . . . [Moreover], Milton's style was not modified by
> his subject. . . . Of him, at last, may be said what Jonson says of
> Spenser, that "he wrote no language," but has formed what
> Butler calls "a Babylonish Dialect," . . . harsh and barbarous.[27]

Nevertheless, when in the greater works the peculiar harshness of
his style subserves noble or sublime conception, our judgment,
"softened by the beauty" or "awed by the dignity of his thoughts,"
"sinks in admiration." In the greater works the style, "in itself
harsh and barbarous," is made by "exalted genius and extensive
learning the vehicle of so much instruction and so much pleasure
that, like other lovers, we find grace in its deformity" (*Lives*, 1:191).
The style, though full of pedantic and perverse tricks, passes safely
through the treacherous narrows of criticism when the divinity of
its cargo hedges it about. The poetry, considered as a "mental
operation," obtains a special dispensation for the barbarous nature
of its porter, the carrier of the thought to our understandings.

Although the thought cannot be known except by means of a
temporal encounter with the particular words by which it is
expressed (i.e., the particular units of expression are the cause of
our knowing the thought and thus, in an important sense, are not
isolable from the thought), the particular words have value, significance, and power from the thought that they subserve, which is
strictly (i.e., logically) speaking the cause of their selection, use,
and value; the specific features of style are significant relative to
their functions in the expression, and their functions are determined by the thought, which is, thus, the subsuming, formal
principle of the meaning of the expression. From Johnson's point of
view then, the beauty or power of the thought is independent of—or
is not necessarily dependent upon—the beauty of the parts by
which it is conveyed, at least in the sense that the sublimity of the
thought can survive defects in the particulars of its expression.

From this conception of relations it follows that the parts, however beautiful (melodious, sonorous, etc.) when considered independently, are not in their personal and private capacities inherently capable of elevating to dignity or endowing with beauty mean or common thought. On the other hand, since the products of artistic endeavor are comprised of independently variable components, requiring of the author choices among better and worse possibilities all along the line, the parts may be independently beautiful (apart from the thoughts) and thus worthy of being singled out for special commendation (as, for example, the parts of versification are singled out for praise in Johnson's remarks on Pope's *Pastorals*).[28] Where there is in the thought little to enchain interest, enlarge comprehension, elevate fancy, or excite pleasure, there may nevertheless be in the parts peculiar merits deserving praise, and Johnson, conscious that felicitous originality is rare and significant progress slow, hardly ever misses an opportunity to identify sources of pleasure or excellence, wherever located or however localized. With *Lycidas* it is unfortunately the case (as it is not with *Paradise Lost*, in which licentious diction is incapable of overcoming the feeling that we are captives of a "higher and nobler mind") that the thought, lacking in native dignity, cannot divert the critical eye from the meanness of its carriage; in this poem harshness begs ineffectually from the sentiments an obscurity that the sentiments—which in themselves force dissatisfaction on the mind—are not empowered to bestow.

When the wider implications of the term *harsh* are understood and when a moment's reflection reminds us that Johnson—the compiler of an extraordinary illustrative dictionary—was uncommonly fit for the task of discerning unusual modes of verbal usage, the judgment passed upon the diction of *Lycidas* loses, I think, all taint of absurdity. At any rate, the preceding should at least make clear that Johnson's response is grounded in principles informed by reflection and experience.

To scan the text of *Lycidas* from the point of view that an adequate conception of *harsh* makes possible is to discover asperities everywhere in the landscape. For example, using the standards of *Idler* 77 as our guide to harshness, we find in the category of *transposition* the regular inversion of word order, justified not by exigencies of rhyme or thought, but by no more exalted value than "quaintness," of Thomas Warton's honoring of which Johnson says: *"Gray* evening is common enough; but *evening gray* he'd think fine."[29] In the category of *harsh and daring figures* we find such gorgeous terms as *blind mouths, swart star, enameled eyes,* and the like; in the category of *unusual acceptations of words, scrannel* (1. 124), *use* (meaning "to frequent" in 1. 137 and adjudged "obsolete" in this signification by Johnson), *swart* (1. 94), *freaked* (1. 144; Johnson's only illustration is taken from Thomson, and it is termed a Scotticism), and so on.[30]

Beyond these categories, we may note with Warren Fleischauer that to Johnson the syntax of *Lycidas* is often "violent, i.e., 'harsh,' as in such lines as Walter Alexander Raleigh singled out . . . as characteristic of its style: 'But now my oat proceeds,/And listens to the Herald of the Sea.' "[31] Moreover, Milton's diction in *Lycidas* contains "other elements repulsive to Johnson's norms for poetic style, [elements that] may here be briefly listed: (1) participial epithets (e.g., 'the mellowing year,' 1. 5, and 'honour'd flood,' 1. 85); (2) expletives (e.g., 'doth,' 1. 16, and 'did,' 1. 60); (3) stock adjectives ending in *y* (e.g., 'watry,' 1. 12, and 'watry' again, 1. 167); and (4) harsh elisions (e.g., 'th' abhorred shears,' 1. 75)."[32] As Fleischauer says,

> Taken singly, none of [these items] would have been sufficient cause for Johnson's strictures on the *Lycidean* diction; but, lumped in the aggregate and considered with other elements more obviously "harsh" in the Miltonic style, they made the poem seem to him, with his disciplined taste and sensitivity to style, an absolute abomination.[33]

In sum, such smoothness and easiness as elegy requires are nowhere to be found in *Lycidas* when it is surveyed through the refined lenses of Johnsonian criticism.

Even as the last sentence is pronounced, we hear the congregated debunkers buzzing in unison: "See what comes of *choosing to forget* that *Lycidas* is a 'pastoral' elegy and that, as such, its style is *deliberately* harsh; of forgetting that Milton, writing to the demands established for this kind of composition, *intended* the style of this his 'dorick lay,' with its poetical berries harsh and crude plucked by fingers rude, to be 'harsh.' To these remarks, it is only possible to repeat that to Johnson, the poet, no less than the critic, is to work from principles having their foundation in the nature of things; pastoral poets are not compelled (and have no "natural" authorization) to "degrade the language of pastoral by obsolete terms and rustic diction which they very learnedly call Dorick [and, thus, to] become authors of a mingled dialect, which no human being ever could have spoken" (*Rambler* 37). And, be it noted, Milton's sylvan swain not only speaks a mingled dialect, but also, adding improbability to absurdity, talks about matters rusti- cal, political, and ecclesiastical in modes lyrical, rhetorical, and satirical. If to Johnson's remarks it is objected that the salient characteristics of *Lycidas* are all owing to Milton's being conver- sant with the pastoral tradition from Mantuan to Spenser and that there is little in the poem without a precedent, Johnson must reply: "What is that to the purpose, Sir? If I say a man is drunk, and you tell me it is owing to his taking too much drink, the matter is not mended."[34]

We can perhaps best penetrate to the solid sense of Johnson's comment by imagining what the quizzical or intrepid listener, not totally abashed by Johnson's peremptory manner of delivery, might next say: "Surely, Sir, it is not unimportant that Milton, conscious of pastoral conventions, adopted for his own purposes material of which established practice had guaranteed the legiti- macy." And we might imagine a Johnsonian response to this effect: "No, Sir, it is not unimportant, but if we hope to advance opinion to knowledge, we must first learn to identify the questions that we are and are not in fact dealing with and not confuse one kind of inquiry with another. At the moment, we are concerned with reasoning from our manifest displeasure to the causes of that displeasure in the material nature of the poem. If we were to inquire after one of the causes of the cause of our displeasure, we would certainly wish to know something about the fellows with whom Milton chose to associate, since such information is relevant to an understanding of the circumstantial determinants of the presence of the offensive material in the poem, but we derive no more genuine pleasure from the poem as a result of our having this information, because the conditions on which our dissatisfaction is based are unaffected by this information, and we are still obliged to say that 'in this poem there is no nature, for there is no truth; there is no art, for there is nothing new.' If a man were to behave rudely and unmannerly at table, the cause of our displeasure would be his deportment; however, if, as a consequence of his behavior, we were to take action, either to enlighten by instruction or to remove by force, we would first seek to know whether the man acted out of ignorance or in spite of knowledge, whether he were a Scot or a scoundrel. But to whatever cause his behavior is assigned, the fact remains that a meal was ruined by a rude and unmannerly fellow. Let us have done with this. 'Surely, no man could have fancied that he read *Lycidas* with pleasure had he not known its author' or had he no special knowledge of the achievements of Milton's predecessors on which to found a comparison of the peculiar facility with which a line of poets handled materials incapable, either individually or collectively, of satisfying the general conditions of pleasure."

To Johnson the pastoral tradition within which *Lycidas* is placed subsumes poems that are able to evoke only what we may for convenience term "coterie pleasure," a pleasure determined by a special state of knowledge in a select audience. Such poems are self-reflexive, and however excellent they may individually be when—after allowing for their inherent incapacity in general to bring to and sustain in our minds those realities on which our pleasure principally depends—compared with one another in terms of the peculiar beauties of their separate components of meter, rhyme, diction, and argument, they are, like West's *Imitations of Spenser*,

> not to be reckoned among the great achievements of intellect, because their effect is local and temporary; they appeal [primarily] not to reason and passion, but to memory, and presuppose an accidental and artificial state of mind. . . . Works of this kind may deserve praise, as proofs of great industry and great nicety of observation; but the highest praise, the praise of genius, they cannot claim. The noblest beauties of art are those of which the effect is coextended with rational nature . . . ; what is less than this can be only pretty.[35]

In his critique of *Lycidas* Johnson does not forget to remember what the Renaissance pastoral really was; instead, he chooses to measure a particular poem—exorbitantly praised by those who, like Dick Minim, watch for cues to hiss and applaud specific performances in the barometric reading of a name as it is affected by the variable weather of popularity—against his general criteria of excellence for poetry, of whatever kind. And I suspect that virtually every teacher, every student, and every Miltonian (if caught off duty) would admit that apprehension of the peculiar beauty of *Lycidas* is necessarily contingent upon some form of archaeological reconstruction of the "tradition" to which the poem belongs.

Happily (for my purposes), James Holly Hanford has stepped forward, thus precluding recourse to a hostile witness. Hanford acknowledges that

> it is doubtful whether anyone, approaching *Lycidas* for the first time, fails to experience a feeling of strangeness, which must be overcome before the poem can be fully appreciated; and not infrequently the pastoral imagery continues to be felt as a defect, attracting attention to its own absurdities and thereby seriously interfering with the reader's enjoyment of the piece itself. The reason for this attitude lies in the fact that we have today all but forgotten the pastoral tradition and quite lost sympathy with the pastoral mood.[36]

That there are in the poem characteristics seriously interfering with our enjoyment of the piece itself, Johnson readily acknowledges, but that familiarity with the pastoral tradition would remove all obstacles to our pleasure, he is unwilling, on principle, to grant. To Johnson familiarity with the pastoral tradition, however extensive or comprehensive, can do nothing to overwhelm or dissipate that displeasure which has its basis in expressions that neither excite sympathy nor confer honor. When learning has done its utmost to enlarge our understanding of poetic conventions, we are still unable, according to Johnson, to reconcile our minds to the disproportion between the performance and the occasion, or between what we are obliged to suppose and the language (i.e., the sentiments and imagery) by which that supposition is to be sustained. Whatever scholarship may invite us to remember, it cannot oblige us to forget that we have in the poem neither rational praise nor natural lamentation, the special ends of elegiac composition, upon the realization of which our pleasure in this kind of writing depends. Deriving his principles of judgment from reason (i.e., from reflecting upon the nature of the occasion, the natural operations of our intellect, and the general conditions of pleasure) rather than from precedent, Johnson simply applies what reason cannot resist to the case immediately at hand, *Lycidas*, refusing to abrogate the rights of reason in the interests of a name.

When we turn from an examination of Johnson's views on pastoral, elegy, diction, music, and rhyme to the critique of *Lycidas*, we find nothing less than a series of terms, statements, and distinctions perfectly consistent with what, on the level of principle, is implicated in his discussions of those forms and material components of poetry and completely consonant with the coherent theoretical framework from which he regularly operates. We may like *Lycidas* more than Johnson did, but his critique of the poem is no quaint misfire; it is the natural consequence of a coherent conception of literature and, as Keast has said, a coherent body of assumptions concerning both its practice and evaluation. If it is shock, it is the shock of recognition that we experience when we read:

> One of the poems on which much praise has been bestowed is *Lycidas;* of which the diction is harsh, the rhymes uncertain, and the numbers unpleasing. What beauty there is, we must therefore seek in the sentiments and images. It is not to be considered an effusion of real passion; for passion runs not after remote allusions and obscure opinions. Passion plucks no berries from the myrtle and ivy, nor calls upon Arethuse and Mincius, nor tells of rough *satyrs* and *fauns with cloven heel*. Where there is leisure for fiction, there is little grief.
>
> In this poem there is no nature, for there is no truth; there is no art, for there is nothing new. Its form is that of a pastoral, easy, vulgar, and therefore disgusting: whatever images it can supply, are long ago exhausted; and its inherent improbability always forces dissatisfaction on the mind. When Cowley tells of Hervey that they studied together, it is easy to suppose how much he must miss the companion of his labours, and the partner of his discoveries; but what image of tenderness can be excited by these lines!
>
> > We drove a field, and both together heard
> > What time the grey fly winds her sultry horn,
> > Battening our flocks with the fresh dews of night.
>
> We know that they never drove a field, and that they had no flocks to batten; and though it may be allowed that the represen-

tation may be allegorical, the true meaning is so uncertain and remote, that it is never sought because it cannot be known when it is found.

Among the flocks, and copses, and flowers, appear the heathen deities; Jove and Phoebus, Neptune and Aeolus, with a long train of mythological imagery, such as a College easily supplies. Nothing can less display knowledge, or less exercise invention, than to tell how a shepherd has lost his companion, and must now feed his flocks alone, without any judge of his skill in piping; and how one god asks another god what is become of Lycidas, and how neither god can tell. He who thus grieves will excite no sympathy; he who thus praises will confer no honour.

This poem has yet a grosser fault. With these trifling fictions are mingled the most awful and sacred truths, such as ought never to be polluted with such irreverent combinations. The shepherd likewise is now a feeder of sheep, and afterwards an ecclesiastical pastor, a superintendent of a Christian flock. Such equivocations are always unskilful; but here they are indecent, and at least approach to impiety, of which, however, I believe the writer not to have been conscious.

Such is the power of reputation justly acquired, that its blaze drives away the eye from nice examination. Surely no man could have fancied that he read *Lycidas* with pleasure, had he not known its author.[37]

As has been demonstrated, there is nothing in this critique that cannot be easily adjusted to the framework of Johnson's critical thought. Before I bring this study to conclusion, however, it might be worth adding that there is, indeed, fluctuation in these remarks, that Johnson does, in fact, move back and forth between topics, without at the same time—I hasten to mention—deviating from or abandoning the theoretical bases of his judgment. Although Johnson refers to diction, rhymes, and numbers, it should be recognized that his primary focus is on *Lycidas* as a *mental operation;* in considering the poem as a mental operation, Johnson's attention is directed away from diction, rhyme, and numbers. (The reader should recall that in providing a justification for *harsh, uncertain,* and *unpleasing,* I was obliged to draw my evidence from "external" sources and then show how the peculiar characteristics of *Lycidas* participate in the classes of infelicity generally condemned by Johnson. In the critique itself Johnson supplies no justification for the judgments on the components of versification that he confidently asserts). To consider *Lycidas* as a mental operation is to emphasize sentiments and images, inasmuch as the pleasure that we are capable of deriving from a poem of this sort depends principally upon the poet's handling of sentiments and imagery, and only secondarily upon his handling of diction, rhyme, and numbers. The general conditions of pleasure are satisfied to the extent that we can credit (or accept as creditable under the given conditions) the sentiments and images as congruent with the motivating occasion of the poem, the nature of the human relationship, and the natural operations of intellectual nature. As a mental operation, the poem is examined in the light of its psychological causes and effects. Johnson, starting from an empirically identifiable effect, in this case displeasure, reasons to the necessary causes of that effect in the poem, in this case the sentiments and images as selected and ordered by Milton. And as the critique unfolds, Johnson moves back and forth in each paragraph between a consideration of sentiments and a consideration of images. If it is fluctuation that we are after, it can be found in this—and only in this—alternating movement of interest. But this fluctuation is intelligible only when it is understood as a natural consequence of Johnson's habitual practice of reasoning about literary materials from a stable conception of the general conditions of pleasure.

If there is anything slightly uncharacteristic in the critique, it is what appears to be Johnson's unusually rigid division of labor among the parts, his uncommonly sharp distinction among the parts as to their functions in satisfying our demands for truth and novelty, *truth* being assigned to sentiments and images, and *novelty*, it seems, to diction, rhyme, and numbers (though images are considered under the heading of *novelty* in those sections in which Johnson notes that whatever images the "pastoral form may supply are long ago exhausted" and that they are such "as a College easily supplies"). This is not the place to launch into a general and extensive discussion of the ways in which various poetic parts are generally evaluated in relation to Johnson's criteria of pleasure (namely, truth and novelty or variety, under the headings of which we would list such correlative, associative, or adjunct terms as new, familiar, diversity, copiousness, originality, etc., and such particularized terms of response as recognition, surprise, wonder, etc.), but some brief indication of general tendencies might be useful.

Sentiments may be true and both true and novel: true, of course, when they express what we can recognize or be made to understand as being faithful to the probabilities and possibilities of nature or human experience; true and novel when they are, say, peculiarly appropriate to the nature of the speaker, or the nature of the particular situation of the speaker, or the peculiar nature of the occasion, or when they, say, make us "remember" or know what we, without the expression, did not know we knew, when, in short, they are sentiments to which "every bosom returns an echo" and which, though original, every reader "persuades himself that he has always felt them." (Sentiments provide merely "novel" pleasure when, under particular circumstances, they charm by inoffensive oddity, sprightliness, etc.) Images too may be true and both true and novel: true when they, say, square with our general experience of the world (give us recognizable "pictures" of the material world); true and novel when they are peculiarly appropriate "pictures" of things, justified by felt exigencies in action, character, thought, situation, *et cetera,* or when, say, the image called to the mind is both true to our experience of the world and without a precedent in our literary experience (for example, it is clear that reference to the "gray" leaves of the weeping willow by an observer represented as lounging on his back beneath the tree would be both a true and novel image if a particular reader had never before encountered it in literature or if it had never been mentioned in literature before). Images provide merely "novel" pleasure when they bring vividly to mind "pictures" charmingly inoffensive to the immediate context or the whole work in which they appear, or when they are the means by which "imaginary" scenes or beings are endowed with vivid particularity. Diction, music, and rhyme, allowing truth only referentially, if at all (e.g., diction is true—i.e., appropriate—to character, occasion, state of mind, etc.), are capable of providing pleasure by virtue of their variety or novelty and—in place of truth—familiarity.

In general Johnson, while acknowledging that genuine pleasure can be traced to separate realizations of truth, novelty, and variety in any of the discrete, variable parts of a composition, insists that most pleasure is derived from the happy coadunation of truth and novelty or variety, or of the new and the familiar, a coadunation realizable in some form in virtually all the distinguishable parts. That Johnson discusses so few parts in the critique can be attributed to the nature of the poem. There are no references to action, unity of fable, characterization, and the like, all of which provide opportunities for the conjunction of truth and novelty (or of the new and the familiar), because the poem deals with a single speaker in a closed situation (i.e., one in which there is no interchange of views and no specific auditor implied), a speaker who is obliged by the implicit imperatives of the occasion to excite sympathy for and to confer honor upon a deceased friend.[38] Johnson concentrates on sentiments and images because the particular ends of this kind of composition are realized or not depending upon what the sentiments and images bring to our minds. It should be recognized that, in discussing truth in relation to sentiments and novelty in relation to the "devices" of art, Johnson deviates not at all from the bases of his critical judgment, and also that the "unusual" division results from no narrowing of Johnson's views but from the nature of *Lycidas* itself. Johnson is not here engaged directly in defining what is necessary to the perfection of a kind of writing; rather, he is isolating the material bases of our dissatisfaction and indicating on what possible qualities of the composition we might be able to found our praise.

Had there been nature and hence truth in the sentiments, it would have been vain to blame the poem for harshness, uncertainty, and unpleasantness in the diction, rhymes, and numbers; the truth of the principal part would have more than compensated for the deficiencies of the "incidental" parts. Since the occasion of the poem is common and since elegiac performances on the common occasion have been many, we willingly repress our expectations for novelty of versification and settle our hopes on some felicitous expression of those sentiments which the common occasion excites in the particular man, Milton, reflecting on a particular schoolfellow. We expect truth, if not novelty. If we had truth, we would have a sufficient foundation for praise. On the other hand, had Milton introduced in the diction, rhymes, or numbers some new species of beauty (as Pope does when, in his *Pastorals*, he exhibits "a series of versification, which had in English poetry no precedent"), we would have been able to locate causes of pleasure insufficient perhaps to compensate for the absence of that pleasure founded on truth, but sufficient to justify praise of the poem; we would have established a small but nonetheless rational foundation on which to rest our esteem for this Miltonic production. Had Milton artfully combined the new and the familiar in the parts, our pleasure would have been augmented in proportion to his success. But in the absence of truth, praise, on the brink of destruction, should be able to cling at least to some clump of novelty for its self-preservation. Unfortunately, there is in this poem no art, for there is nothing new. In the critique Johnson is not suggesting that novelty is exclusively the province of art and truth the province of sentiments; he is speaking to the characteristics of a particular poem and asserting that to please at all there must, as a bare minimum, be truth in the sentiments or novelty in those adjuncts of poetry not necessary to it as a *mental operation*.

It is perfectly natural that a critic with Johnson's priorities and working from his conception of the special demands of the elegy would focus on the sentiments and images of the poem. And when *Lycidas* is examined in the light of those priorities and that conception, it everywhere reveals an "utter disregard both of life and nature" and a plethora of "mythological allusions," "incredible fictions," and "sentiments which neither passion nor reason could have dictated, since the change which [Christianity] has made in the whole system of the world."[39] For example, no "image of tenderness" can be excited by these lines: "We drove a field, and both together heard. . . ." These lines have power only as they provoke reflection on the shared experiences of youthful association; however, the particularity with which the pastimes and employments are described works against what on the level of generality the lines would establish, since from the particulars we can infer nothing precisely relevant to the association of Milton and King. What sympathy can be evoked by reflecting on their inability to do in the future what we do not know them to have done in the past? How is our interest in King enhanced and the sense of Milton's loss communicated by lines insisting that King can no longer be engaged in activities connected with pastoral superintendence? Wherever we look, sympathy is not excited and honor is not conferred. The speaker of the poem simply does not "speak by the influence of those general passions and principles by which all minds are agitated, and the whole system of life is continued in motion" ("Preface to Shakespeare").

Johnson's attention is directed to sentiments and images, of course, even at the end of the critique, when he inveighs against the *grosser* fault of the poem. Johnson quite reasonably expects Milton to be serious over the grave. However, the poem would be offensive in its commingling of orders of religious reference even if "sacred truths" were not at issue, for, like Virgil's "Sixth Pastoral," *Lycidas* adds absurdity to improbability by presenting a shepherd uncomplicatedly at home in pagan and Christian worlds (in, i.e., temporally distinct periods). What is merely offensive in "The Silenus" is odious in *Lycidas;* Milton's poem moves beyond poetic injudiciousness and approaches impiety. In this poem there is not only no nature and hence no truth, but also no unpolluted Truth. And it should be understood that the *grosser* fault, its indecency notwithstanding, makes a powerful contribution to the ineffectuality of the poem as an elegy. Trifling fictions are mingled with sacred truths to no good purpose on any occasion, but the combination is particularly disturbing on an occasion calling for reflection on the actual death of a real friend. Again, wherever we look we find exhausted images such as a college easily supplies and sentiments that neither passion nor reason could have dictated, and for purposes not entirely clear—but certainly not consistent with the ends of elegy—we discover in this poem that "probability is violated, life is misrepresented, and language is depraved" ("Preface to Shakespeare").

When we come to the critique of *Lycidas,* as we have in this study, from an examination of the specific questions, assumptions, and principles of reasoning underlying Johnson's criticism and of the differentiating characteristics of pastoral and elegy as constituted by and hence as necessarily implicated in a coherent conception of literary theory and practice, we must recognize that the critique could signal a transition from apodictic standards to the standards of the heart; that it could exemplify a fluctuating commitment to antithetical critical emphases, an unstable devotion to conceptions of literature as rhetoric and as self-expression; that it could represent a naive demand for sincerity; that it could shine with fitful but nevertheless unmistakable glimmerings of those doctrines which would blaze with dazzling brilliance in the writings of Coleridge and Wordsworth; that it could do all these things only if Johnson had written other than he has, using terms other than those he has employed, working from assumptions other than those governing his discussion, and arguing from a theoretical base other than that which informs his judgment here and elsewhere, early and late, and which endows his various terms and doctrines with determinate meaning and significance.

The critique of *Lycidas* is no critical *faux pas,* no quaint misfire; it is the ineluctable consequence of those assumptions and principles which early and late guided Johnson's judgment of particular works. Within the large corpus of critical material produced by Johnson, the critique of *Lycidas* amounts to little more than a footnote, but the "note" is no less the natural offspring of Johnson's genius than is the "Preface to Shakespeare," having its theoretical ground in the same conception of literature that underlies the "Preface." Johnson does indeed occupy a conspicuous place in critical and intellectual history, but we can no more identify that place by noting doctrinal similarities and differences in his isolated statements and in similarly isolated statements of his predecessors and successors than we can determine the relationship of *Othello* to other works of art by noting that, like, say, *Sir Gawain and the Green Knight* and *Finnegans Wake,* it is rich in imagery or, more specifically, clothing imagery. Only by seeing the various critical productions and pronouncements in relation to the peculiar ends, problems, and methods of reasoning habitual to Johnson, in relation to the determinate framework of principles and assumptions underlying his posing and resolving of questions, can we know something certainly about the distinctive place in critical history that Johnson has marked off for himself and the permanently valuable contribution that he has made to critical inquiry.

By principle Johnson is not particularly interested in distinguishing among genres or in delineating in detail the special pleasures derivable from various distinct classes of works. By principle he works with broad, generalized conceptions of genre, specific limitations on artistic freedom of choice in any of the genres being governed by the features of "nature," the capacities of authors, and the general psychological conditions of pleasurable response in the reader, with lasting pleasure being relative to the congruence between the expression or representation and what the general reader can accept, under certain conditions, as creditable by referring to general human experience or to probabilities naturally contained, by implication, within that experience. Thus, as we have seen, the definition of true pastoral emerges from a consideration of human life as modified, qualified, or restricted by the special conditions of rural existence. From this conception of "form," we arrive at differentiations of imagery (rural) and topics (such as are not likely to interest rural people less than others). Similarly, the generalized conception of elegy emerges from a consideration of the occasion, from which we derive the natural ends of such writing, namely, to excite sympathy for and to confer honor upon the deceased, all other characteristics of the type being subsumed by these purposes and subject to independent specification. Thus a "pastoral" elegy is distinguished from other elegies only by its confinement to rural imagery.

Distrustful of abstract speculation and all dialectical systems of reasoning, in which coherence is a consequence of "ideas" being pushed into necessary relations by the exigencies of a ruling hypothesis (systems, that is, that are self-validating but that cannot account for the events or materials to which they refer being exactly as they are and no other way), Johnson depends upon established principles of judgment that derive from a consideration of the psychological bases of pleasure. And starting always from some inductively achieved and empirically identifiable effect (i.e., pleasure or displeasure), he reasons to the necessary and sufficient conditions of that effect in the truth, novelty, or variety of the various parts, discriminating the details responsible for the pleasure we obtain from novelty or variety (in quest of which the common satiety of life sends us all) from those details responsible for the pleasure we obtain from the exhibition or expression of "nature" or passion running level with our experience or creditable as naturally incident, under certain circumstances, to our state of life.

No writer who talks coherently can escape involvement in theory; statements presuppose questions, and questions presuppose a means of dealing with them in some terms and with some assumptions. The enduring value of Johnsonian criticism is attributable to the fact that Johnson, accustomed to think distinctly and to speak precisely, worked from a coherent body of assumptions and consistently asked certain questions and addressed certain problems. Johnson puts no great emphasis on distinctions of genre; his principles of judgment are not precipitates of a consideration of the special status of art or the processes of creation; he is not interested in determining the principles of construction necessitated by the adoption of particular "points of view" or manners of representation, or in identifying synthesizing principles of form controlling the necessary relations among the various parts, or in any number of other legitimate critical concerns. All is ordered in relation to the general conditions of pleasure, and since works are made up of variable parts, all independently capable of better or worse realization, each distinguishable aspect of any work may be separately valued as an instance of excellence; value, for example, can be placed on new thoughts, sentiments, diction, imagery, a new series of versification, some "new" psychological complexity, and so forth. Thus, Pope's *Pastorals* offer something without a precedent in versification, Gray's *Elegy* something new in sentiment.

Johnson could address only those problems which fall within the range of his theoretical framework, but that framework is one perfectly suited to the task of dealing with significant aspects of literature. And as long as those aspects of literature are interesting to critics, Johnson's principles will be useful to them, for his critical framework is no historical or intellectual curiosity; it is rather a powerful critical instrument, enabling anyone who chooses to use it to inquire, to know, and to prove.

Appendix

Principles of Criticism: Individual Talent and Coded Media

As I noted in chapter 2, Fussell is convinced that Johnson's *two* senses of literature—as self-expression and as rhetoric—are special reflections of the conflict intrinsic to the "facts of writing" and that Johnson wavers uncertainly between the two antithetical senses, making determinations as he leaps unpredictably to one or the other polarity. The two senses of literature attributed to Johnson emerge from a definition of the facts of writing sponsored by particular theoretical premises:

> The theory of literature I am relying on to shed some light on Johnson's life of writing is simple, empirical, and quite unoriginal. It derives largely from three well-known places: Harry Levin's essay of 1946, "Literature as an Institution"; Northrop Frye's speculations, in *Anatomy of Criticism,* about the autotelic world of literary forms; and E. H. Gombrich's demonstration, in *Art and Illusion,* of the indispensability of a "coded" or prestructured or systematized medium if artistic communication is to take place at all. What I assume is that we recognize a piece of writing as literature only through our prior acceptance of the convention that its genre is literary: otherwise we do not notice it, or we do not notice it artistically.[1]

Before attempting to deal with the larger theoretical problems implicated in Fussell's assumptions about the dependence of "literariness" upon identification of genre, I should like to comment briefly on an aspect of Gombrich's "demonstration." It is important to recognize at the outset that Gombrich has specified the conditions essential to communication of any kind, including "artistic communication"; a "coded," prestructured, or systematized medium is indispensable to communication as such (even though speakers and writers are constantly changing the code as they use it, through metaphor and neologism, and as a result of situational necessity). At the primary level, coded medium is a particular language with its lexicon, its rules for syntactic arrangement, and so on. And although every language allows an infinite variety of specific speech acts, all particular statements in any given language must convey meanings if communication is to take place (if particular meanings are to be shared), that are possible to that language. Additionally, there is a vast number of limitations on expression that may be understood as "conventions" for specific utterances, writings, or writers, "conventions" that limit the meanings of particular speech acts and that, upon recognition, may trigger in the reader or listener more or less determinate expectations of subsequent meaning possibilities. For example, we could classify as "conventional" all traits that we could identify as belonging to a genre, as constituting the peculiar terminological preferences of particular times, geographical locations, "schools," and so forth, as signalizing individual authors (reflecting their habits of thought, their abiding interests in certain topics, subjects, or issues, their reliance on certain images, locutions, or figurative devices).[2] The more extensive our knowledge of those "conventions," the more precise our expectations and determinations (whether justified, finally, or not) of specific meaning.

To the preceding it is necessary to add that all conventions (including the "subsidiary" conventions mentioned above) admit an area of indeterminacy, and fuzziness, making allowance thereby for tolerable incongruity; otherwise "meaning" would be virtually predictable prior to—or early on in—actual statement (as it is, for example, in many casual exchanges with barbers, gas station attendants, colleagues), and genuinely surprising, novel, "original" statement would be virtually impossible. Each expectation may be invalidated, each "convention" subverted by the specific, local decisions of individual writers or speakers. (As readers we recognize "subversion" when we run bump into recalcitrant material, into material that cannot immediately or quickly be accommodated within the framework of our expectations, our working hypotheses of meaning possibilities.) Now, for "new" meaning to be conveyed and understood, it is further necessary that the area of indeterminacy be filled in according to known and common processes, that the incongruity occur within known and knowable limits of toleration, and that the decisions invalidating expectations be of a specific nature. Every convention (or tendency), in short, must allow for the new, and the new can emerge only by maintaining some form of contact with the old; otherwise the new is hopelessly ambiguous. The processes involved in this emergence are those of "metaphor," namely, extension, analogy, amalgamation. On this matter, E. D. Hirsch has written:

> Every new verbal type is [in a manner of speaking] a metaphor that required an imaginative leap. The growth of new genres is founded on this quantum principle that governs all learning and thinking: by an imaginative leap the unknown is assimilated to the known, and something genuinely new is realized. This can happen in two ways: two old types can be amalgamated . . . or an existing type can be extended. . . . Both processes depend on metaphor—that is, on the making of a new identification never conceived before.[3]

To that of Hirsch we may add the testimony of Frank Kermode: " . . . the forms of art—its language—are in their nature a continuous extension or modification of conventions entered into by maker and reader, and this is true of very original artists so long as they communicate at all."[4]

With this much established, we can return to Fussell's case. On the face of matters Fussell's ruling hypothesis ("What I assume is that we recognize a piece of writing as literature only through our prior acceptance of the convention that its genre is literary: otherwise we do not notice it, or we do not notice it artistically") would not seem to provide very easy access to the particular problems that Johnson addressed or the special principles from which he argued. Initially, I am not entirely sure I know what it means to notice something artistically. More important, Fussell's assumption, as formulated, would seem to direct us away from matters of crucial importance in Johnson's criticism. A more detailed expression of the assumption, "an act of what observers will consent to consider literature can take place only when an individual talent engages and, as it were, fills in the shape of a preexisting form that a particular audience is willing to regard as belonging to the world of literature,"[5] does not bring us any closer to Johnson's primary critical standards or first-order categories of judgment. And this is true even if we happen to agree with Fussell. Johnson simply does not spend much time wondering whether a piece of writing is literature or not. Writing of whatever kind was more generally considered in terms of its capacity to provide pleasing instruction and hence in terms—as Keast and others have remarked—of its psychological causes and effects.

What distinguishes Johnson from many of his predecessors is the extent to which his critical priorities enable him to recognize and define the value of works that for some others had no legitimate or estimable literary status—tragicomedy, for example. To get at the distinguishing features of Johnson's criticism, we must first recognize that his critical efforts regularly lead him

> to forsake the view of art as manifesting itself in distinct species, a view presented in great detail in the treatises of his predecessors, for the ampler domain of nature, in which, as he conceives of it, distinctions and definitions hitherto thought inviolable and "natural" can be shown to be rigidities, arbitrary constrictions, or, at best, ideal manifestoes.[6]

Among other things, Johnson, starting from distinct and knowable principles, is interested early and late in revising commonly accepted notions of what "prestructured" differentia (to use one of Fussell's terms) are indispensable to effective and valuable writing, in reducing the number of specific requirements "essential" to various types of expression, and in transferring attention to the common sources of pleasure in truth and novelty. Johnson takes issue, not with the indispensability of "coded" media to communication (though he rather assumed than affirmed the indispensability; he, of course, did not talk in such terms), but with the specificity with which the various genres had been defined. The more elaborate, detailed, and specific the prescribed limitations on diction, character, subject matter for each of the genres, the less frequent are the opportunities for the production and recognition of something new in literary expression, for the transcendence of previously established limits, and for the acquisition of new knowledge about the capacities of man.

Again, Johnson found the principles for reasoning about art, not in the various forms of art, but in the universal psychological bases

of human pleasure. And he disagreed with many of his predecessors about the exact nature of the "preexisting forms" that a writer,
by individual talent, was obliged to fill in; he did not accept as
necessary to appropriate artistic effect many requirements of
genre, upon the satisfaction of which recognition of literary status
was, for many, contingent. He regularly objects to

> the arbitrary edicts of legislators, authorized only by them-
> selves, who, out of various means by which the same end may be
> attained, selected such as happened to occur to their own reflec-
> tion, and then, by a law which idleness and timidity were too
> willing to obey, prohibited new experiments of wit, restrained
> fancy from the indulgence of his innate inclination to hazard and
> adventure, and condemned all future flights of genius to pursue
> the path of the Maeonian eagle. (*Rambler* 158)

Further, to Johnson most limitations on forms of writing derive
from the nature of the subject matter to which they were restricted,
from the manner of presentation to which they were naturally
limited, from the general effect that the common reader could
naturally expect them to produce; for instance, occasional poetry
was limited in subject matter, in large measure, by the occasion for
which it was produced; the manner of drama is not that of narrative
poetry; pastoral poetry, "being the 'representation of an action or
passion, by its effects upon a country life,' has nothing peculiar but
its confinement to rural imagery, without which it ceases to be
pastoral";[7] a comic composition must raise mirth, and so on. In
general, however,

> the performances of art [are] too inconstant and uncertain, to be
> reduced to any determinate idea. It is impossible to impress
> upon our minds an adequate and just representation of an object
> so great that we can never take it into our view, or so mutable
> that it is always changing under our eye, and has already lost its
> form while we are laboring to conceive it. . . . Imagination, a
> licentious and vagrant faculty, unsusceptible of limitations, and
> impatient of restraint, has always endeavored to baffle the
> logician, to perplex the confines of distinction, and burst the
> inclosures of regularity. There is therefore scarcely any species
> of writing, of which we can tell what is its essence, and what are
> its constituents; every new genius produces some innovation,
> which, when invented and approved, subverts the rules which

the practice of foregoing authors had established. . . . any man's reflections will inform him that every dramatick composition which raises mirth is comic; and that, to raise mirth, it is by no means universally necessary, that the personages should be either mean or corrupt, nor always requisite that the action should be trivial, nor ever, that it should be fictitious. (*Rambler* 125)

It is to broad, general, "natural," universal requirements that Johnson makes appeal, and it is these requirements that function, in his criticism, as natural limitations on specific writings. Moreover, he appeals to them because he is interested in determining the general bases of pleasure and in tracing effect to cause; he is not preoccupied with genre distinctions or devoted to perpetuating many of the generic "rules" that, taken together, determine the specific natures of the "preexisting forms" that "a particular audience" may be "willing to regard as belonging to the world of literature." Furthermore, it is essential to understand that there is intrinsic to Johnson's conception of writing no latent strife between "individual talent" and "preexisting forms." If there is strife in writing, it is that which naturally attends any act of deliberate composition and is a necessary consequence of a writer's struggle to find language adequate to his conception or purpose. Fussell imposes his own categorical imperatives on Johnson when he traces "inconsistencies" in Johnson's critical thought to the inevitability of this strife between talent and form. (Johnson leans, according to Fussell, in the direction of individual talent when he asks for "self-expression" and of "preexisting forms" when he appeals to the "received formulations and devices" of rhetoric).

Whatever the merits of Fussell's position in its generalized formulation, it should be recognized that all criticism does not spring from the sorts of questions for which Fussell seeks to provide solutions or from the kinds of assumptions from which he argues, and that whenever specific acts of writing (i.e., Johnson's criticism) are described in the terms occasioned by a prior definition of the "facts of writing," the definition itself achieved under the auspices of and obedient to the imperatives of a particular "theory" of literature (in fact, of course, Fussell confuses a set of doctrines with theory), the specific acts will inevitably exhibit traits of the class logically implicated in the sponsoring definition (the agent of discovery). If description is based on a discrete set of a priori assumptions about the nature of the thing to be described, then the thing, in its nature, is tautologically included in the assumptions from which investigation begins. In short, to describe anything in the terms that determinations prior to experience make available is to disclose in that thing traits of those determinations.

Fussell, of course, does only what any critic does when he reasons from a hypothesis, stated or implied, about the nature of things. To the extent that particular decisions are implicitly contained in the principles, terms, and assumptions from which reasoning begins, all acts of interpretation partake of the tautological. However, if it can be shown that Fussell's decisions are answerable rather to his assumptions than to the details for which they purport to account, or if it can be demonstrated, on the other hand, that Johnson's decisions cannot be subsumed by Fussell's assumptions, then it can reasonably be asserted that Fussell's assumptions are inadequate to the task of disclosing the nature or bases of Johnson's critical activity.[8]

There is, I submit, nothing axiomatic about the assumption, from which Fussell begins his reasoning. It is perhaps true that some readers have recognized and that some continue to recognize "a piece of writing as literature only through [a] prior acceptance of the convention that its genre is literary," but a moment's reflection on past and present critical diversity convinces us that recognition is not now and has not been in the past necessarily contingent upon such an acceptance. A comprehensive examination of the various ways critics have differentiated literature from "nonliterary" pieces of writing is well beyond the scope of this essay, but a few words on general tendencies might be useful.

Once we assume that literature can be differentiated from other forms of verbal communication (as Fussell does, at least implicitly), we can proceed to make our actual discriminations by appealing to one or more of many possible differentia. Thus if I assume that all writing is preeminently a sign of mental powers or activity and further assume that the production of literature, as distinct from that of other forms of verbal communication, requires in the writer either special faculties or general faculties in a special degree, then I may determine the literary or nonliterary status of any piece of writing, whatever its kind, by noting whether or not the faculties in the requisite kind or degree are manifestly present (or, as is more often the case, by so reading the material as to disclose in it the distinctions on which my critical ingenuity has fastened). If, on the other hand, I derive my primary distinctions not from a consideration of the writer (or of the writing as a sign of the writer), but from a consideration of audience response, then I may recognize a piece of writing, whatever its kind, as literature whenever a work elicits the preferred response (or whenever I can so read a work as to attribute the preferred response to it), recognition here being the ineluctable consequence of my prior acceptance of the convention that a response distinct in nature or degree is peculiarly appropriate to literature (to which I could attach the distinguishing title, "literary response").

Again, literature may be identified by the special means it employs, recognition proceeding on the assumption that literature has a special language, relies on special resources of language, uses language in special ways to convey meanings not possible to "nonliterary" discourse. Similarly, we may conceive of literature as having a special subject matter and thus provide another basis for its recognition. This list of the ways we may go about the business of discriminating literature from other forms of discourse could be greatly extended, but the essential point is that recognition is a function of our basic differentia; we recognize as literature what our differentia compel us to recognize as literature, and as our differentia change, so also do our powers of recognition. Fussell's definition might have some value if we could confidently assume that all critics (or at least all critics of any distinguishable historical period) shared the same critical principles, argued in similar ways from a commonly shared body of assumptions, and so forth. However, since the means of recognition are various, the objects identified by the various means are similarly various. In order to know the objects of recognition, we must first discover the intellectual bases of differentiation, since literature or, say, *Hamlet* is not independent of our a priori determinations.

The more one thinks about Fussell's primary assumption, the more perplexing it becomes. Not only do many critics treat as literature writings that belong to no recognizable or traditional literary class (writings, in fact, that many have recognized, for various reasons, as belonging to such particular branches of inquiry as history, philosophy, religion, science, etc.), but they also betray no signs of having been induced to treat (and hence to recognize) these writings as literature as a result of having first found the means by which to subsume such works, at least temporarily, under legitimate literary genres.

On quite different grounds from those mentioned above, many critics would be unwilling to allow the assumption, because, it is asserted, we can discover in literature no single attribute or set of attributes that distinguishes it from nonliterary discourse. As soon as we ascribe distinctiveness to an attribute, we find either that it inheres in all word-bound works (or in many that no one had ever recognized as literature), or that it inheres in too few, thus excluding from "literature" many works that the generality of readers, in different periods, had accepted as literature.

Moreover, even those modern critics who have done most to refine our notions of literary genre—the so-called Chicago or neo-Aristotelian critics—would not be inclined to concur with the assumption. Indeed, since theirs is essentially an *ex post facto* criticism, they would unequivocally reject, on principle, any critical position that attempted to fix (or assumed the fixation of) the forms that writings must assume in order to be considered as literature and all notions that implied that a piece of writing could be recognized as literature only through our prior perception of it as an example of an *existing* literary genre. On precisely this matter Crane has written:

It will be sufficient for all our purposes if we begin, simply, by taking as "poems" or "works of literary art" all those kinds of productions which have been commonly called such at different times, but without any supposition that, because these have the same name, they are all "poems" or "works of literary art" in the same fundamental structural sense. . . . And for such [diverse productions as *The Divine Comedy, The Faerie Queene, King Lear, Othello,* etc.] we shall need to assume, in addition, only one common characteristic: that they are all works which, in one degree or another, justify critical consideration primarily for their own sake, as artistic structures, rather than merely for the sake of the knowledge or wisdom they express or the practical utility we may derive from them, though either or both of these other values may be importantly involved in any particular case. . . . [The task of criticism is to make] formal sense out of any poetic work before us on the assumption that it may in fact be a work for whose peculiar principles of structure there are nowhere any usable parallels either in literary theory or in our experience of other works.[9]

Formal literary structures may be types, but it is clear, to Crane at least, that some types may be known by only one example (once the work is created, other works, of course, may be constructed on the same formal principles), and that "typing" is not immediately prerequisite to recognition as literature, since, as Crane repeatedly affirms,[10] we have not begun to define (and hence to understand and recognize) the forms of a substantial number of pieces of writing that we have consented to treat as literature.

And if we terminate the enumeration of theoretical objections to Fussell's primary assumption and test it against common experiences uninformed by precept, we still find skepticism refusing to submit to credulity. In practice the way we go about recognizing a piece of writing as literature is actually both simpler and more complex than is commonly assumed. In general we treat as literature what we are asked or what, for one reason or another, we are inclined to treat as literature. There is, in short, no form of writing that in at least one of its incarnations cannot be discussed and recognized as literature, industry or ingenuity being as perverse as the understanding is tolerant and as the class *literature* is hospitable to divergent formulations.

As soon as anyone decides to discuss a selected piece of writing (say, the remarks on the back of a particular record jacket, the *Bible*, a specific State Department paper, a particular sermon) in "literary" terms, according to "literary" criteria, as embodying particular "literary" devices, on its "literary" merits, under the governance of any terms, categories, or priorities that have been generally associated with the analysis or description of literature, we are willing, if only tentatively and temporarily, to recognize the legitimacy of calling that work, in response to the critic's specified conditions, literature, even though we may happen to disagree with his distinctions, analysis, or description, and we do this without once forgetting that the work under discussion is yet a sermon or a record-jacket commentary, and without confounding the *Iliad* with a State Department paper, or, say, *Rasselas*. We may treat a sermon or a group of sermons as literature without believing for a moment that sermons *necessarily* constitute a literary genre. And a student blissfully ignorant of any concept of genre may nevertheless be willing to recognize that *Beowulf* is literature. Indeed, a man may glide through life accepting the literary status of works that he could not classify by genre, even upon being informed that unremitted and everlasting torment was the price of ignorance. We need not make our appeal to the "ignorant" and "uneducated," however; even the dedicated literary critic or scholar may devote a lifetime to the study, contemplation, and discussion of a particular literary work without ever determining to his own satisfaction to which genre it properly belonged.[11]

The fact is that *literature* is not a determinate class, delimiting in any meaningful way the forms of writing that may or may not be included within its legitimate jurisdiction. In acceding to any critic's request to consider a particular piece of writing as literature, we consent in general only to attend to his special way of construing a work for the purpose of disclosing in it what he takes to be (or what have traditionally been taken to be), for one reason or another, devices, powers, attributes, or effects, of literature. If we do not concur with his assumptions or conclusions or grant that he has isolated attributes differentiating literature from other kinds of writing, we still stand ready to acknowledge that some particular sermon, say, may be considered as literature. And it is because *literature* is not a distinct category of writing with a determinate set of universal attributes that we can be so tolerant.

Our reasons for accepting a piece of writing as literature are as manifold and diverse as are the terms, categories, doctrines, and principles that we employ in our discussions of literature. Like water, literature is largely known through the intellectual operations that we happen to apply to it. Water, construed in one manner, is a medium for swimming, whereas under the construction sponsored by threatening flames, water is understood to be a fire extinguisher (even though quite a different construction of water has informed us that it is compounded of one element that sustains fire and another that is flammable.)[12] Thus literature is a protean entity that alters as it alteration finds in the observer (i.e., in the constitutive categories of observation). Nevertheless, even if we do not approach texts with a limiting and hence restrictive conception of what differentiates literature from other forms of verbal discourse, we can still consent to recognize any piece of writing as literature (at least provisionally), if only because we can think immediately of no compelling reason not to think of it as such, if only because it is included in a "literature" course, if only because we sacrifice no intellectual principles, abrogate no argumentative prerogatives, invalidate no fundamental principles in allowing the designation.

The preceding discussion provokes, of course, many questions that it refrains from answering, but for all its shortcomings it does at least cast doubt, I think, on the adequacy of the notion that we recognize a piece of writing as literature *only* through our prior acceptance of the convention that its genre is literary. It is perfectly possible for someone to recognize (or claim to recognize) literature by this means, but the means do not appear to have achieved any widespread acceptance or to be capable of accounting very adequately for common practice.

In approaching Johnson's writing (including his critical writing), instead of beginning with the actual questions that Johnson regularly addresses, with the actual assumptions on which he commonly relies, with the actual method of reasoning about subjects that he generally employs, with the actual purposes that his arguments serve, with, in short, the actual intellectual bases of his practical judgments (all of which may be known directly or inferred from his practice), Fussell begins with a pronouncement concerning the elementary "facts of writing," this procedure being justified, presumably, on the not totally unreasonable assumption that any subsequent analysis of actual "acts of writing" will be greatly facilitated by a prior analysis of the inescapable "facts of writing." Acts are simply the places where the facts show up. Oddly enough, the first question that Fussell asks is not "What is writing?" but rather "What constitutes literature?" The answer[13] is strikingly obvious. "Simply this: the decision of an audience that a piece of writing is 'literary.' "

This answer is banal to the point of innocuousness. It is, in fact, a crisper version of my equally true and equally banal assertion that we recognize as literature what we are asked, or what for one reason or another we are inclined, to recognize as literature. Had Fussell been content to rest here, we all could have gone peacefully back to the contemplation of our thumbs, but he goes on to add by way of clarification that

> an act of what observers will consent to consider literature can take place only when an individual talent engages and, as it were, fills in the shape of a pre-existing form that a particular audience is willing to regard as belonging to the world of literature.[14]

Now, since no particular audience will consent to consider every piece of writing as literature, we must, to cover the ground, make explicit the corollary that is not articulated here: "An act of what observers will consent to consider 'nonliterature' can take place only when an individual talent engages and, as it were, fills in the shape of a preexisting form that a particular audience is willing to regard as belonging to the world of 'nonliterature.' "[15] Combined, these statements define the battleground or the playground on which the warfare or sport of writing takes place. Unfortunately, by prior definition the encounter between talent and tradition culminates in a predictable result. If talent does not yield to tradition (i.e., preexisting form), we are placed in the awkward position of being witnesses to the thing which is not; the field must always be a playground, never a battleground. Yet the definitions force us (at least, invite us) to conceive of the possibility of a battleground and of the forces of talent carrying the day.

The basic problem can perhaps be clarified by considering the subservience of talent to form. When individual talent encounters tradition, it must find the means to confine its rambunctious impetuosity within the limits prescribed by preexisting forms. If, for example, eleven forces of talent run out on the field wearing football uniforms after preexisting form has yelled "baseball," then, of course, the forces of talent must immediately make some significant adjustments; otherwise the crowd would become unruly and, as one man, cry: "What the hell is going on here" (or something to that effect). After witnessing talent yield to preexisting form, we can consent to call the result either literature or nonliterature. If, on the other hand (and this is certainly a hypothetical possibility), individual talent steadfastly and adamantly refuses to submit to the demands of any preexisting form and decides, rather, to make, say, two or more preexisting forms bow before its strength, then, by definition, the audience must frankly admit the existence of a logical impossibility—admit, that is, that it has met a piece of writing that is neither literature nor nonliterature, a piece of writing that is not a piece of writing. The game-warfare analogy, of course, breaks down sooner than the idea supporting it, namely, that if talent does not engage with and fill in the shape of a preexisting form, then, by definition, we cannot consent to consider the actual piece of writing that results as either literature or nonliterature. This paradox is not insoluble, of course, but the first step toward solution involves, at the very least, a modification of the definition of what constitutes literature.

Oddly enough, Fussell finds support for his definition even in facts that tend or would seem to invalidate it. For example, seeking confirmation for his position, Fussell appeals to Stuart Gilbert's discussion of the reception in England of the "Sirens" episode of *Ulysses:* " . . . when it was sent by the author from Switzerland to England during the First World War, the Censor held it up, suspecting that it was written in some secret code. Two English writers (it is said) examined the work and came to the conclusion that it was not 'code' but literature of some eccentric kind."[16] As soon as we ask how they came to their conclusion, we immediately recognize that it could not have been achieved by relying on Fussell's explanation of what constitutes literature. Their decision was reached before they had access to the whole work and presumably before they knew that the episode was indeed an episode, a fragment of a whole, complete work, in advance, that is, of sufficient "genre" clues. Moreover, Gilbert's description tells us that the two writers did not think that Joyce had filled in the shape of a preexisting form (the work was "eccentric," belonging to no recognizable form) that they were willing to regard as belonging to the world of literature. On the contrary, they were willing for one reason or another to regard as belonging to the world of literature a piece of writing that they could not identify by genre; decision preceded rather than followed genre identification.

Fussell goes on a little later to inform us that "it takes a mature and experienced sensibility . . . to do what Norman Mailer has done, to appropriate a genre not considered literary—the news story, the 'report,' the eyewitness account—and make it serve literary purposes."[17] But, in calling, say, *Armies of the Night* literature, we must apparently subordinate our notions of genre to what for lack of other terms we are willing to call, vaguely, "literary purposes." Recognition is based, not on identification of literary genre, but on detection of "literary purpose." Mailer has not filled in the shape of a preexisting form that we are willing to regard as belonging to the world of literature. On the contrary, we are willing to regard as literature, on the basis of its "purpose," a piece of writing that belongs to a "genre" that, by prior consent, we do not recognize as literary. Moreover, it is clear that Mailer's success does not oblige us to add the "report," the news story, to the list of literary genres.

In fact, of course, Mailer has not filled in the shape of a pre-existing form (literary or otherwise); he has found the means to transcend, bypass, transgress the formal limitations (whatever they are exactly) of the news story, creating in the process a piece of literature that we are content for the time being to call (with Mailer's prompting) "novel-history, history-novel," a "new" genre. Mailer has written a news report with a difference, a difference depending upon and exemplifying the processes of metaphor; a new type (even perhaps a unique type) has emerged from the dynamic coadunation of preexisting types (in much the same way that *highway* and *man* achieve something other than highway-ness and man-ness in *highwayman*). In the end we have not this form plus that form, but a dynamic whole demanding recognition in its own terms and governed by imperatives tending toward a peculiar, formal completion. In sum, we understand that *Armies of the Night* is both like and unlike a news story, a report, and that Mailer has done more than appropriate a preexisting, nonliterary genre in order to make it serve literary purposes.

Shortly before commenting on Mailer, Fussell notifies us that, "like other sorts of public notices, what literature is at any moment depends wholly on conventions which appear and depart, wax and wane, fructify or deaden."[18] But how can these fluctuations take place? Fussell's definition does not allow for waxing and waning. (Indeed, one wonders how any piece of writing ever came initially to be identified as literature, if a particular audience can consent to recognize that, and only that piece of writing as literature which takes a form previously acknowledged to be literary.) We cannot logically agree both with this statement and with Fussell's prior definition, since the definition contains no implicit means by which to account for the comings and goings of recognizable forms of literature. At bottom the basic point here seems to be only that some forms are popular in one age, some in another. To this innocuous truth we must add the qualification that the preferences of writers in these matters determine in no necessary or absolute sense what we are willing, at any historical moment, to call literature. For example, the fact that no one today may choose to write heroic dramas or pastoral elegies does not prevent me from recognizing the literary status of works written in the past in those forms. Similarly, if someone today should choose to write a pastoral elegy, I would immediately recognize its "form," even though no one else today was writing in that form. The only thing I cannot do, of course, is recognize the literary status of an unformed form (existence precedes recognition), though I certainly recognize that new literary forms may in the time to come emerge.

Underlying the whole argument is the assumption of generic stability, for without any stable grounds of "genre" differentiation there can clearly be no sharp separation of talent from preexisting form, of what is inside from what is outside the writer. We are thus brought to the identification of "coded medium" with literary genre.

> The idea of the 'coded medium' is a modern way of conceiving of a relatively fixed literary genre [fixed relative to individual talent, presumably]. *This coded medium comes inevitably from outside the writer:* otherwise it fails to transmit signals recognizable to the observer. Which is another way of saying what Northrop Frye has said: 'The *forms* of literature can no more exist outside literature than the forms of sonata and fugue and rondo can exist outside music.' The medium is a public property which is not inside the writer.[19]

Our assent to Fussell's remarks would be less hesitant if he did not repeatedly fall into a loose way of talking. In a sense there is no startlingly new information offered here; part of the drift of the quotation seems to be that a writer fashions material already at hand into a shape that the material, left to its own devices, would not naturally assume. (Of course, the architect, cabinet-maker, composer, potter, painter, seamstress all work under the same conditions.) But (leaving aside the problem of what any particular audience may or may not be willing to call the thing fashioned into a shape) I am reluctant to grant much of what goes beyond the obvious in these remarks. Why should we equate "coded medium" with relatively fixed literary genre and talk about a *form* of writing (a genre) as though it were a *medium* of writing? (What "media" are necessary to the realization of the form-medium?) Why should we interpret genre as the primary (only) medium with which an author (individual talent) engages? Why wouldn't it make more sense to talk about language as *the* (or *a*) medium used in the fashioning of a form of literature, a genre? Why should we stress the vulnerability of the writer and the rigid toughness of the genre? Could we not just as easily stress the strength of authorial will and the vulnerability of genre, since genre is finally subservient to the particular aims, purposes, and governing conceptions of the writer? How do we go about determining the extent to which artistic purpose yielded to a particular writer's *conception* of genre requirements (and it is essential to remember that with various writers we are dealing with varying conceptions of genre), or the extent to which *understood* genre requirements yielded to artistic purposes? How, in short, do we go about the job of adjusting vulnerabilities? Can we not more safely say that whenever a writer discovers that specific genre requirements inhibit rather than promote expression, whenever a writer finds that aspects of the specific genre in which he has *chosen* to write no longer serve as fundamental conditions of artistic freedom, enabling him to embody powerfully, vividly, and precisely his conception, he chooses rather to violate the rules or to disregard the generic imperatives than to revise his composition or to disrupt the ongoing integrity of his work? (Even so timid and rule-conscious a man as Joseph Addison, who was willing to change much that his friends took exception to in *Cato*, chose rather to defend a violation of poetic justice than to conclude his play with the success of Cato.) Rules guide practice only as long as they free expression and serve artistic purpose.

Moreover, is it not the case that knowledge of the genre[20] in which a writer is working is frequently the least useful information we can have about a particular work? Is it not also true that in *choosing* to write in a particular genre (as he understands its nature and requirements), a writer frequently solves very few practical problems of composition? To understand Dryden's *Astraea Redux*, for example, we must know a good deal more than that it belongs to the *genre* "occasional poetry"; we must know, in addition, more than what particular event occasioned the poem. To know that it was designed to celebrate the return of Charles II to England is to know very little about the poem, about how the poem is obliged to work, and very few real problems were solved by Dryden in choosing to write on the return of Charles. The expression of Dryden's individual talent was restricted or limited less by the occasion itself than by how he construed the problems involved in dealing with the return of Charles; his problems were immediate and practical: how to represent the exile as fortunate for Charles and for the people of England without offending Charles and disturbing the people; how to make Charles acceptable to the people and the people acceptable to Charles without creating fictions in which nobody could believe; how to suggest the way Charles should behave upon his return without appearing to be impertinent; and so on. To understand *Astraea Redux* is to experience the resolution of problems such as these in the systematic, coherent whole that is the poem.

It is worth noting here, I think, that occasional poetry is really not the exceptional, but the paradigmatic case. Every poem, however denominated, is for the reader like a new game, the rules for which he cannot presume to know prior to reading but must discover and learn by playing, that is, by reading.[21] Every particular work (not a mere copy and successfully terminated) is a "unique" product owing its peculiar coherence to the playing out of those local options that a writer's successive, specific choices have activated. To play the writer's game we must pick up, as we go along, clues resonating with significance, intuiting as we proceed temporally "meanings" (or "wholes") more complete than the as-yet-disclosed information will fully justify, and altering our working hypotheses[22] in response to our perception of changing relations; briefly, reading forces us to formulate and revise hypotheses, which are tentative, heuristic intuitions of whole meanings in advance of full evidence, as we encounter the work in its linear unfolding.

Our confidence in the explanatory power of a particular hypothesis increases as we get closer to the end of the work, and this is the case because fewer choices (fewer possibilities and more necessities) are available to the writer at the end than at the beginning, and because our latest hypothesis is accountable to more actual material than the earliest. Even if the earliest and latest are substantially the same—which is frequently the case, since all hypotheses are constitutive, are peculiarly inclined, that is, to direct attention to details compatible with their natures—the latest is to the earliest as hindsight is to foresight, as quarterbacking on Monday is to quarterbacking on Saturday afternoon; one is taken to be an account of what has happened, whereas the other is a more or less coherent sense of what ought or might be expected to happen. The latest, of course, may not be adequate to the richness and complexity of the work examined, but something that I am willing, for lack of a better or more precise term, to call a *hypothesis* is necessarily involved in the understanding or experiencing of any extended piece of writing, since without it the reader would be flooded with an incredible assortment of discrete units (monads) lacking relation, emphasis, or hierarchical importance. Without any hypothesis (an impossibility), the reader is simply confused, overwhelmed, assaulted by data that cannot be assimilated or retained in the memory.

If reading is tainted by interpretation from the beginning and hypotheses, as prophecies, tend to be self-fulfilling, what prevents reading from being an exercise in self-imposition, a game in which each player takes out of the magic circle exactly what he has diligently put into it? Frequently, of course, nothing checks the steady progress of a self-initiated, self-sustaining, and self-justifying game. But in general the best readers are quick to modify their hypotheses as they confront new details, because they run crashing into recalcitrant material, because most early hypotheses are tentative, open to falsification as well as confirmation, because of a felt tension between the details and the means of accounting for them. Throughout, we recognize that our task is to learn the rules that somebody else has devised for a game that we cannot be sure we know; the writer, in a manner of speaking, is our adversary, one who may regularly subvert the ongoing integrity of *our* controlling intuition by making choices that cannot properly be contained within the legitimate boundaries of our intuition. When this happens, we as readers have at least the following three options available to us: we can attempt (1) to demonstrate that the

new details are insignificant, unimportant, adventitious, gratui-
tous, irrelevant, and so on; (2) to prove that they are "bad" choices,
artistic flaws, mistakes, signs of carelessness, of textual corrup-
tion, compositorial ineptness, and so on; or (3) to construct a new
hypothesis, in which such details function as necessary, contributing parts of an entirely different, whole structure, the sufficiency of
our conception of which may again be tested (invalidated or con-
firmed) by subsequent disclosures. In the course of reading we
perhaps rarely contemplate our intuitions in any self-conscious,
deliberate way, but, as stated earlier, if our experience with a work
involves something more than an extended series of discrete, disjunct impressions (without history or future), then the ground of
significant response is necessarily some more or less coherent
cognition; otherwise, we could never know what we know, persuade others of the value or nature of our knowledge and our means
of knowing, or test, falsify, or corroborate what we know.

If we happen to be interested in "formal" criticism, we have an
obligation to reason back from a specific, achieved hypothesis
about the distinct nature of the whole work to the details of the text,
attempting to demonstrate that only this hypothesis can adequately
account for the text in all its particularity; the parts, while prior to
the whole they collectively achieve, are seen and discussed as
necessities following from the hypothesis that generates their
sequential unfolding, the hypothesis (an account of principles of
construction) here standing in relation to the details of the text as
the meaning of a sentence stands in relation to the individual words
of the sentence. (We know a meaning because of the words, but the
meaning is the cause of the words being said as they are said.)[23] We
may then go on to note class correspondences obtaining between
this work and several other works to which a "genre" name has
been assigned, but "genre" distinctions (and here and elsewhere I
use the term *genre,* as we all generally do, loosely) control the
artist's selection and the audience's responses in only a minimal
sense, whereas the peculiar, constitutive principles of form control
(determine the nature and effect of) a particular work, classifiable
by genre, in a maximal sense. As one critic has said:

Sonnet form, for instance, is a perfectly comprehensible class
term, but it implies very little for the form of any sonnet. It

designates formal components which are largely fixated and do not interact. . . . While a critic recognizes a sonnet by virtue of features which sonnets possess in common, he is usually not concerned to show that these features . . . are significant of anything in relation to the whole.[24]

On what grounds can we legitimately say that "the making of literature is a matter of the engagement of a vulnerable self with a fairly rigid coded medium. . . . "? How much "give" does the genre have? What minimal requirements must a work meet in order to be placed in a specific genre? And so on. The history of literature indicates that genre is more open than closed, flexible rather than rigid. Are Jane Austen and James Joyce engaging with the same "coded medium," namely, the novel? As soon as we start to designate the attributes of a genre, we find that we have inadvertently excluded works that, in spite of our categorical specifications, seem to belong to the genre. Underlying Fussell's remarks, I think, is the false assumption that in any given period there is substantial agreement about what characteristics constitute the several distinct genres. A perfunctory examination of critical practice suggests that nothing could be farther from the truth. Just as critics distinguish literary from "nonliterary" discourse in various ways, so they differentiate among genres in various ways. Some critics define genre in terms of some more or less specific *quality* thought to be inherent in all works of the type—tragic quality, comic quality, satiric quality, ironic quality, and so on, so that narrative poems, long lyrics, novels, and dramatic works may all be classified as, say, tragedies. Others fix upon subject matter as the discriminating sign of genre, so that we have, for example, domestic tragedy, bourgeois tragedy, social tragedy, and so on, exemplified in dramatic works and extended prose and verse narratives. Still others define according to kinds of probability—fantastic, realistic, naturalistic, surrealistic, and the like. Others differentiate on the basis of the kinds of techniques and conventions employed, for example, conventions of narration (omniscient author, first-person narration, stream of consciousness). And so on. The grounds of differentiation are many and various. And if critics discriminate among genres in many ways, writers also conceive of generic limitations in many radically disparate ways. In the absence of any consensus concerning the specific nature of genre limits or powers, there can, of course, be no general agreement about the ways in which talent adjusts to preexisting form.

I should now like to look briefly at the equation of coded medium with genre and to amplify earlier remarks. In the first place, it seems to me that only confusion is served by talking about a "kind," a "form" as though it were a "medium," a "material" to be shaped, especially when genre is elsewhere described as the shape that the writer fills in. If a medium is also a form, we have a right to know how this comes about. Putting this aside for a moment, let us look at the concept of a "coded medium." Now, the world of language, not to mention the worlds of painting, music, sculpture, and so on, is full of coded media, and considerable loss of precision results when we reduce media to medium. The fact is, of course, that any distinguishable and conventionally determinate set of linguistic units can be called a coded medium, material, that is, that achieves specific form relative to pressures or controls exerted upon it, not pressures and controls intrinsic to or emanating from within the set. For example, phonemes are brought under the control of words) phonemes are formed into shapes—words—that they would not assume if left to their own devices); words are controlled by "grammar" and syntax; grammar and syntax by sentences; sentences by whole compositions. This sequence, of course, does not exhaust the possibilities of matter-form relationship, since between sentences and whole compositions a variety of conventions (including what we loosely call genre conventions) may be brought under the governance of the overall shaping principle of the whole composition, which principle determines the formal relations of all the parts and the hierarchy of importance among them; however, the sequence does indicate how form at one level of organization may become matter at another level.

What is essential to this argument can perhaps best be illustrated by noting that whereas a detailed, objective (though highly incomplete) knowledge of the antecedent units may be derived from the whole composition, no knowledge, however comprehensive, of the constituent parts will enable us to infer the whole composition. From a whole composition we can derive knowledge—albeit limited—of sentences, from sentences a knowledge of syntax, from syntax a knowledge of words, from words a knowledge of phonology, but we cannot infer a vocabulary from a knowledge of phonemes, a grammar from a familiarity with vocabulary; a grammar may limit the kinds of things that may be said, but it cannot predict or by itself generate sentences; and a whole composition, comprised of many sentences and ordered to a distinct end, cannot be derived from a knowledge of the individual sentences making up the whole. (Put all the sentences of, say, *Hamlet* in a box and then ask any student to return at the end of the term with a great play in hand.) Of course, we may construct a hypothetical language that begins with phonetics and comes to term in the production of a particular discourse or piece of writing, but in such a model evolution still depends upon the regular imposition of formal restraints upon a regular succession of matters.

For present purposes, let us assume, that the basic medium with which a writer deals is a particular language (with its lexicon and rules governing the values and the organizational possibilities of words), which is not of his own devising and hence may be understood as belonging to his (as we say) "speech community." Language is the primary "coded medium." At this point we may invoke the aid of Fussell and Frye, applying what they say of genre to language: *"This coded medium comes inevitably from outside the writer:* otherwise it fails to transmit signals recognizable to the observer. . . . The medium is a public property which is not inside the writer."[25] What a man actually says or writes in a particular language, however, does not exist outside the speaker or writer (a language or "speech community" cannot speak or write). A statement is fashioned out of the materials of a particular language, and we immediately recognize the statement as possible to the language; from the outset we know whether or not the writer is using a language that we understand. On the other hand, we do not always know either immediately or ultimately what genre a writer is engaging with, and furthermore, no realized work identifiable by genre, no result achieved by the specific choices of a writer can be said to be outside the writer, if we conceive of genre, not as material (a medium), but as a synthesis of material achieved by means of some shaping principle, since by definition a form is the result of forces exerted upon materials that would not by themselves assume a distinctive shape.[26] But this statement needs to be refined, for even when the end peculiar to a particular genre can be clearly stated—a shoe is formed in such a way as to fit a foot, a certain kind of tragedy to effect the catharsis of pity and fear, for example—it is clear that every production not a mere copy of something already existing embodies artistic choices that culminate in a unique realization of the ends specified for the genre, in much the same way that every new declaratory sentence is a unique realization of the ends peculiar to that type of sentence.

In a radical sense, it is impossible for a writer to fill in the shape of a "preexisting form." Form is the result of specific acts of selection and arrangement. The characteristics of a genre, how-ever designated, are so many conditions to be met or so many limitations on the vagaries of imagination, but a unique synthesis of material, classifiable perhaps by genre, can emerge only as a result of *a writer's* taking advantage of those opportunities for choice in a genre which are consonant with and instrumentally useful to his peculiar artistic purpose; otherwise we would have statements of conditions and limitations, but no actual writings. If the conditions are met, we may be willing to recognize the work as an example of a certain genre, but the conditions cannot generate any specific form classifiable by genre. For example, we can say that any sculptor in clay interested in representing a man is severely limited, first, by the "material" with which he has chosen to work and, second, by the "form" which he has chosen to represent (the "form" of a man is not the "form" of a toadstool). But no sculptor can represent the form of a man without at the same time forming a man. The range of possible forms that the "form" of man may assume is virtually infinite, just as the range of possible forms that, say, a novel may assume is virtually infinite. In relation to clay, "man" is a formal restraint; in relation to "man," a particular representation is a formal restraint. By way of refinement, we can narrow with increasing precision the type to which the "formed" man belongs. Thus, from man we can move to thin man, to thin man wearing a business suit, to thin man wearing a business suit, sitting and smoking a pipe, to the same man qualified by signs of age, emotion, and so on, thus arriving at a type that includes one member. But whatever the final product, the formed man will be a unique synthesis of parts.

We can discuss genre requirements as coded media, but it is important to keep in mind that "genre" is not a primary coded medium, in the sense that a language is a primary coded medium, since (if for no other reason) there is no consensus concerning genre requirements and since no genre requirements can be specified—for writing—that cannot be realized in language; in short, the material foundation of the genre requirements is language. And the meaning or purpose of any composition, whatever its genre, must be statable in or inferrable from the language. Moreover, "genre," as we generally understand the term, is not a form, but a set of conditions deemed necessary to the creation of form. Genre requirements are *material* limitations on the form of the whole. In a manner of speaking, we can say that when a writer *chooses* to write in one genre rather than in another, he subordinates the various possibilities for formal development intrinsic to language to the control of genre requirements (the laws that apply to language achieve functional value in relation to the rules specified for the genre). The rules or laws of genre (however defined) are in turn *material* limitations on the intrinsic form of a specified work, but that intrinsic form does not derive from the rules of genre; rather, the rules become functional in relation to restraints imposed upon them by intrinsic form.

Now in relation to the overall form of a work everything is material, including genre requirements and much that is not normally comprehended (or, because of our loose way of talking about such matters, may not be comprehended) under our conception of genre. In "realistic" works, for example, a writer's working conception of the nature of external reality limits what can be said or done in a work and what sorts of probabilities can be actively contemplated. "Reality," as conceived, is then a "coded medium." With regard to "thought," limits are provided by the problems, ideas, and topics entertained, specifically by the particular manner of construing those problems, ideas, and topics;[27] hence, the *thought* in the work, as limited in its aspects and subservient to artistic purpose, can be considered in terms of a coded medium. If a writer happens to rely regularly on specific devices or techniques, not demanded or required by the genre, then we can examine those techniques and devices as coded media (they, too, are *means* to a determinate end). Similarly, imagery, symbolism, and so forth may be considered as so many coded media subservient to the peculiar formal imperatives of a particular work. In short, any distinguishable system of parts can be discussed as a medium. In slightly different terms, we may speak

> of the words of a poem as the material basis of the thought they express, although the words also have form as being ordered in sentences and rhythms; and similarly we may speak of thought as the matter of character, of character and thought in words as the matter of action and emotion, and so on up to but not including the overall form which synthesizes all these elements, formally effective in themselves, into a continuous poetic whole.[28]

What a definition of genre, however detailed, cannot do, of course, is specify the nature, number, or value of all the various coded media with which a writer may actively engage in the production of a distinct piece of writing. Effective communication depends upon the employment of coded media, but it is a mistake to assume that all the coded media used by a writer in making a particular work can be construed as so many aspects of a pervasive medium called "genre" or to imply that whatever is not comprehended under a particular conception of genre is an attribute of the writer's "individual uniqueness."[29] In every work tending toward completion, every choice made along the way limits the range of possible alternative choices that may be made subsequently, but few crucial choices (choices on which the peculiar artistic integrity of the work depends) are necessarily implicated in what we may abstractly identify as the attributes of a specific genre,[30] even though it is also true that many particular choices are of a kind peculiar to the genre in which the writer happens to work. (The extent to which a writer is conscious of the generic nature of any choices is relative to his particular conception of genre and of its concomitant requirements; the critic, of course, with the whole work before him may discuss the work in terms of generic necessities that emerge from a conception of genre radically different from that of the writer.)

In the end what Fussell takes to be the fixed poles of the literary enterprise—talent and preexisting form—are no more than hypostatizations. Armed with these categories, no critic could come to a detailed understanding of any particular work, if only because he could not reason from these ground terms to necessary literary particulars. The cognitive weakness of the hypothesis, however, is not on the side of *scope,* since every act of writing is comprehended under its polarities, but on the side of *precision,* since the necessary relations obtaining in any single piece of writing simply cannot be known by means of his preferred categories. Additionally, he assumes throughout what even casual acquaintance with the history of literary criticism and practice would not seem to justify, that the persistence of names for types of writing (novel, lyric, tragedy, etc.) is a guarantee of the persistence of a commonly shared understanding of the meanings or significations of those names, and that this understanding provides a rational basis for discriminating between what in any piece of writing belongs to code and what derives from a writer's uniquely vulnerable self.

To know something about the power with which access to the "facts" of writing endows us, the reader is invited to lay aside his Goethe for a moment and consider how skillfully and subtly I am managing in this sentence to exercise my individual talent within the externally imposed limits of the coded medium in which I have elected to write—the declarative English sentence. Now, from this sentence the reader may move to whole works and examine, say, *Tom Jones, Great Expectations, Finnegans Wake,* and *Naked Lunch* (all four being works that particular audiences have been willing to regard—for some reason or other, according to some criteria or other—as novels) as exemplifications of the felicitous conjunction of self and code. What we must inevitably recognize, I think, is that a distinction between self and code does not provide us with the first principles of either writing or reading; the terms of this distinction are not enabling terms, terms that enable us, without the specification of additional principles or categories, to reason to necessary, inescapable conclusions about literary "facts."

The more general our sense of genre criteria, the more we necessarily attribute to individual talent; the more precise our generic criteria, the less we attribute to talent, but in either case critical inquiry cannot go much beyond the naming of the parts. More important, even if there were general agreement as to the precise nature of the specific *forms* of writing which, in the absence of adequate definitions of literary *forms*, we tend to classify under such inclusive types as novel, lyric, tragedy, an so on, we would still have to deal with the fact[31] that native force (or the uniquely vulnerable self) is not directly, immediately, or necessarily inferable from the observable traits of the work itself, many of those traits exhibiting the effects of forces just as external to the writer as the coded medium is assumed by Fussell to be. In short, some traits may be precisely what they are as a result of training, models, reading, social-political events, and the like; *genre*, however defined, is simply not the only element of writing with which an individual talent engages.

In its unimpeachable form (that is, to write anything a writer must employ a coded medium—actually media), Fussell's point is, for the writer or critic, without value, since the polarity on which it is based can achieve determinate meaning only when it is subordinated to a particular and coherent critical framework, incorporating primary assumptions about the nature of literary materials, forms, purposes, values, ends, et cetera. What Fussell is offering us, finally, is his own peculiar version of what has virtually become a habitual mode of critical reasoning, the dialectical mode, based on an a priori conception of literature as discourse admitting of discussion in terms of content and form, content apparently being for Fussell ideas, feelings, or attitudes in the writer (the verbal exemplification of his uniquely vulnerable self) and form being coded media, which are identified with genres in their general significations (whatever they are). The "theory" underlying the discussion of Johnson's writing is simply a cognitively inadequate tool of analysis.

In sum, it seems clear that an adequate understanding of genre can only proceed from the formal analysis of literary particulars. Once a particular work has been constructed and once it has been understood through formal analysis as the result of an artist's imposing some form upon some material in some fashion for some purpose, the realized or achieved form can be discussed in relation to other works that are similarly formed by similar means for similar purposes and, hence, formally associated with those works or construed as a representative of a distinguishable class of works. Formal analysis, which seeks to explain all artistic choices by reference to principles of construction, precedes generic classification. Generic classification involves the comparative analysis of works in terms of degrees of likeness/difference obtaining in the materials, manners, forms, and purposes of particular works.

Notes

Introduction

1. Oliver F. Sigworth, *Eighteenth-Century Studies* 1 (1967): 159-68.

2. Paul Fussell, in *Samuel Johnson and the Life of Writing* (New York: Harcourt, Brace, Jovanovich, 1971), pp. 35-61.

3. Arieh Sachs, *Passionate Intelligence: Imagination and Reason in the Work of Samuel Johnson* (Baltimore, Md.: Johns Hopkins Press, 1967).

4. *Eighteenth-Century Studies*, 4 (1971): 184-98.

5. Sigworth, "Johnson's *Lycidas*," pp. 164-165.

6. Fussell, *Life of Writing*, p. 60.

7. Ibid., p. 43.

8. Sachs, *Passionate Intelligence*, p. 21.

9. Ibid., p. xi.

10. Krieger, "Fiction, Nature, and Literary Kinds," p. 186.

11. Ibid., p. 188.

12. Ibid., p. 197.

13. Sigworth, "Johnson's *Lycidas*," pp. 167-68.

14. Jean H. Hagstrum, *Samuel Johnson's Literary Criticism* (Minneapolis: University of Minnesota Press, 1952), p. vii.

15. *Rambler* 208.

16. E. D. Hirsch, Jr., *The Aims of Interpretation* (Chicago and London: University of Chicago Press, 1976), p. 80.

17. An appendix, "Principles of Criticism: Individual Talent and Coded Medium," follows chap. 6. The appendix is to some extent an independent essay; it is included, however, because it is concerned with aspects of Johnson's theory and practice. In addition, it is instigated by issues raised in the chapter of Fussell's book on which I focus attention in chap. 2. Essentially, the appendix deals with Johnson's notions of genre and with broad problems of definition of genre.

Chapter 1

1. Paul Fussell, *Samuel Johnson and the Life of Writing* (New York: Harcourt, Brace, Jovanovich, 1971), p. 57.

2. Oliver F. Sigworth, "Johnson's *Lycidas*: The End of Renaissance Criticism," *Eighteenth-Century Studies* 1 (1967): 165.

3. Ibid., pp. 164-65.

4. Fussell, *Life of Writing*, p. 60.

5. Sigworth, "Johnson's *Lycidas*," pp. 167-68.

6. Ibid., pp. 160-61.

7. Ibid., p. 168.

8. Ibid., p. 165.

9. I discuss emotions in relation to Johnson's critical priorities at some length in section 2.

10. Sigworth, "Johnson's *Lycidas*," p. 165.

11. "Preface" to the *Dictionary*.

12. It is undoubtedly to this demand for passion to which Sigworth is alluding in part when on p. 160 he asserts that "the criticism of *Lycidas* can offer a line of interpretation illuminating in a new perspective some of the inconsistencies of Johnson's critical thought." If the demand were regularly made then Johnson would, of course, not be guilty of inconsistency. At any rate, the relationship between personal suffering and criteria of artistic excellence is at best a tenuous one, and as far as general speculation is concerned, it is perhaps just as reasonable to assume that a lifetime of suffering would induce a man to demand from literature, not real passion, but flights of fancy, delightful diversion, romantic enchantment, or airy fictions, which by steady insinuation would entice a troubled mind from the relentless harshness of everyday life.

13. *Rambler* 92.

14. Samuel Johnson, *The Lives of the Poets*, ed. G. B. Hill. 3 vols. (Oxford: Clarendon Press, 1905), 1:410.

15. *Rambler* 208.

16. *Rambler* 92.

17. *A Journey to the Western Islands of Scotland*, ed. Mary Lascelles (New Haven and London: Yale University Press, 1971), p. 40.

18. Sigworth, "Johnson's *Lycidas*," pp. 164-65. What exactly is the sense of the term for us?

19. In *Johnsonian Studies*, ed. Magdi Wahba (Cairo, 1962), pp. 235-56.

20. Walter John Hipple, Jr., *The Beautiful, The Sublime, and the Picturesque in Eighteenth-Century British Aesthetic Theory* (Carbondale: Southern Illinois University Press, 1957).

21. Robert Marsh, *Four Dialetical Theories of Poetry* (Chicago and London: University of Chicago Press, 1965).

22. Robert D. Hume, *Dryden's Criticism* (Ithaca: Cornell University Press, 1970), p. 154.

23. In taking exception to George Watson's claim, in *The Literary Critics*, that Dryden's "Heads of an Answer to Rymer" is "the one critical document in English between the Restoration and Johnson's Shakespeare in which the *Poetics* of Aristotle are [sic] attacked frontally and without qualification," Robert Hume comments: "We might dismiss something like Sir Robert Howard's objection to rules in the 'Preface' to *The Duke of Lerma* (1668) as too early to be important, but in 1694 Charles Gildon's *Miscellaneous Letters and Essays* explicitly rejects rules, the French, and the authority of Aristotle with a vehemence far surpassing Dryden's private questionings of seventeen years earlier" (Hume, *Dryden's Criticism*, p. 156). And if we ask, with Robert Hume, whether we have not "set too early a

date for the triumph of neoclassical orthodoxy," we must respond by ruling the question, as formulated, out of order and, after perusing the critical diversity and "iconoclasm" in the period, conclude "that the neoclassical monolith had fractured before it congealed" (Hume, *Dryden's Criticism*, pp. 156-57).

24. The critic proceeds to proofs by asserting, for example, "that there [*is*] something both new and out of harmony with neoclassical doctrine in Dryden's discussion of the Roman satirists in terms of 'historical factors and the conditions of the age'; or that Pope's allusion in the *Essay on Criticism* to the 'nameless graces which no methods teach' is a sign of his not being a representative, pure and simple, of the neoclassical school'; . . . or that Johnson was helping to 'dispose' of neoclassicism when he condemned 'mere formal imitation of earlier masterpieces' and asserted that 'No man as yet ever became great by imitation'; or that another fundamental principle of neoclassicism [*is*] being denied by Maurice Morgann and others in the later eighteenth century when they contended that there is 'something mysterious' in poetry, something more than a 'mere formal art'; or that it was a conception of poetry 'newly won' in the eighteenth century which made its values consist, not in its appeal 'to the intellect alone,' but in its power to move the feelings, 'its impassioned utterances and aesthetic effects' " (R. S. Crane, *The Idea of the Humanities* [Chicago and London: University of Chicago Press, 1967], 2:161. Crane is here dealing with the procedure as it is manifested in J. W. H. Atkin's *English Literary Criticism: 17th and 18th Centuries*).

25. Even allowing for the hypothetically possible but extreme case in which, in the course of lengthy essays, two writers, working independently, make exactly the same statement, we simply cannot assume from this identity—in the absence of any consideration of the intellectual framework underlying the passages—that they are expressing identical or even compatible views. The converse is also true: there is no absolute or even necessary disagreement between critics whose writings yield contradictory statements.

26. Of course, the practice of romanticizing Johnson is not a new fashion. It alternates, it seems, with the identification of neoclassical traits in his writings.

27. Sigworth, "Johnson's *Lycidas*," p. 165.

28. "Preface to Shakespeare"; emphasis added.

29. It is worth remarking that Johnson expected the writer who intended either to express or to excite emotion also to be in his senses, since he is obliged, under the common conventions of linguistic communication, to find language that is adequate to the occasion, to the speaker, and to our conceptions of the possible or probable operations of the mind under the specified conditions of stress; grief, for example, to be communicated and communicable, would have to go beyond any simple standards of the personal and sincere; nothing is perhaps more personal and sincere than uncontrollable weeping, but weeping, as weeping, cannot be embodied in literature. If it is ineffable, then there's an end on't. If the grief is "idiosyncratic," then it is, for the reader, little more than a form of noise, because its expression cannot be recognized as a particular instance of a general class of emotional conditions, justified in its form by local circumstances; consequently, it fails to provoke in the reader or spectator appropriate response. There can be no full empathetic participation in grief that cannot be recognized as such.

30. *Rambler* 60.

31. R. S. Crane, "English Neoclassical Criticism: An Outline Sketch," in *Critics and Criticism: Ancient and Modern*, ed. R. S. Crane (Chicago: University of Chicago Press, 1952), p. 382. Considering the appeal to great works and to principles of nature, Crane notes that "except for the distribution of their emphases, Johnson and Reynolds, writing in the

1770's, were no different from Dryden, writing a hundred years before, so that if Johnson could accuse Cowley [during the same general period when the *Life of Milton* was written] of 'not sufficiently enquiring by what means the ancients have continued to delight through all the changes of human manners,' Dryden could, conversely, insist in 1679 that a dramatist who would move the passions must, in addition to possessing a lofty genius, be skilled 'in the principles of Moral Philosophy' " (Crane, "An Outline Sketch," p. 382). This is the same Dryden who in the preface to his *State of Innocence* notes: "It requires philosophy as well as poetry to sound the depth of all the passions: what they are in themselves, and how they are to be provoked," adding significantly that "in this science the best poets have excelled." Early and late in the period critics looked to the conditions of human life for the principles of art. Moreover, "It was in terms of . . . 'natural reasons,' stated sometimes as mere factual probabilities, sometimes as explicit deductions from psychological causes, that Horace had vindicated the importance of vivid sentiments and truthful characters, that Quintilian had urged the effectiveness of a temperate and timely use of metaphor, that Dryden had argued for the unities of time and place, that Hume had accounted for the delight we receive from tragedy in spite of its painful images, that Johnson had explained why Butler's *Hudibras*, wanting that variety which is the great source of pleasure, is likely to weary modern readers" (Ibid. p. 379).

32. Sigworth, "Johnson's *Lycidas*," p. 161; taken from *The Poems of Alexander Pope*, ed. John Butt (New Haven, 1963), pp. 119-20.

33. Sigworth, "Johnson's *Lycidas*," p. 161.

34. Ibid., p. 161; emphasis added.

35. Ibid., pp. 161-62; emphasis added.

36. Ibid., p. 164; emphasis added.

37. Ibid., p. 165; emphasis on "forgetting" added. I have already made reference to Johnson's examination of the unities, where Sigworth detects Johnson in the act of "forgetting the literary form as an abstract artistic construct." After hearing of all this forgetting, the reader is perhaps too ready to despair of finding in Johnson any significant powers of recall, but in the essay's eleventh hour, Sigworth does not omit to remember—fortunately for Johnson and conveniently for Sigworth's thesis—that at the end of his life Johnson had managed to forget "nothing of the suffering" he had experienced. Considering Johnson's condition, posterity can only fruitlessly wish that Boswell had found an opportunity to abduct a flapper from Swift's Flying Island for domestic service in Johnson's household.

38. The nature of Johnson's standards will be discussed in detail later; see especially chap. 4. To accuse Johnson of forgetfulness here is tantamount to accusing Aristotle of neglecting to remember that Greek tragedy, as Francis Fergusson somewhere says, is organized into units of "purpose, passion, and perception" and designed to meet the ritual expectations of the Greek audience, or, alternatively, that such tragedy, like literature in general, must inevitably reflect the social and economic conditions of the age in which it was written. In describing the structure of tragedy in terms of all the causes, in their order of importance, necessary to the production of a whole, complete action achieving a distinct emotional effect, Aristotle was restricted to an examination of those matters logically contained within his critical purposes and his principles of critical reasoning, just as any critic fulfills in time the imperatives formally implicated in his ground terms and his specific (and hence restrictive) formulation of problems and of the means adequate to their solution.

39. *Lives*, 3:224-25; emphasis added. In his essay Sigworth quotes only "evidently means rather to shew his literature than his wit." I am not at all certain that when Pope describes

the care he took to imitate "some good old authors," he intends to include Renaissance masters under the denomination of old authors. Johnson, at any rate, locates Pope's models in antiquity, not in the Renaissance. In distinguishing the pastorals of Pope from those of Ambrose Philips, he says: "Philips had taken Spenser, and Pope took Vergil for his pattern" ("A. Philips," *Lives*, 3:319). And in this passage it should be noted that Johnson refers to the "poems of antiquity," not to the poems of Renaissance masters.

40. A full exposition of the meanings embedded in "there is no nature, for there is no truth; there is no art, for there is nothing new" would lead us inevitably to an examination of the theoretical bases of Johnson's critical thought and of the crucial significance of such primary terms as *new, familiar, truth, nature, pleasure, novelty, copiousness*, etc. to that thought. That examination will be deferred until section 2.

41. If the reader were to look in Johnson's writings for an exemplification of what is demanded, implicitly and explicitly, from *Lycidas*, he would find it in "On the Death of Dr. Robert Levet" (written a few short years after the *Life of Milton*), which Sigworth nowhere mentions. Here is real passion, personal and sincere, but the power of personal feeling is transmitted in terms that both transcend and preserve the particular, that fix our attention on "officious" Levet ("Well tried thro' many a varying year") while conveying to us the speaker's sense of loss, terms that both chasten and exalt our common humanity, and that, in celebrating Levet's release from bondage, make life for us, finally, more valuable and endurable. Here is real loss and real consolation, for Johnson and ourselves.

42. He asks the question in this form in *Rambler* 156.

43. In *Rambler* 93 Johnson notes that "the faults of a writer of acknowledged excellence are more dangerous, because the influence of his example is more extensive; and the interest of learning requires that they should be discovered and stigmatized, before they have the sanction of antiquity conferred upon them, and become precedents of indisputable authority."

44. Jean H. Hagstrum, *Samuel Johnson's Literary Criticism* (Minneapolis: University of Minnesota Press, 1952), pp. 45-46.

45. In chaps. 2 and 6 I attempt to demonstrate that *sincerity* is not a first-order critical principle to Johnson.

46. "Shakespeare and the Drama," *Tolstoy on Art*, trans. A. Maude (Oxford: Oxford University Press, 1924), pp. 445-46.

47. Sigworth, "Johnson's *Lycidas*," p. 168.

48. Ibid., p. 167.

49. Hipple, *The Beautiful*, p. 308.

50. *Spectator* 29.

51. *Pivot*, by the way, strikes me as no very exalted position to occupy in critical history; as applied to Johnson, the term reduces him to an intellectual curiosity, interesting primarily for his auspicious anticipations of future standards of taste.

52. Sigworth, "Johnson's *Lycidas*," p. 168.

53. In *The Sacred Wood*, T. S. Eliot informs the modern reader that "poetry is not an expression of personality; it is an escape from personality; it is not an outpouring of emotion; it is a suppression of emotion. . . ."

54. After having said all this, I do not think that I am being entirely whimsical when I also say that, at bottom, Sigworth is justified in emphasizing the importance of real passion to Johnson. In my view, Sigworth misrepresents the case primarily by stressing pivot, by linking Johnson to the future on the basis of vague, general terms, and by refusing to discuss Johnson's critical thought in terms of the theoretical principles underlying it.

Chapter 2

1. Paul Fussell, "The Facts of Writing and the Johnsonian Senses of Literature," in *Samuel Johnson and the Life of Writing* (New York: Harcourt, Brace, Jovanovich, 1971), p. 35; emphasis added.

2. Ibid., p. 37; emphasis added. See the appendix, where I discuss the cognitive inadequacies of Fussell's assumptions and examine the theoretical implications and the practical consequences of his critical approach, which, as a method of inquiry and a logical system of inference, belongs to that class of criticism commonly denominated *dialectical* and which, while always with us, is once again becoming the most common mode of critical reasoning.

3. Fussell, *Life of Writing*, p. 39; emphasis added..

4. Ibid., p. 60; emphasis added.

5. Indeed, if the demand for "self-expression" were fully realized, one wonders not only what "monster" would be produced, but how Johnson, by Fussell's definition, could recognize the product as literature, inasmuch as recognition is contingent upon an individual talent's filling in the shape of a preexisting form that the generality of readers will collectively conspire to regard as literature. How can Johnson ask for a literature that, if produced, he could not recognize as literature?

6. Fussell, *Life of Writing*, p. 42.

7. Ibid., p. 43.

8. Ibid., p. 43.

9. See section 2, esp. chaps. 4 and 6.

10. *Lives*, 1:2.

11. *Johnsonian Miscellanies*, ed. G. B. Hill (Oxford: Clarendon Press, 1897), 1:287.

12. Madame d'Arblay, *Diary and Letters*, ed. Charlotte Barrett (London: Macmillan & Co., 1904-05), 2:271-72.

13. The conversation is completed in the following manner: " 'Sir, the man who has vigour, may walk to the east, just as well as to the west, if he happens to turn his head that way.' *Boswell*. 'But, sir, 'tis like walking up and down a hill; one man will naturally do the one better than the other. A hare will run up a hill best, from her fore-legs being short; a dog down.'—*Johnson*. 'Nay, sir; that is from mechanical powers. If you make mind mechanical, you may argue in that manner. One mind is a vice, and holds fast; there's a good memory. Another is a file; and he is a disputant, a controversialist. Another is a razor; and he is sarcastical.' " With what mechanical operation of the mind Johnson would associate Boswell, we must leave to speculation.

14. Fussell, *Life of Writing*, p. 50.

15. In *Rambler* 25 Johnson calls attention to one of the dangers following from the inculcation of the notion of a peculiar genius: "But of all the bugbears by which the *Infantes barbati*, boys both young and old, have been hitherto frighted from digressing into new tracts of learning, none has been more mischievously efficacious than an opinion that every kind of knowledge requires a peculiar genius, or mental constitution, framed for the reception of some ideas, and the exclusion of others; and that to him whose genius is not adapted to the study which he prosecutes, all labour shall be vain and fruitless. . . ."

16. Fussell, *Life of Writing*, p. 3.

17. Ibid., p. 43.

18. Ibid., p. 43. In all of this I do not mean to suggest that Johnson's interest in the law was casual or that he did not actively consider law as a profession. We know otherwise, of course. My point is simply that Fussell is inducting into the service of his controlling hypothesis particulars that would not volunteer for active duty if left to choose for themselves.

19. I have taken the quotation from Fussell, p. 44. For the identification of the justice as Saunders Welch and the full context of the passage, see Marshall Waingrow, ed., *The Correspondence and Other Papers of James Boswell relating to the Making of the Life of Johnson* (New York: McGraw-Hill, 1969), p. 249.

20. Fussell, *Life of Writing*, p. 46.

21. For my discussion of the passage from the *Journal*, see above, chap. 1.

22. Fussell, *Life of Writing*, p. 46.

23. "Uncoded self-expression" is no easy concept to apply to literature (or to writing of any kind), and in what sort of work such an impulse could culminate, I am unable to guess. See Appendix.

24. Incidentally, there is nothing in *Rambler* 152 that is inconsistent with the principles of literary judgment informing Johnson's discussions of tragedy, comedy, and rules in *Ramblers* 125, 156, 158. In all these essays we detect a steady preoccupation with a common set of critical questions and issues, a coherent set of assumptions about literature, and a persistent method of reasoning to conclusions from a discrete set of critical principles.

25. See Fussell, *Life of Writing*, pp. 47-48.

26. Ibid., p. 47.

27. R. W. Chapman, ed., *The Letters of Samuel Johnson* (Oxford: Clarendon Press, 1952), 2:228, no. 559. Hereafter references to Johnson's letters will be to this edition, and letters will be cited by number.

28. Fussell, *Life of Writing*, p. 47.

29. Ibid., p. 48.

30. Working from such a conception, he determined whether the work exhibited powers within or beyond the antecedently established range of accomplishment. It is by means of such a conception that Johnson is inclined to suspect—quite wrongly, as it happens in this case—that the *Tale of a Tub* was not written by Swift. This sort of conception operates throughout the *Lives*.

31. And, of course, we generally expect serious moral and didactic works to be expressions of positive belief, without assuming at the same time that the writer always exemplifies in practice what his work seriously recommends or endorses.

32. According to Fussell, Johnson's literary sensibility, "for all its appearance of judiciousness, is really madly irrational, unsystematic, impulsive, and untidy."

33. I realize that Fussell's critical method, limited to the inferential possibilities inherent in dialectical reasoning, does not encourage him to test his hypothesis against alternative hypotheses relating to the same material, but he might have enhanced the attractiveness of his self-expressive position by noting in detail how persistently over the years Johnson demands "self-expression" from a rich multiplicity of literary works.

34. Fussell, *Life of Writing*, p. 52.

35. Ibid.; brackets in original.

36. Even Fussell's aside is not self-evidently true. Johnson, to be sure, regularly attempts to determine whether works much praised owe their celebrity to intrinsic merits or to accidental, adventitious factors, but the plain, easily verifiable fact is that much praise does not *always* (or even regularly) trigger his skeptical contrariness. For example, like a great many of his predecessors, Johnson values the test of time (even though he does not always defer to its decisions); to Johnson, that work which, through variations of taste and changes of manners, continues to please can be accepted at least tentatively as having its basis of lasting appeal in an agreeableness to nature, in a conformity to truth. (Of course, if literature were answerable only to time, criticism, as Johnson well knew, would be both unnecessary and useless; the test of nature must oversee the decisions of time.) Subscription to any such notion as that advanced by Fussell would result in our being continually startled by the frequency with which Johnson concurs with general opinion; to read the *Lives of the Poets* under this ordinance would be too turbulent an experience. The aside, however, does serve Fussell's purposes; it brings to our minds a compulsively irascible and cantankerous Johnson whose judgments emanate not from critical principles, but from a contentious, querulous sensibility. (Johnson rarely "talks for victory" in *print*, if by talking for victory we mean the Johnsonian tendency to close debate by fair means or foul.)

37. Fussell, *Life of Writing*, pp. 52-53.

38. Ibid., p. 53.

39. *Adventurer* 92, slightly altered.

40. Fussell, *Life of Writing*, p. 53.

41. Ibid., p. 54.

42. Ibid.

43. Ibid., pp. 54-55.

44. If nothing else, Fussell has here cleared the way for the admission of a massive number of new prosodic distinctions into our glossaries of literary terms: as we discern (i.e., diagnose) variations in metrical practice, we may add to the regular diastolic-systolic meter such items as arrythmic meter, bradycardiac meter, endomyocardiac meter, extrasystolic meter, and discuss metrical problems, of course, in terms of febrillation and myocardial infarction. Of course, Fussell's particular critical condition would have to be diagnosed as "hardening of the categories." (This delightful phrase has been borrowed—appropriated—from M. H. Abrams's *The Mirror and the Lamp*.)

45. It is interesting that both Sigworth and Fussell attempt to gain points at the expense of Johnson's memory.

46. Fussell, *Life of Writing*, p. 55.

47. Apparently for the sake of brevity, Fussell, quoting next a long section of the critique of *Lycidas*, italicizes those words and phrases which betray how the "antithetic critical emphases . . . interweave as Johnson proceeds" (we are to divine which of the italicized items belong to which of the emphases) to produce a fabric of mixed texture, "like a fabric made by weaving together the inorganic [rhetoric? affective?] and the organic [self-expressive?], steel filaments with silk:

> When Cowley tells of Hervey that they studied together, it is easy *to suppose* how much *he must miss* the companion of his labors and the partner of his discoveries; but what image of tenderness *can be excited by* these lines:
>
>> We drove afield, and both together heard
>> What time the grey fly winds her sultry horn,
>> Batt'ning our flocks with the fresh dews of night.
>
> *We know that they never drove afield, and that they had no flocks to batten;* and though it be allowed that *the representation* may be allegorical, the true meaning is so uncertain and remote that *it is never sought* because *it cannot be known* when it is found.

I shall not preempt discovery by unseasonable disclosures, like Fussell, but rely instead on the perspicacity and assiduity of the reader to disentangle the several threads of antithetic significance in the passage. Fussell abandons argument altogether here and entertains the reader with rough verbal equivalents of pictorial "slides," each italicized item a "shot" of one or the other distinctive landscape of Johnson's critical mind.

48. This is the first and only indication we have, by the way, that Johnson could have taken the *whole* poem as either expression or artifact.

49. Fussell, *Life of Writing*, pp. 56-57; emphasis added.

50. In this particular poem, of course, the "religious" fault is intimately related to the "psychological" fault, since, for Johnson, the inherent improbability of this combination of trifling fictions and awful truths on a serious occasion at this point—postpagan point—in human history naturally brings dissatisfaction to the mind of the general reader, living at this point in human history; by this commingling Milton does not so much corrupt common understanding as violate its knowledge.

51. The truths to which Johnson refers make no contact with the world of rhetoric, and he nowhere suggests that such combinations might incline the reader to think that pagan myth and Christian truth are of "equal efficacy," that such combinations might embolden people on the verge of theological commitment to subscribe to the articles of faith inherent in pagan myth. What he denounces is the implicit, if unintended, impiety and indecency of the combination. Johnson's focus is on Milton's unintentional impiety, not on the jeopardy in which the reader's soul may be placed as a result of reading the poem. Whenever I read the section of the critique on the "grosser" fault—and so much else by Johnson—I am reminded of a distinction that Kenneth Burke made years ago (having forgotten where—in one of the "Motives" books, I think—I perhaps misremember its significance also) between *tone* and *voice, tone* being essentially suasive, hortatory language, language that, appealing to our will, understanding, or emotion, serves the end, however subtly or indirectly, of affecting our feelings, directing our behavior, or altering our views, and *voice* being that language which has an unanswerable *ipse dixit* quality about it, that language which, even when personally disagreeable to us, does not in any way look for its fulfillment and certification in our "O.K." "In the beginning was the word and the word was God" is, for example, pure voice. Having no immediate or overriding anxiety about the subtle theological harm that *Lycidas* might cause, Johnson, speaking in full-throated ease, simply "vocalizes" what,

make no mistake about it, is the case. What many modern readers, especially under-graduates, find particularly offensive about Johnson (as he is usually encountered in selected portions of the *Life*) is precisely his vocality. Attentive as we all are to the promises of the fatal charmer, undergraduates are peculiarly inclined to listen with credulity to the whispers of hope and to neglect or deride the plain-spoken, hard, yet finally comforting and energizing wisdom of the *voice* of experience, thus failing through deafness or vociferation to recognize that only he who has listened closely to the *tonality* of experience can speak with its *voice*.

52. Fussell, *Life of Writing*, p. 57.

53. Ibid., p. 42.

54. That Fussell is inordinately impressed by Johnson's inconsistencies, however, is con-firmed in part by what he says after mentioning Johnson's fondness for an honest registra-tion of empirical reality: "Boswell was fascinated with Johnson's massive inconsistencies, and it is the theme of those inconsistencies that provides him with his fully orchestrated conclusion to the *Life of Johnson*, a book which is really a series of variations on Boswell's point that 'Man is, in general, made up of contradictory qualities.' " Anyone who reads Boswell's *Life* through, coming finally to

> Such was Samuel Johnson, a man whose talents, acquirements, and virtues were so extraordinary, that the more his character is considered, the more he will be regarded by the present age and by posterity, with admiration and reverence,

must surely be made uncomfortable by Fussell's offhanded but characteristic remarks, since it is clear, I think, that the *Life* would not have the powerful effect it has upon us if its multifarious details were not governed by Boswell's complex, but single and coherent conception of Johnson's distinct moral and intellectual character. In my view Ralph Rader has brought us very close to a full understanding of the synthesizing formal principle of Boswell's massive achievement:

> The subject of Boswell's book is not the life of Johnson but the *character* of Johnson as revealed in the facts of his life; and his purpose is to make us feel that admiration and reverence which is the natural emotive consequence of full empathetic perception of character. . . . [Boswell] had within his mind not a series of disjunctive photographic impressions but a single dynamic image of Johnson which, though it derived from innumerable manifestations of Johnson's character, was nevertheless quite independ-ent of any particular manifestation and even independent of their sum. . . . the par-ticulars are not a heterogeneous collection of facts but a homogeneous presentation of character. Each of the particulars is displayed by Boswell, to the degree which each inherently permits, as an epiphany of an infinitely varied but always single character. Boswell's image of Johnson is the selective, constructive, and controlling principle of the *Life*, the omnipresent element which vivifies and is made vivid in the whole. The image is the unity—the real and living unity—of the *Life*.

("Literary Form in Factual Narrative: The Example of Boswell's Johnson," in *Essays in Eighteenth-Century Biography*, ed., Philip Daghlian (Bloomington: Indiana University Press, 1968), pp. 6, 7, 9.) In *Hester Lynch Piozzi* James L. Clifford offers an assessment of Boswell's achievement that is compatible with Rader's judgment: "Boswell's superiority over his rival biographers . . . lies not only in the completeness of his picture of Johnson, but also in the *significant definition*, the delicate shading, and the *general coherence* of his portrait" (p. 357; emphasis added).

55. Fussell, *Life of Writing*, p. 58.

56. Ibid.; emphasis added.

57. Of course, adequacy of expression may certainly be facilitated by genuine emotional turbulence—we can always feel more than we can imagine; and, conversely, inadequacy of expression may certainly be read, in many instances, as a sign of inauthentic, feigned emotion, since the man actually in love will presumably give expression to what we can credit as possible or probable to a man in love.

Chapter 3

1. Jean H. Hagstrum, *Samuel Johnson's Literary Criticism* (Minneapolis: University of Minnesota Press, 1952), p. 45.

2. Walter Jackson Bate, *The Achievement of Samuel Johnson* (Oxford: Oxford University Press, 1955), p. 219.

3. Arieh Sachs, *Passionate Intelligence: Imagination and Reason in the Work of Samuel Johnson* (Baltimore, Md.: Johns Hopkins Press, 1967).

4. Donald J. Greene, review of *Passionate Intelligence* by Arieh Sachs, *Studies in Burke and his Time* 9 (Winter 1968) pp. 877-78; my brackets. Of another critic's playing this sort of game with another common pair of opposites—generality and particularity—W. R. Keast has written: "His adoption of an opposition between generality and particularity as the focus of his analysis, and his simple extension of the context of statements by Johnson containing these words to include a group of critics so miscellaneous as Longinus, Dennis, Addison, and Blair concentrates attention on the material similarities of vocabulary and doctrine among critics but disregards the essential differences in ends, problems, and methods by which vocabulary becomes significant and doctrine intelligible." (W. R. Keast, review of "The Background and Development in English Criticism of the Theories of Generality and Particularity," by Scott Elledge, *Philological Quarterly* 27 (April 1948); p. 132.

5. Greene, review, p. 879.

6. In fairness to both Greene and Sachs, it should be noted that in his review Greene also says: "Mr. Sachs is often right about Johnson, and his *apercus* are frequently more accurate than those of earlier writers on Johnson." Nevertheless, as Greene persistently makes clear, Sach's "rightness" is not a consequence of either his critical principles or his method of reasoning.

7. In *Eighteenth-Century Studies* 4 (1971): p. 184-98.

8. Krieger, "Fiction, Nature, and Literary Kinds," p. 186. Of course, in neither Hume nor Johnson is the "belief" in general nature founded on rationalist assumptions, and we have absolutely no reason to believe that under the guise of an empiricist Johnson was a receiver of stolen Cartesian (i.e., rationalist) goods. To both Johnson and Hume, general human nature was a matter of fact and experience, not a matter of "reason."

9. Krieger, "Fiction, Nature, and Literary Kinds," p. 187; emphasis on "aberration" added.

10. Ibid.; emphasis added.

11. Ibid., p. 188.

12. What Krieger offers us here is not *exegesis*, but *eisegesis*.

13. It may well be that in the real world Icarus plummets to his destruction while we go about our business indifferent to his fate, but we become disengaged from our indifference as he engages our attention. (Otherwise what would be the point of Brueghel's painting or Auden's

poem?) In the real world a great deal happens at once, but as we selectively attend to the same "happenings," we happen to be similarly affected by them. In the face of literature, we attend to what the writer forces upon our attention, and we are similarly moved by what we notice because, for the most part, we share the same opinions concerning what it is that we are attending to. And we share the same opinions because the generative principles, the structural bases of our natures are generally the same, because the "transformational rules" for our emotional inferences are essentially the same. Johnson's judgments are so frequently accurate precisely because he so clearly discerns the uniform operations of our minds in the endless variety of proportion and innumerable modes of combination.

14. I do not entirely understand why a particular would necessarily cease to be a "true" particular if I took it into my head to discuss it in terms of the kinds of relations in whch it did or could participate. And if all were indeed particular—if all particulars resolutely insisted on their own particularity—how could any particular be made up of parts (where would particularity begin), and how would I arrive at any notion of *the particular* or be able to discuss *particulars?* The fact is that if any man really believed what Krieger attributes to Johnson, he would simply not be able to express his belief in terms—in a language—that would not give the lie to what he was saying. If he found the terms, who would be capable of understanding them?

15. What kind of a particular is a *mode*, especially a mode "of combination"?

16. Krieger, "Fiction, Nature, and Literary Kinds," p. 88; emphasis on "forgetting" added. Like Sigworth and Fussell, Krieger catches Johnson in the act of forgetting.

17. As Keast said long ago, "the infinite accidental modifications in the actual manner in which the passions do their uniform work afford novelty and variety" to representations of life—novelty and variety, that is, of the sort comprehended under a system of natural human probabilities, of general operations of the mind. ("The Theoretical Foundations of Johnson's Criticism," in *Critics and Criticism*, ed., R. S. Crane [Chicago: University of Chicago Press, 1952], p. 400.)

18. Krieger, "Fiction, Nature, and Literary Kinds," p. 189.

19. Ibid.

20. Ibid., p. 191.

21. Johnson assumes, of course, that Shakespeare could frequently have made such a distribution or shown such a disapprobation without deviating from nature or probability.

22. Krieger, "Fiction, Nature, and Literary Kinds," p. 191.

23. Ibid., p. 193.

24. Ibid., p. 194.

25. Ibid.; emphasis added.

26. In spite of the evidence of the text, we are to assume that throughout the "Preface" Johnson is working on Krieger's aesthetic-metaphysic problem; in spite of the fact that Johnson is addressing specific and distinct problems in the "unities" section, in spite of the fact that nothing that Johnson says here about consciousness of fiction invalidates, undermines, or conflicts with what he has said earlier, we are to assume that antecedent issues would have been quickly settled if Johnson had not forgotten his consciousness of our consciousness of fiction.

27. Krieger, "Fiction, Nature, and Literary Kinds," pp. 196-97.

28. Ibid., p. 197. Of course, both the "existentially blind unity" and the "anarchic variety" are functions of Krieger's categorical imperatives.

29. Krieger, "Fiction, Nature, and Literary Kinds," p. 198.

30. With a little ingenuity, Johnson, by this method of reasoning, could be quartered with Sidney, Aristotle, Arnold, Boileau, Frye, Dennis, Eliot, etc.

31. Just as there is no reason to assume, prior to analysis, that two psychological critics share any assumptions about the nature of mind, ask similar questions about the relations between psychology and literature, or employ in their respective arguments similar systems of inference, so there is similarly no reason to assume that between two writings within the broad class of "qualitative" criticism there is any substantive agreement.

32. What is true of two writings by different writers is likewise true of two writings by the same writer; i.e., we cannot simply assume, on the basis of surface similarities, that two passages from different contexts enforce the same point or, on the other hand, assume, on the basis of surface dissimilarity, that two passages from different contexts contradict one another.

33. The tragic nature of these plays is established when various aspects of the "thought" in the plays can be read in such a way as to reveal, at some level of abstraction, distinguishable kinds of "good." There may be some disagreement among critics about the "goods" involved, but no critic adopting this position could possibly walk away from these plays (and countless others) without finding his tragic "goods."

34. Crane, *Idea of the Humanities,* 2:30. I have substituted *interpreter* and *criticism* for Crane's *scholar* and *research.*

35. Throughout this section on the cognitive adequacy of hypotheses I have been indebted to Stephen Pepper's *World Hypotheses: A Study in Evidence* (Berkeley and Los Angeles: University of California Press, 1942), p. 118 et passim.

Chapter 4

1. Jean H. Hagstrum, *Samuel Johnson's Literary Criticism* (Minneapolis: University of Minnesota Press, 1952), pp. vii-viii.

2. The full statement is: "Mr. Leavis is not a critic who works by elaborated theory. As between Coleridge, on the other hand, and Dr. Johnson and Matthew Arnold, on the other, he has declared his strong preference for the two latter—for the critic, that is, who requires no formulated first principles for his judgment but only the sensibility that is the whole response of his whole being." "The Moral Tradition," *New Yorker,* September 24, 1949, p. 89.

3. In "Johnson as Monarch," *Essays in Retrospect: Collected Articles and Addresses* (New Haven, Conn.: Yale University Press, 1948), p. 28.

4. Keast, "Theoretical Foundations," p. 390.

5. Fussell, *Life of Writing,* p. 60.

6. "Johnson's Dictionary," in *New Light on Dr. Johnson,* ed., Frederick W. Hilles (New Haven, Conn.: Yale University Press, 1959), p. 71.

7. "Dr. Johnson's Spectacles," in *New Light on Dr. Johnson,* pp. 177-87.

8. Hagstrum, *Johnson's Criticism,* pp. vii-viii.

9. R. S. Crane, *The Languages of Criticism and the Structure of Poetry* (Toronto: University of Toronto Press, 1953), p. 58. On the same matter, Crane, in slightly more specific terms, says: "It is noteworthy . . . that Johnson tended to discuss pastoral, comedy, and tragicomedy chiefly in terms of reasons common to all poetry or even all discourse and derived from his characteristic distinction between general and particular nature and his insistence on resolving all poetic value, whatever its species, into a union of truth (in the meaning of 'sentiments to which every bosom returns an echo') with novelty and variety." *Critics and Criticism*, p. 384.

10. "Preface to Shakespeare."

11. *Johnsonian Miscellanies*, 1:187.

12. Sigworth, "Johnson's *Lycidas*," p. 160. Incidentally, the evidence on which this claim is principally based is an alleged contradiction between views expressed in the critique of *Lycidas* and in *Rambler* 36, on pastoral poetry; as we shall see shortly, Sigworth has made an unfortunate choice, since there is nothing in the critique incompatible with the *Rambler* essay.

13. It is worth remembering that not one of our critics gives us sufficient reasons to believe that the contradiction or polarity attributed to Johnson either obtains or is characteristic of his thought. In general, the conflict or discrepancy is assumed, and the prosecution rests its case after exhibiting several passages, believing that further testimony is unnecessary and that the only business remaining is to listen, with approval, to the verdict that is consistent with the "self-evidential" facts of the case.

14. In *Homage to John Dryden*.

15. Because, as Keast says, "the kinds of critical problems with which he deals, the particular doctrines and judgments he puts forward, the stands he takes on the leading critical issues of his day, and the methods of argument he habitually employs can all be traced . . . to a coherent view of literature and a coherent body of assumptions concerning both its practice and evaluation." "Theoretical Foundations," p. 391.

16. In *Critics and Criticism*, ed., R. S. Crane (Chicago and London: University of Chicago Press, 1952), pp. 389-407.

17. Keast, "Theoretical Foundations," p. 393.

18. Ibid. For example, comedy must deal with characters of low rank; the speakers in pastoral poems must use rustic diction, etc.

19. Keast, "Theoretical Foundations," p. 394.

20. In *Rambler* 121, for example, Johnson notes: "The roads of science are narrow, so that they who travel them, must either follow or meet one another; but in the boundless regions of possibility, which fiction [Johnson's specific references in this paper are to poems] claims for her dominion, there are surely a thousand recesses unexplored, a thousand flowers unplucked, a thousand fountains unexplored, combinations of imagery yet unobserved. . . ." See also *Rambler* 158.

21. Keast, "Theoretical Foundations," p. 395.

22. Ibid.

23. Ibid.

24. Ibid.; emphasis added.

25. Ibid., pp. 398-99.

26. Ibid., p. 399.

27. *Rambler* 92.

28. Keast, "Theoretical Foundations," p. 399; emphasis added.

29. Ibid.

30. Ibid., p. 400.

31. Ibid., p. 401.

32. See ibid., pp. 402-3.

33. For Keast's full discussion of the author, see ibid., pp. 403-4.

34. The reader should recognize that in presenting Keast's argument in an abbreviated, truncated form, I have restricted myself to the bare bones of his case, omitting much of the evidence on which he relies and some of the major points he makes, points not immediately relevant to the following discussions of pastoral, elegy, and the critique of *Lycidas*. (For example, I refer only obliquely to Keast's examination of Johnson's reliance on the "circumstantial method" to determine what manifest excellence may be attributed to the native powers of the author.) To understand Keast's full argument, the reader must, of course, consult the original essay.

Chapter 5

1. By *ideas* Johnson, of course, means not so much "thought" as "sense impressions of objects," i.e., imagery or images.

2. Keast, "Theoretical Foundations," p. 401.

3. In the "Life of Waller," Johnson says: "From poetry the reader justly expects, and from good poetry always obtains, the enlargement of his comprehension and the elevation of his fancy. . . ." (*Lives*, 1:292)

4. "Preface to Shakespeare."

5. It is well to remember that Johnson did not look upon the ocean until he toured Plymouth with Reynolds in 1762, during their trip to Reynold's native Devonshire.

6. Johnson is referring to writers of modern English pastorals.

7. Since it might possibly be asserted, in opposition to Johnson's judgment, that because contests in life are often decided in favor of a contestant who has displayed no conspicuous superiority of ability, the poem, measured by Johnson's own standards, deserves praise—our pleasure should follow immediately upon our recognition of the truth of the representation—it is worth noting that Johnson nowhere endorses the "imitative fallacy"; i.e., he nowhere suggests, for example, that to convey boredom properly the writer must "excite" boredom in the reader. An event or sentiment to which we are indifferent in life will be greeted with frigid indifference when it is presented in writing. The pleasure that we derive from a sentiment is relative to the degree that "it is both true and unobvious, to the inherent human relevance of its substance, and to the concision and force of its expression" (Rader, *Essays in Eighteenth-Century Biography*, pp. 20-21). If what is said is both true and obvious, what it lacks in dignity of thought must be compensated for in the happiness or novelty of its expression. A represented action or passion will be pleasing to the extent that the writer awakens our interest in the subject (i.e., a person with a morally determinate character) of the action or passion. The representation of what would provoke pain in the spectator if it

were "really" happening is pleasurable under certain circumstances, for a variety of reasons: for example, a painful circumstance may provide the occasion for the display of a character's essential virtue, which display is naturally pleasing—our pleasure in Beowulf's actions is, to a large extent, proportionate to the dreadfulness of his situation and the strength and ferocity of his hateful antagonist; his actions ratify his wisdom and virtue and gratify our hopes and expectations. Also, our consciousness of fiction, when we view tragedy, for example, at once allows us to be excited by those emotions which would actually be activated by "real" events and blocks any impulse to take steps to alleviate the witnessed distress or to interrupt the action; our freedom from responsibility—realities are brought to mind, not witnessed, and thus we do not have to place ourselves in jeopardy or, more important, suffer the reflective consequences of inaction—permits us to witness, without self-recrimination, the fulfillment of our hopes and expectations, which are, in general, directed toward the best—however painful or terrible—that is possible, under the circumstances, for those whose character and behavior have engaged our kind interest and concern. And so on. Faithful descriptions of physical nature please immediately because they square with common experience and mediately because they trigger pleasant associations.

8. See Reynolds's "Discourse" for 1778.

9. I here refer, of course, to one of the most famous passages of the *Essay:*

> True wit is nature to advantage drest,
> What oft was thought, but ne'er so well exprest,
> Something, whose truth convinc'd at sight we find,
> That gives us back the image of our mind.

(11. 297-300)

10. *Lives*, 3:441-42; emphasis added.

11. Keast, "Theoretical Foundations," p. 400.

12. "Pope," *Lives*, 3:235.

13. *Lives*, 3:316-19.

14. The inherent improbability forces dissatisfaction on our minds.

15. *Lives*, 3:324; emphasis added.

16. For example, those critics who have been led into their hypothesis "by considering pastoral, not in general, as a representation of rural nature, and consequently as exhibiting the ideas and sentiments of those, whoever they are, to whom the country affords pleasure or employment, but simply as a dialogue or narrative of men actually tending sheep" in that age when "the care of . . . flocks was the employment of the wisest and greatest men" (*Rambler* 37).

17. It might be useful to recall what Johnson says of Arcadia in the "Life of Gay": "There is something in the poetical Arcadia so remote from known reality and speculative possibility, that we can never support its representation through a long work. A Pastoral of an hundred lines may be endured; but who will hear of sheep and goats, and myrtle bowers and purling rivulets, through five acts? Such scenes please barbarians in the dawn of literature, and children in the dawn of life; but will be for the most part, thrown away as men grow wise, and nations grow learned" (*Lives*, 2:284-85).

18. "Waller," *Lives*, 1:271.

19. *Rasselas*, chap. 47.

20. Of description, characterization, and so forth.

21. James Boswell, *The Life of Samuel Johnson*, ed., George Birkbeck Hill, rev. L. F. Powell (Oxford: Oxford University Press, 1934-50), 4:175 n. 4.

Chapter 6

1. Warren Fleischauer, "Johnson, *Lycidas* and the Norms of Criticism," in *Johnsonian Studies*, ed., Magdi Wahba (Cairo, 1962), p. 247.

2. I do not accept Arthur Sherbo's attribution of "An Essay on Elegies" to Johnson. I am convinced by my own examination of "An Essay" and by the evidence and arguments that have accumulated in response to Sherbo's case that Johnson could not have written the work. The critical principles and assumptions informing "An Essay" simply are not compatible with those underlying Johnson's criticism in general or his conception of elegy in particular. Those readers who wish to examine the particulars of the controversy should read Sherbo's "The Uses and Abuses of Internal Evidence," Ephim G. Fogel's "Salmons in Both, or Some Caveats for Canonical Scholars," and "A Reply to Professor Fogel." These articles are conveniently available in *Evidence for Authorship: Essays on Problems of Attribution*, ed., David V. Erdman and Ephim G. Fogel (Ithaca, N.Y.: Cornell University Press, 1966). Two subsequent articles should also be consulted: Robert Folkenflik's "Johnson and 'An Essay on Elegies,' " and Sherbo's "A Reply." Both of these pieces are in the *Bulletin of the New York Public Library* 77 (Winter 1974): 188-99; 200-204.

3. In this chapter I concentrate on funeral elegies, since I am leading to a discussion of *Lycidas*. I say little about mournful "elegiac" poems of the disappointed love or the "tragic" nature of life variety or about the various verse and rhyme patterns of "elegiac" poetry. Throughout I focus on those aspects of sentiment, imagery, diction, rhyme, and numbers which bear in some way on funeral elegy and on Johnson's examination of *Lycidas*. Most of Johnson's remarks on "elegy" are restricted to laments for the death of a friend or loved one; he is relatively silent on "amorous elegies." If we reject the attribution of "An Essay on Elegies" to Johnson, then Johnson's most extensive comments on amorous elegy and the elegiac stanza are found in the last three paragraphs of the "Life of Hammond." Johnson finds in Hammond's *Love Elegies* "neither passion, nature, nor manners," and he "finds it difficult to tell" why "Hammond or other writers have thought the quatrain of ten syllables elegiack" (*Lives*, 2:315-16).

4. Emphasis added throughout.

5. Some of the peculiar distinctiveness of the epitaph is attributable to its being an inscription on a tomb and its location in or near a church; in only one essential respect is the epitaph differentiated from the elegy, according to Johnson: an epitaph "debars the admission of all lighter or gayer ornaments. In this it is that the style of an epitaph necessarily differs from that of an elegy." The epitaph has throughout an "air of solemnity," but although the elegy admits some lightness and gaiety, it is, by virtue of the seriousness of its occasion—which it shares with the epitaph—always "superior to the *glitter of slight* ornaments." The epitaph prohibits entirely what the elegy admits sparingly and in moderation. For Johnson, the chief difference between the two is primarily technical. I am here quoting from Johnson's "Essay on Epitaphs" in *The Works of Samuel Johnson* (Oxford, 1825), 5:262. All quotations from the "Essay" are taken from this edition. The phrase *superior to the glitter of slight ornaments* is from the "Life of Shenstone" (*Lives*, 3:355).

6. "Dryden," *Lives*, 1:442.

7. "Hammond," *Lives*, 2:315.

8. "Milton," *Lives*, 1:163.

9. "Cowley," *Lives*, 1:37.

10. The Earl of Chesterfield, according to Dr. Maty.

11. "Hammond," *Lives*, 2:314-15; emphasis added.

12. In the end, I suspect that—like those grown men in the shadows of whose conscious-nesses there always lurks some inexplicable and unshakeable guilt, animated undoubtedly years ago by some fearful lesson concerning the infinite corruptibility or concupiscence of the flesh—we today shudder guiltily and automatically at the sight of Johnson's "sincerity" as a result of some horrible story heard long ago about the "intentional fallacy."

13. Claudius, in Act 1 of *Hamlet*, for instance.

14. *Lives*, 1:20; emphasis added.

15. *Poetics*, chap. 17. See *The Basic Works of Aristotle*, ed., Richard McKeon (New York: Random House, 1941). p. 1472.

16. "Shenstone," *Lives*, 3:355.

17. Ibid.; emphasis added.

18. Johnson's preference is for pauses at the fourth or sixth syllables: "The noblest and most majestic pauses which our versification admits, are upon the fourth and sixth syllables, which are both strongly sounded in a *pure* and *regular* verse [i.e., an iambic pentameter verse], and at either of which the line is so divided, that both members participate of harmony. . . . But far above all others, if I can give any credit to my own ear, is the rest upon the sixth syllable, which taking in a complete compass of sound, such as is sufficient to constitute one of our lyrick measures, makes a full and solemn close. Some passages which conclude at this stop I could never read without some strong emotions of delight or admiration" (*Rambler* 90). With matters of poetic music, as with larger issues, Johnson has his principles from reason (in this case, as a result of reasoning on the nature of the English language) and experience. *Rambler* 90 (and other writings as well) should remind us that Johnson had a fine ear for the music of poetry, especially those of us who tend to find in Johnson's defective auditory organs convenient excuses or justifications for his "metrical" opinions. The reader of poetry, no more than the composer or reader of a musical score, lives under no tyrannic domination of the "physical" ear; the competent reader hears with his mind, not his ear.

19. In the "Life of Roscommon," Johnson says: "Blank verse left merely to its numbers has little operation on the ear or mind: it can hardly support itself without bold figures and striking images" (*Lives*, 1:237).

20. "Milton," *Lives*, 1:192-93; emphasis added. It is important to remember that Johnson concludes this section by saying: "But whatever be the advantage of rhyme, I cannot prevail on myself to wish that Milton had been a rhymer, for I cannot wish his work to be other than it is [Johnson is, of course, speaking generally; there are some pieces that he could wish to be other than they are, both doctrinally and metrically]; yet like other heroes he is to be admired rather than imitated. He that thinks himself capable of astonishing may write blank verse, but those that only hope to please must condescend to rhyme."

21. A full exposition of the prosodic principles informing Johnson's approach to poetry as "metrical composition" would cast additional light on his characteristic habit of reasoning

from effects to their necessary, empirically identifiable causes but, unfortunately, take us well beyond the central concerns of this essay. Those, however, who are inclined to believe that, for such technical discussions, Johnson merely applied to the cases at hand what the authority of, say, Edward Bysshe's *Art of English Poetry* would justify, should run the risk of being disabused of their opinions by considering, at the very least, Johnson's remarks on mixed measures, elision of vowels, the distribution of pauses, and representative meter in *Ramblers* 86, 88, 90, 92, 94.

22. The editors of the Yale edition of *The Rambler* correctly observe that Johnson's "discussion of inversion of accent is typical of eighteenth-century prosodic theory. Initial inversion [as in 'maker omnipotent'] is always sanctioned [though certainly not *always* by Johnson] (cf., e.g., John Mason, *Essay on the Power of Numbers*, 1749, p. 43; John Newberry, *Art of Poetry*, 1762, I. 11; Lord Kames, *Elements of Criticism*, 1762, II. 384-485); while medial inversion is usually more strongly censured than it is by SJ (cf. e.g., Edward Bysshe, *Art of English Poetry*, 4th ed., 1710, pp. 5-6; Daniel Webb, *Observations*, 1769, p. 107 n)." Note to *Rambler* 86; see *The Rambler*, ed. W. J. Bate and Albrecht B. Strauss (New Haven: Yale University Press, 1969), 4:92.

23. Fleischauer, "Norms of Criticism," pp. 242-43.

24. Ibid., p. 243.

25. Joseph Epes Brown, *The Critical Opinions of Samuel Johnson* (New York: Russell and Russell, 1961), p. 126.

26. In *Spectator* 297.

27. "Milton," *Lives*, 1:189-91.

28. By the time Pope wrote his Pastorals he had "obtained sufficient power of language and skill in metre to exhibit a series of versification, which had in English no precedent . . ." (*Lives*, 3:224-25).

29. Boswell, *Life*, 3:159.

30. For this list I am indebted to Fleischauer's article and Johnson's *Dictionary*.

31. Fleischauer, "Norms of Criticism," p. 246.

32. Ibid.

33. Ibid., p. 247. Throughout this discussion of diction, I have relied on Fleischauer's article, especially on his analysis of *harsh*. The reader interested in pursuing the matter of "harshness" further should, if he aspires to thoroughness, set out with Fleischauer's article and Johnson's *Dictionary* in hand. Commenting on one aspect of Milton's style, Keats writes: "I have given up *Hyperion*—there were too many Miltonic inversions in it—Miltonic verse cannot be written but in an artful or rather artist's humour. I wish to give myself up to other sensations. English ought to be kept up." See John Keats, *Selected Poems and Letters*, ed., Douglas Bush (Boston: Houghton Mifflin Co., 1959), p. 355.

34. Boswell, *Life*, 3:158-59.

35. "West," *Lives*, 3:332-33.

36. "The Pastoral Elegy and Milton's *Lycidas*," *PMLA* 25 (1910): 403.

37. "Milton," *Lives*, 1:163-65.

38. I have borrowed "single speaker in a closed situation" from Elder Olson; see "An Outline of Poetic Theory," in *Critics and Criticism*, ed., R. S. Crane (Chicago: University of Chicago Press, 1952), pp. 546-66.

39. *Rambler* 37.

Appendix

1. Fussell, *Life of Writing*, p. 63.

2. Here I would treat all manifestations of the habitual or customary as *conventional*.

3. E. D. Hirsch, Jr., *Validity in Interpretation* (New Haven and London: Yale University Press, 1967), p. 105. Incidentally, Hirsch finds confirmation for the general point in Gombrich's *Art and Illusion* (New York, 1960), p. 25: Gombrich "quotes approvingly Quintilian's remark, 'which craftsman has not made a vessel of a shape he has never seen?' and comments: 'It is an important reminder, but it does not account for the fact that even the shape of the new vessel will somehow belong to the same family of forms as those the craftsman has seen.' This tendency of the mind to use old types as the foundation for new ones is, of course, even more pronounced when communication or representation is involved. Not every convention could be changed at once, even if the craftsman were capable of such divine creativity, because then his creation would be totally incommunicable. . . . The point is stated pithily by Gombrich: 'Variants can be controlled and checked only against a set of invariants.' " See Hirsch, p. 104.

4. Frank Kermode, *The Sense of an Ending* (New York: Oxford University Press, 1967), p. 102.

5. Fussell, *Life of Writing*, p. 35.

6. Keast, "Theoretical Foundations," p. 395.

7. *Rambler* 37.

8. See chap. 2 for a full discussion of Fussell's approach to Johnson's criticism.

9. R. S. Crane, *The Languages of Criticism and the Structure of Poetry* (Toronto: University of Toronto Press, 1953), p. 165-68.

10. In the chapter from which the above remarks were taken, "Toward a More Adequate Criticism of Poetic Structure."

11. If only because he, along with so many others, is not interested in questions of genre or in genre distinctions.

12. Part of this illustration has been taken from Julián Márias's "Philosophic Truth and the Metaphoric System," in *Interpretation: The Poetry of Meaning*, ed., Stanley Romaine Hopper and David L. Miller (New York: Harcourt, Brace, and World, 1967), pp. 40-53.

13. Fussell has forewarned us that the facts of writing, "Like 'the facts of life' . . . may seem at first glance a little startling, but like those other facts, once we're in on the secret, we wonder how we could have been so ignorant before."

14. Fussell, *Life of Writing*, p. 35.

15. Of course, to be truly faithful to Fussell's position, we would have to supply the corollaries for writings belonging to the worlds of science, history, philosophy, psychology, etc., but in deference to Occam, let us resist the temptation to multiply propositions.

16. This quotation is taken from Fussell, *Life of Writing*, p. 36.

17. Fussell, *Life of Writing*, p. 37.

18. Ibid.

19. Ibid. In substituting *medium* for Frye's *form* Fussell is perhaps not confirming Frye's point. At any rate, Fussell here equates form and medium.

20. In general, "knowledge of genre" involves little more than the association of some few "material" aspects of works with various class names. When we think of *novel*, for example, we generally have very few differentiating characteristics in mind.

21. No poem, of course, plays by completely unique rules (we, at least, could not participate in—i.e., understand—a game played by such rules), but by "rules" that we have the capacity to understand, by virtue of our linguistic skills and cognitive abilities (which enable us, as we successively "guess at" a writer's "intentions," to rule meaning possibilities and potentialities both in and out). Moreover, our cognitive and linguistic powers and limitations are also those of the writer. The range of meanings that the writer can express is limited, ultimately, by precisely the same intellectual forces that control our understanding and, proximately, by the "type" imperatives that are set in motion by his successive choices. For writer and reader alike, early decisions impose severe restrictions on the subsequent development (or, in the case of the reader, understanding) of a work.

22. Our conception, that is, of the whole to which we assume that the successive details stand in necessary or meaningful relation. Whether they do or not, we assume, I think, that linguistic details gathered together in one discrete piece of writing somehow belong together, that words so gathered together stop following one another for some reason at some appropriate point, that, in short, words set in motion, presumably, for some purpose, tend naturally toward a point of stillness, where nothing more can or needs to be said.

23. I have taken this concept from Elder Olson's "William Empson, Contemporary Criticism, and Poetic Diction," which appears in *Critics and Criticism*, pp. 45-82.

24. Arthur K. Moore, "Formalist Criticism and Literary Forms," *Journal of Aesthetics and Art Criticism* 19 (Fall 1970): 23.

25. Fussell, *Life of Writing*, p. 37.

26. I am referring here to "artificial" forms (plays, lyric poems, sonatas, paintings, etc.), not to "natural" forms (trees, shrubs, horses, men, etc.).

27. For example, no character discusses jealousy as such, but only as much of the topic as is dictated by his particular dilemma or his particular way of construing the topic and its implications.

28. Crane, *Languages of Criticism*, p. 154.

29. If a writer happens to accept as valid or appropriate certain conventions sponsored by particular notions of propriety or decorum—that in a tragedy, for example, a king should speak in a "high" style and exhibit no habits of thought or behavior that general opinion associates (again as a result of particular notions of propriety and decorum) with "low" characters—he is still faced with the practical problem of making a determinate character functional in his play and necessary to its sequence of events; i.e., the conventions define a more or less specific boundary of permissibility (beyond which is the area of the artistic

"thou shalt not"), but they do not determine how the area of legitimacy is to be filled in. A critic, if he happens to be interested in such matters, may recover the reasoning governing the way the writer actually filled in that area, but he cannot arrive at any very useful grounds of necessity in the actual details by reasoning from what is stated or implied in the conventions. In other words, knowledge of these "genre requirements"—and I consent to call them such because they have been treated as such by some writers and critics—may tell you why a king did *not* do something other than what he did (why Cato was not a drunk), but not why he behaved as he did.

30. In passing, one wonders how the critic can possibly go about the business of separating the features of genre from the individual realization of them in a specific work, inasmuch as those features are not self-realizable or self-generating.

31. As Johnson so regularly did when—in an effort to determine "how far man may extend his designs, or how high he may rate his native force" ("Preface to Shakespeare")—he employed the "circumstantial method" to separate the native power of the artist from "all external assistance or obstruction" (Keast, "Theoretical Foundations," p. 406).

Selected Bibliography

Abrams, Meyer H. "Dr. Johnson's Spectacles." In *New Light on Dr. Johnson: Essays on the Occasion of His 250th Birthday*. Edited by Frederick W. Hilles. New Haven, Conn.: Yale University Press, 1959.

———. *The Mirror and the Lamp: Romantic Theory and the Critical Tradition*. Oxford: Oxford University Press, 1953.

Alkon, Paul Kent. *Samuel Johnson and Moral Discipline*. Evanston, Ill.: Northwestern University Press, 1967.

Barrett, Charlotte, ed. *Diary and Letters of Madame D'Arblay*. Vol. 2. London: Macmillan & Co., 1904-5.

Bate, Walter Jackson. *The Achievement of Samuel Johnson*. Oxford: Oxford University Press, 1955.

———. *Samuel Johnson*. New York: Harcourt, Brace, Jovanovich, 1977.

Bond, Donald F., ed. *The Spectator*. 5 vols. Oxford: Clarendon Press, 1965.

Boswell, James. *The Life of Samuel Johnson, LL. D., with A Journal of a Tour to the Hebrides with Samuel Johnson*. Edited by G. B. Hill. Revised by L. F. Powell. 6 vols. Oxford: Clarendon Press, 1934-50.

Bronson, Bertrand H. *Johnson and Boswell: Three Essays*. Berkeley and Los Angeles: University of California Press, 1944.

Brown, Joseph Epes. *The Critical Opinions of Samuel Johnson*. New York: Russell and Russell, 1961.

Bush, Douglas, ed. *John Keats: Selected Poems and Letters*. Boston: Houghton Mifflin Co., 1959.

Chapin, Chester F. *The Religious Thought of Samuel Johnson*. Ann Arbor: University of Michigan Press, 1968.

Congleton, J. E. *Theories of Pastoral in England*, 1684-1798. Gainesville: University of Florida Press, 1952.

Crane, R. S. "English Neoclassical Criticism: An Outline Sketch." In *Critics and Criticism: Ancient and Modern*. Edited by R. S. Crane. Chicago: University of Chicago Press, 1952.

———. *The Idea of the Humanities*. 2 vols. Chicago: University of Chicago Press, 1967.

———. *The Languages of Criticism and the Structure of Poetry*. Toronto: University of Toronto Press, 1953.

Curley, Thomas M. *Samuel Johnson and the Age of Travel*. Athens: University of Georgia Press, 1976.

Damrosch, Leopold, Jr. *The Uses of Johnson's Criticism*. Charlottesville: University Press of Virginia, 1976.

Eliot, T. S. *On Poetry and Poets*. New York: Farrar, Straus, and Cudahy, 1957.

Empson, William. *Some Versions of Pastoral*. Norfolk, Conn.: New Directions, 1960.

Fleischauer, Warren. "Johnson, *Lycidas*, and the Norms of Criticism." In *Johnsonian Studies*. Edited by Magdi Wahba. Cairo, 1962.

Fogel, Ephim G. "Salmons in Both, or Some Caveats for Canonical Scholars." In *Evidence for Authorship: Essays on Problems of Attribution*. Edited by David V. Erdman and Ephim G. Fogel. Ithaca, N.Y.: Cornell University Press, 1966.

Folkenflik, Robert. "Johnson and 'An Essay on Elegies.'" *Bulletin of the New York Public Library* 77 (1974): 188-99.

Fussell, Paul. *Samuel Johnson and the Life of Writing*. New York: Harcourt, Brace, Jovanovich, 1971.

Gray James. *Johnson's Sermons: A Study*. Oxford: Clarendon Press, 1972.

Greene, Donald J. *The Politics of Samuel Johnson*. New Haven, Conn.: Yale University Press, 1960.

Hagstrum, Jean H. *Samuel Johnson's Literary Criticism*. Minneapolis: University of Minnesota Press, 1952.

Hanford, James Holly. "The Pastoral Elegy and Milton's *Lycidas*." *PMLA* 25 (1910): 403-47.

Heninger, S. K., Jr. "The Renaissance Perversion of Pastoral." *Journal of the History of Ideas* 22 (1961): 254-61.

Hill, G. B., ed. *Johnsonian Miscellanies*. 2 vols. Oxford: Clarendon Press, 1897.

Hilles, Frederick W. and Bloom, Harold, eds. *From Sensibility to Romanticism: Essays Presented to Frederick A. Pottle*. New York: Oxford University Press, 1965.

Hipple, Walter John, Jr. *The Beautiful, the Sublime, and the Picturesque in Eighteenth-Century British Aesthetic Theory*. Carbondale: Southern Illinois University Press, 1957.

Hirsch, E. D., Jr. *The Aims of Interpretation*. Chicago: University of Chicago Press, 1976.

———. *Validity in Interpretation*. New Haven, Conn.: Yale University Press, 1967.

Hume, Robert D. *Dryden's Criticism*. Ithaca, N.Y.: Cornell University Press, 1970.

Johnson, Samuel. *A Dictionary of the English Language*. 1755. Facsimile reprint. Hildesheim: Georg Olms.

————. *A Journey to the Western Islands of Scotland*. Edited by R. W. Chapman. London: Oxford University Press, 1924.

————. *The Letters of Samuel Johnson, with Mrs. Thrale's Genuine Letters to Him*. Edited by R. W. Chapman. 3 vols. Oxford: Clarendon Press, 1952.

————. *The Lives of the Poets*. Edited by George Birkbeck Hill. 3 vols. Oxford: Clarendon Press, 1905.

————. *Rasselas*. Edited by R. W. Chapman. Oxford: Clarendon Press, 1927.

————. *Samuel Johnson's Prefaces and Dedications*. Edited by Allen T. Hazen. New Haven, Conn.: Yale University Press, 1937.

————. *The Works of Samuel Johnson, LL. D.* 11 vols. (Oxford, 1825).

————. *The Yale Edition of the Works of Samuel Johnson*. Edited by Allen T. Hazen and John H. Middendorf. New Haven, Conn.: Yale University Press. Vol. 1, *Diaries, Prayers, and Annals*, edited by E. L. McAdam, Jr., with Donald and Mary Hyde, 1958. Vol. 2, *The Idler and The Adventurer*, edited by W. J. Bate, J. M. Bullitt, and L. F. Powell, 1963. Vols. 3, 4, 5, *The Rambler*, edited by W. J. Bate and Albrecht B. Strauss, 1969. Vol. 6, *Poems*, edited by E. L. McAdam, Jr., with George Milne, 1964. Vols. 7, 8, *Johnson on Shakespeare*, edited by Arthur Sherbo, with an Introduction by Bertrand H. Bronson, 1968. Vol. 9, *A Journey to the Western Islands of Scotland*, edited by Mary Lascelles, 1971. Vol. 10, *Political Writings*, edited by Donald J. Greene, 1977. Vol. 14, *Sermons*, edited by Jean H. Hagstrum and James Gray, 1978.

Keast, William R. "Johnson's Criticism of the Metaphysical Poets." *English Literary History* 17 (1950): 59-70.

————. "The Theoretical Foundations of Johnson's Criticism." In *Critics and Criticism: Ancient and Modern*. Edited by R. S. Crane. Chicago: University of Chicago Press, 1952.

Kelley, Richard. "Johnson Among the Sheep." *Studies in English Literature* 8 (1968): 475-85.

Kermode, Frank. *The Sense of an Ending: Studies in the Theory of Fiction*. Oxford: Oxford University Press, 1967.

Krieger, Murray. "Fiction, Nature, and Literary Kinds in Johnson's Criticism of Shakespeare." *Eighteenth-Century Studies* 4 (1971): 184-98.

Lawry, Jon S. " 'Eager Thought': Dialectic in 'Lycidas.' " *PMLA* 75 (1962): 27-32.

Leavis, F. R. "Johnson as Critic." *Scrutiny* 12 (1944): 187-204.

McAdam, E. L., Jr. *Dr. Johnson and the English Law*. Syracuse, N.Y.: Syracuse University Press, 1951.

McKeon, Richard, ed. *The Basic Works of Aristotle*. New York: Random House, 1941.

Márias, Julián. "Philosophic Truth and the Metaphoric System. In *Interpretation: The Poetry of Meaning*. Edited by Stanley Romaine Hopper and David B. Miller. New York: Harcourt, Brace, and World, 1967.

Marsh, Robert. *Four Dialectical Theories of Poetry*. Chicago: University of Chicago Press, 1965.

Moore, Arthur K. *Contestable Concepts of Literary Theory*. Baton Rouge: Louisiana State University Press, 1973.

Olson, Elder. "An Outline of Poetic Theory." In *Critics and Criticism: Ancient and Modern*. Edited by R. S. Crane. Chicago: University of Chicago Press, 1952.

———. "William Empson, Contemporary Criticism, and Poetic Diction." In *Critics and Criticism: Ancient and Modern*. Edited by R. S. Crane, Chicago: University of Chicago Press, 1952.

Pepper, Stephen C. *World Hypotheses: A Study in Evidence*. Berkeley: University of California Press, 1942.

Pope, Alexander. *The Prose Works of Alexander Pope*. Edited by Norman Ault. Oxford: Shakespeare Head Press, 1936.

———. *The Twickenham Edition of the Poems of Alexander Pope*. edited by John Butt. New Haven, Conn.: Yale University Press. Vol. 1, *Pastoral Poetry and An Essay on Criticism*, edited by E. Audra and Aubrey Williams, 1961. Vol. 2, *The Rape of the Lock*, edited by Geoffrey Tillotson, 1940. Vol. 3.1, *An Essay on Man*, edited by Maynard Mack, 1950. Vol. 3.2, *Epistles to Several Persons*, edited by F. W. Bateson, 1951. Vol. 4, *Imitations of Horace*, edited by John Butt, 1939. Vol. 5, *The Dunciad*, edited by James Sutherland, 1943. Vol. 6, *Minor Poems*, edited by John Butt, 1964. Vols. 7, 8, *The Iliad*, edited by Maynard Mack 1967. Vols. 9, 10, *The Odyssey*, edited by Maynard Mack, 1967. Vol. 11, *Index*, edited by Maynard Mack, 1969.

Rader, Ralph W. "Literary Form in Factual Narrative: The Example of Boswell's *Johnson*." In *Essays in Eighteenth-Century Biography*. Edited by Philip B. Daghlian. Bloomington: Indiana University Press, 1968.

Reade, Aleyn Lyell. *Johnsonian Gleanings*. 11 vols. Privately printed, 1909-52.

Reynolds, Joshua. *Discourses on Art, with Selections from the Idler*. Edited with an Introduction by Stephen O. Mitchell. Indianapolis, Ind.: Bobbs-Merrill Co., 1965.

Richter, David H. *Fable's End: Completeness and Closure in Rhetorical Fiction*. Chicago: University of Chicago Press, 1974.

Rosenmyer, Thomas G. *The Green Cabinet: Theocritus and the European Pastoral Lyric*. Berkeley: University of California Press, 1969.

Sachs, Arieh. *Passionate Intelligence: Imagination and Reason in the Work of Samuel Johnson*. Baltimore, Md.: Johns Hopkins Press, 1967.

Sacks, Sheldon. *Fiction and the Shape of Belief: A Study of Henry Fielding with Glances at Swift, Johnson, and Richardson.* Berkeley and Los Angeles: University of California Press, 1964.

Schwartz, Richard B. *Samuel Johnson and the New Science.* Madison: University of Wisconsin Press, 1971.

————. *Samuel Johnson and the Problem of Evil.* Madison: University of Wisconsin Press, 1975.

Sherbo, Arthur. "A Reply." *Bulletin of the New York Public Library* 77 (1974): 200-04.

————. "A Reply to Professor Fogel." In *Evidence for Authorship: Essays on Problems of Attribution.* Edited by David V. Erdman and Ephim G. Fogel. Ithaca, N.Y.: Cornell University Press, 1966.

————. "The Uses and Abuses of Internal Evidence." In *Evidence for Authorship: Essays on Problems of Attribution.* Edited by David V. Erdman and Ephim G. Fogel. Ithaca, N.Y.: Cornell University Press, 1966.

Sigworth, Oliver F. "Johnson's *Lycidas:* The End of Renaissance Criticism," *Eighteenth-Century Studies* 1 (1967): 159-168.

Sledd, James H. and Kolb, Gwin J. *Dr. Johnson's Dictionary: Essays in the Biography of a Book.* Chicago: University of Chicago Press, 1955.

Snell, Bruno. *The Discovery of the Mind: The Greek Origins of European Thought.* New York: Harper Torchbooks, 1960.

Tolstoy, Leo. "Shakespeare and Drama." In *Tolstoy on Art.* Translated by A. Maude. Oxford: Oxford University Press, 1924.

Trickett, Rachel. *The Honest Muse: A Study in Augustan Verse.* Oxford: Clarendon Press, 1967.

Tuve, Rosemond, *Images and Themes in Five Poems by Milton.* Cambridge, Mass.: Harvard University Press, 1957.

Voitle, Robert. *Samuel Johnson the Moralist.* Cambridge, Mass.: Harvard University Press, 1961.

Waingrow, Marshall, ed. *The Correspondence and Other Papers of James Boswell Relating to the Making of the Life of Johnson.* New York: McGraw-Hill, 1969.

Wimsatt, W. K., Jr. "Johnson's Dictionary: April 15, 1955." In *New Light on Dr. Johnson: Essays on the Occasion of His 250th Birthday.* New Haven, Conn.: Yale University Press, 1959.

————. *The Prose Style of Samuel Johnson.* New Haven, Conn.: Yale University Press, 1941.

Index